Pastor C

You were a
great inspiration. With
much love, I thank you!!!

Rose

Tainted

5/19/07

Justice

GIVEN TO ME ON

MALCOLM X Birthday

We want to hear from you. Please send your comments about this book or your own personal story to us in care of the address below. Thank you.

Gadson Jeffries Publishing
PO Box 5416
Hillside, New Jersey 07205
www.gadsonjeffriespub.com

Requests for information on hearings and court documents should be addressed to:

Gadson Jeffries Publishing
P.O. Box 5416
Hillside, New Jersey 07205
United States of America

Or email us at:

info@gadsonjeffriespub.com

Kenneth P. Freeman

Rose Tainted Justice
Privileges, Power, and Internal Affairs

Gadson Jeffries Publishing
Hillside, New Jersey 07205 USA

Rose Tainted Justice: Privileges, Power, and Internal Affairs

Published in 2006 in the United States of America by
        Gadson Jeffries Publishing
        P.O. Box 5416, Hillside, New Jersey 07205-5416
        www.gadsonjeffriespub.com

In cooperation with
        G.L. Honeycutt Consulting, LLC
        P.O. Box 15338, Alexandria, Virginia 22309
        www.honeycuttconsulting.us

Library of Congress Control Number: 2006907690

ISBN   1-934003-27-1
ISBN   978-1-934-003-27-5

10 9 8 7 6 5 4 3 2

Cover Design by Charles Caldwell
Book Design by Gaea L. Honeycutt

Contents

We Won't Forget Your Labor of Love

Politicians will lie to you, saying there're only a few bad apples in any law enforcement agency. Civic organizations will lie on you, declaring there're only a few good officers in the entire world. I'm neither a politician nor do I belong to any civic group, so I'm at liberty to tell you the truth. This book is dedicated to you, the individual officer who through integrity and intelligence, refused to place keeping your job, your status, and the acceptance of top brass (as well as other officers) above doing what is both legal and right.

My heart is sorrowful because I've felt what awaits you at the end of your journey. Only a few will ever be publicly vindicated, most will bear a lifetime of shame from their department and be ostracized by peers, who will only support you in the darkest corners through cautious "atta-boys", away from those they're trying to impress. Anti-social, belligerent, disrespectful, and troublemaker will be tattooed to your foreheads, forever branding you as an officer not worthy of his/her badge.

But take heart. Your integrity will sustain you and it will be your greatest reward. You have persevered a great injustice and are the true winners. Your intelligence inspires you, knowing, as I have come to discover, that one officer *can* shape a department. You may never see the legions of young officers that will follow your individual example from a distance and you may never get the credit that you deserve.

Nevertheless, you are our city's, our state's, and our nation's final frontier against a clandestine tyranny, and abuse of the powers and privileges of your agencies. Thank you for sacrificing your reputation, your social status, and for many of you, your solid careers.

I love you, admire you, and will always pray for you and for your families, who are suffering terribly along beside you. Stand, and keep standing!

Kenneth P. Freeman

This Court Will Come to Order

The Honorable Judge Paulette Sapp-Peterson flaunted her authority, reminding everyone she was a strong, African American woman with power, and choosing not to wait for the return of Judge Andrew Smithson, the presiding judge of record. Judge Smithson, who had called in sick, was well versed in my case and extremely competent. Judge Sapp-Peterson used his absence as her best opportunity to tie up a political lose end, deciding not to take a risk on an unbiased jury.

Judge Sapp-Peterson's robe was unzipped in the front, exposing the wrinkled garments she wore underneath. Those present that day couldn't help but notice the judge wore bedroom slippers in the courtroom. She strolled to her seat on the bench, where she stoically informed both attorneys she was in a rush to get out of there and that they'd better be brief. That admonishment was an unofficial warning to make all arguments short and lay off the lectures. Her decision was already in hand, but the hearing was being recorded. Therefore, giving the appearance that she actually considered what the attorneys argued during the session was paramount.

The New Jersey Attorney General's Office sent six hired

guns in black suits to monitor Deputy Attorney General Saju Mathew that morning. DAG Mathew was, for the most part, honorable. That was considered an extreme liability by a corrupt administration. But, he was familiar with case, and it was too late in the game to replace him.

A dark cloud had engulfed me ever since F.B.I. Agents interviewed the snitch. Our snitch. My investigation exposed a relationship that many wanted to shun. The informant worked well for Internal Affairs, but all of that seemed to pale in comparison to the idea that the Feds thought he might be one of the ringleaders behind the 1993 World Trade Center bombing. Now that Bin Laden and his psychotic crew had reduced our towers to ruble, my motives for protecting our informant were highly suspect. But not to me. I knew what I had done was the right thing to do. Even if Judge Sapp-Peterson allowed McGreevey's headhunters to devour me in the process.

The judge's fatal flaw was that she still had high aspirations. She allowed herself to become a concubine in an effort to be accepted into New Jersey's political country club. In New Jersey, as in western culture, a mistress' affinity for affection and recognition were blinders of her true potential, leaving her soul dissatisfied, always desiring, wishing, wanting to be the official wife. Judge Sapp-Peterson understood that New Jersey winked, as attorney generals became State Supreme Court justices instead of the truly competent and seasoned judges that manned the courthouses daily.

The hearing had to continue along that path. And I had to accept whatever the judge decided was in the interest of justice. A funny word, justice, especially when spoken in the bosom of our nation's Eden of corruption, the Garden State.

After a few "brief", oral arguments had been presented, Judge Sapp-Peterson was ready to formally present her decision. Her statement was captured on the official court transcript:

> *The motion for summary judgment is granted, in all respects and I'm going to place my reasons on the record later, because as I said that I will be leaving and I will not be able to complete my reasons prior to departing.*
>
> *But suffice it to say that the Court is grouping the issues as follows: namely that number one, the temporal proximity on the CEPA claim is lacking.*
>
> *That is that in order to sustain a cause of action based on CEPA, he has to establish that he disclosed or threatened to disclose the activity to a supervisory or public body, that he suffered an adverse employment decision and a causal connection between the two.*
>
> *To the extent that the whistle blowing activities relates to his reporting of 1997, there is number one, no reporting to a supervisor or public body a public official I believe in 1999, but the temporal proximity between the whistle blowing activities and what he did is lacking, and there was no adverse employment action for almost - - for more than two years, because I believe the first charges were in May of 2001?*

DAG Mathew, who was representing the interests of both the State of New Jersey and the Department of Corrections, responded. "Right. . ."

Judge Sapp-Peterson continued her diatribe.

> *That's number one. Number two, the Court also agrees that the doctrines of res judicata do apply, that the O.A.L. (Office of Administrative Law) is positioned to address these issues, and the case that the Court refers to is I think it's the case. . . Inselin versus Township of North Bergen 275, N.J. Super 352.*
>
> *That under Inselin and given the fact that these issues with respect to him being singled out, the racial issues, were raised, that the Administrative Law judge was poised to address those issues, those issues have clearly been litigated.*

> *And finally, with respect to the other incidents, the*
> *specific incidents of retaliation that are based upon*
> *the May 18th charges, the November 9th charges, and*
> *the August charges again, these were all issues factu-*
> *ally that were addressed before the Administrative Law*
> *Judge, so I believe that summary judgment is appropri-*
> *ate, and I will go into further detail on the record, when*
> *I place my reasons on the record.*[1]

With those spoken words, and a premature stroke of her
pen, my quest for justice evaporated in that Mercer County
courthouse. Opposing counsel was just as awed as my attorney,
Ronald L. Washington, Esq.

The judge based her decision on the temporal proximity to
my initial formal notification of an administrative indiscretion.
In short, in order to prove retaliation by a governmental agency,
we had to demonstrate an absolute and direct connection between the very first time I ever notified a single supervisor of
a problem and every time anybody retaliated against me. An
impossible feat. We proved that each act of retaliation was connected to separate official complaints, but a content paramour
protects her lover's home.

"Are you going to appeal her?" DAG Mathew was am-
bivalent to the judge's decision. On the one hand, he won an
enormous motion, and he should have celebrated the way the
half-dozen spies in his entourage were rejoicing. They were on
their cell phones right inside of the courtroom, screeching with
a modest roar, "Congratulations! We got him."

But Saju's integrity oozed from his conscience. Unfortunately for him, Saju was an attorney who actually honored an
attorney's code of ethics. Because of that, he recognized his
skills were misused by the court, making him an unwitting accomplice to a travesty from the bench.

---

1 Transcript of Summary Judgment Motion, Freeman v. State of NJ Department of Corrections, et al, Docket No. MER-L-1208-01, before Hon.
Paulette Sapp-Peterson, J.S.C., February 20, 2004.

"Wouldn't you?" Ron was resolved, and the only questions in his mind dealt with the inherent costs of the appeals process and whether the Appellant Court would attack the Governor McGreevey Machine. Ron didn't lack funds, but he knew I did. After all, as much as he personally believed in my case, it remained a business matter for his firm.

DAG Mathew nodded and smiled.

"Most definitely." Both attorneys, shocked at Judge Sapp-Peterson's decision, exited the courtroom without so much a raised eyebrow. They were anticipating the response of the New Jersey Court of Appeals. Both jurists understood the Appellant Court could invoke a privilege that allowed them to avoid reviewing the case, passing it on to a state Supreme Court, bloated with politically appointed former attorney generals.

The leaders of one of New Jersey's largest agencies had demonstrated their ability to defraud her citizens once again, without so much as a whimper. And then, to have it all swept under a rug further demonstrated New Jersey's official stance on corruption, appropriately enforced by the Attorney General's Office. When the whistle was blown, six of McGreevey's hired guns were deployed to monitor the judge and an unsuspecting DAG.

ONE

Newark in the Summer of 1969

". . . And here he is. In the white T-shirt, Reggie!" "Uh oh!" I thought. "Here comes the boos." The heckles of dissention rang loudly from the feminine crowd. All four of my sisters gave my eldest brother, Kelvin, a rough way to go during our games. Reginald was his middle name, but everybody called him "Reggie" for short.

"Boo!" The chants weren't from hatred, but reflected the fact that Reggie was almost guaranteed victory. He was much taller than my middle brother, Keith, and me, and he was unrelenting as he took full advantage of the six- and eight-years age differences. Keith and I were helpless against the dominance an eleven-year-old wielded. We were truly the underdogs, so the hopes of our household were with us.

My mother played the dramatic announcer. Her diction was precise, formal, and a bit over-the-top when it came to disguising her Athens, Georgia drawl. She moved from Athens to Detroit as a young teen, but hints of Athens imbued her vocal cords, no matter how refined Aunt Bertha wanted her to appear.

"And the challengers, also in their white T-shirts, Keith and Ken!" Let's hear it ladies. . . "Yeah!" Now that's what I'm talking about! Cheer for the underdogs. Our over-sized tanks made me look like I was wearing suspenders on a skirt. I was too small for it, but we thought it made us look cool, and that was enough for me.

Keith and I were about to play a game of "Puff" basketball against Reggie. We used an old small, orange sponge basketball that Keith and I received for Christmas. The basket hoop hung over our closet door, barely within reach of my tosses.

My mother made Reggie play the game while walking around on his knees. That way, she thought, we would have a more sporting contest. Pee-wee Affirmative Action, if you will, to level the playing field.

Yeah, right! As if *that* was going to be enough to overcome Reggie's height and skills. Flagrant elbows, blocked shots, and the omnipotent "iron booty", which was employed when Reggie forcefully thrust his rear end into a defending opponent, smashing our little stomachs, and hurling us into a state of agony. Reggie was merciless when it came to sports and the chance of victory. For Keith and me, it was another loss and tearful eyes. But, cake and ice-cream made the defeats seem bearable.

Keith and I had four of the most beautiful sisters cheering for us as if we were the great Bill Russell and Willis Reed. My sisters, Karen (Kal), Kirisha (Kay), Kawana (Wanie), and Kenita were excellent antagonists and, even at their young ages, could drive any man to drink. Heavily! But Keith and I had them on our side. When their scowls had little affect on Reggie, my sisters would resort to other means of "assistance" such as pushing or tripping Reggie as he dove for a basket.

My baby sister, Kenita (who was six years older than me), would interrupt the game with her own ad hoc diversion tactic. Complete mayhem would break out after she broke wind. And, like clockwork, Kenita's denials signaled the start of a great "Heidi-who-dun-it" mystery in the middle of our own Raiders-Jets game.

Entertaining, but with a script-like predictability, my oldest sister, Kal, designated herself the ghetto version of Sherlock Holmes. Our beloved Dreadlock Holmes was notorious for shutting down everything to institute her own system of Marshall Law. Ol' Dreadlock was determined to detect the offender with the resolve of Malcolm X.

In times past, Dreadlock erroneously interpreted 'By Any Means Necessary' as empowerment to literally "sniff-out" the culprit. Yes, with her nose buried in the crack of each of our sphincters, Dreadlock would inhale, like a stressed-out crackhead on the trail of cocaine-vapors locked inside our pants, giving "Waiting to Exhale" new meaning.

The delay would soon end thanks to Dreadlock's extremely discerning schnauzer. By the end of the evening, a few things were finalized. The culprit was accurately "sniffed-out", Reggie would win the game, gloat over his victory with a corny song and dance, Keith would pout, I would cry, and there would be baked snacks for all.

In retrospect, we were allowed to deceive ourselves during those years. While we enjoyed life inside of our four walls, reality glistened brightly in the lives of one of our neighbors. The man that lived across the street would engage in fistfights with his teenaged stepson in the middle of the street. Their household was estranged from the neighborhood, yet familiar to most from occasional sightings. The father was stronger than his stepson, but clearly not as agile. He rushed the high-school aged kid and got flipped onto the back of his head—a perfect wrestling move. The blood oozed from the back of the man's split scalp and was slowly absorbed into the asphalt on which he'd crashed. Normally, the fights, a terribly sad expression of love, weren't brief at all.

All who either heard or watched the fighting were distressed, except for one noticeable onlooker. The only one unaffected by all of that violence was the wife and mother. She would roll her eyes as the two publicly dueled, the battle spilling from inside their home to the street. You could tell she was almost wishing they would simply hurry up, get it over. The mother was the source of the disputes, and some believed she was the catalyst.

Watching from the driveway of their home while she still wore her robe, she looked bored, as if their combat was nothing more than a commercial between life and whatever else comes this way. She had a look that reminded on-lookers to mind their own business.

After the fighting ended, the two warriors would stagger in their house, pacing themselves to maintain precariously poetic distance from the other, and each receiving a complimentary shoulder pat from the woman as acknowledgement of her unyielding concern. Her face actually looked sincere. That was, until the two disappeared from our ghetto stage. Her fangs flashed as she chided, "The show's over, ol' nosey asses." Her last words before following the man inside gave her comfort, reassurance that her actions were pure, untainted, honorable.

The animosity we saw didn't happen in a box. Tensions all around us were already high, and it wasn't just because of family problems. Our nation had been irreparably wounded, and the people of Newark, New Jersey were mourning over the worst riots ever to violate her—riots which weren't even two summers past. She was also under the constant threat of more destruction. Stories in the news and gossip all had the ring of truth. The thirteen-story Scudder Holmes public housing project was the scene where a woman had either been thrown off or had jumped off the roof, depending on whether you believed the police or your neighbor. Once-thriving businesses along Springfield Avenue were torched and looted. All young black men fit some kind of general police description no matter how secure the alibi. Police beatings and assaults on the police volleyed like championship ping-pong. Who started it all? Maybe it was the chicken, and maybe it was the egg. The only thing that mattered was it had to end.

"We hold these truths to be self-evident that all men are created equal" had a footnote for Newark as well as other urban cities. The citizens of Newark were afraid of the police. The police were afraid of the people. Everybody was afraid of a precarious future. The Kennedy's were abruptly kidnapped from our lives by the stench of misery, along with the souls of Malcolm and Martin.

I was just a preschooler during those times, but I could remember how our big-box, floor-model television, which we kept in the living room, served only as a television stand for a smaller 9-inch, black and white (B&W) television. There were no knobs to turn and "remote control" only meant that whoever was nearest to the set of pliers would use them to change the channel.

The smaller B&W was considered a step-up for us. The big set made everyone think that their eyesight was fading. That was because it used to have a diminishing round, white spot in the center of the screen, signifying the end of the picture tube. Keith and I were forced to squint harshly using our youthful imaginations as we *listened* to Batman and watched the incredibly shrinking, white dot. As time passed, we couldn't see anything inside the white dot except for the white dot. So the little B&W gave us something that only God could have managed—a new respect for Batman and every young boy's dream, Batgirl, in that smooth, tight black suit.

However, not all advances brought pleasant realities. In fact, that small B&W was where my family observed the gentlemen of broadcast, like Cronkite, stoically pontificate the drudgery of war, as well as its impending stalemate, while primetime cameras explicitly honed in on an army helicopter's gunman gleefully shooting a woman and her small children in the tall grass fields of Vietnam.

"Are they supposed to do that, Mommy?" The blades from

the helicopter frantically blew the blades of grass aside as they uncovered the undernourished toddler killed moments earlier.

"Y'all just turn from that, now." My mother's response was one of protection, not indifference. What kind of questions should four and six year olds ask? "Is Bugs is on? Turn the channel." Pliers in hand, our world once again retreated from chaos to tranquility, at least temporarily.

Those were strange and confusing times all around our nation. But, in the midst of it all, our basketball game served as an inexpensive vacation, uniquely controllable, and very entertaining. We were spared, at least for one more moment, from life's crude and cruel realities. Both joy and peace made their home within the boundaries of ours, and we were grateful.

TWO

Where I Was Blind, Now I See

As we would later reflect on our plight, including the levels of degradation that surrounded us, we somehow never felt trapped by it. I mean, the eight of us lived in a two-bedroom apartment, having to share a *single* bathroom. My oldest two sisters slept in the rear bedroom and younger two in the next bedroom. My mother's bedroom was converted from what used to be the dining room, while my brothers slept in the den on pullout daybeds. I shared a bed with whoever wouldn't push me onto the floor that particular night. That was kind of tough, especially since I had a reputation for drooling on everybody's pillows. There's nothing that can compare to the sensation of a three-year-old's drool as it seeped into your ear.

Welfare was nothing new to us and food stamps were common in our neighborhood. After being on welfare for so long, our family got a break when my mother began working as a teacher's aide.

A new government program entitled "Drop In" had been introduced and my mother, who was a high school drop out, 'dropped in' to Central High School where she took night classes. School was a must for us, as my mother desired to improve herself and, simultaneously, set a precedent for the family. The same night Kal graduated high school, finishing academically second in her class, we celebrated a second time as my mother graduated from night school. My mom later enrolled in college where she earned her bachelor's degree, and moved from teacher's aide to head teacher. But, that didn't last because, as fate would have it, a better job offer came her way. Ironically, she was hired as a social worker by the Essex County Division of Welfare, the same agency that used to give us food stamps.

Inspiring things were always around me, but I was growing up in the inner city, which meant that your chin was bound to be tested. Fights would break out for things as ridiculous as not owning a popular style of pants with double-stitching along the seam called "Swedish Knits".

The Bible teaches against fighting, and admonishes believers to "turn the other cheek" if somebody slaps you. My mother believed the Holy Scriptures, without a doubt. However, there's something to be said about a mother's love, and that compelled her to defend her babies. Therefore, that meant that she would prepare us to survive even if some may have considered it disobedient to God's Word.

Well, my mother didn't want us to fight, but she made it clear that we were not to run *from* a fight. Her credo was, "If they hit you, you hit them back harder." It wasn't about being tough, it was about her children having the capacity to survive and not live in a state of fear. Although she may have wished she could always be there to protect us, my mother understood that there would come a time when we would have to stand alone and defend ourselves.

My first serious test of her credo was in the second grade. Hawthorne Avenue School had an overcapacity of students and not enough classrooms, the familiar effect of reduced school funding. So, the school used temporary classrooms in a portion of the upper floor of a local Boys Club, which was approximately a block and a half away from the main school building.

It held all of the second graders that should have been in the main building.

There was a kid we called Big Head Eddie in one of the other second grade classes. Eddie was larger because he had stayed back, which made him a year older than the rest of us. He got his nickname because his head was as big as a stop sign, and he was about as dumb as a stop sign. But because he was so much bigger than everybody else, nobody would dare say it to his face. Eddie was hardened partially because he was adopted and because his older brother beat him sometimes. We knew that he cried some mornings because of the ashy streaks left on his face from the tears. We never felt sorry for Eddie because he had a well-earned reputation beating up second graders, that year and the last time he was in the second grade.

I never had any problems with ol' Big Head. He mostly beat up dark-skinned kids, which was strange, seeing how he was tootsie-roll dark himself. Crazy as it may have seemed, it was all too common to hear black folks associate being dark with being ugly. I just didn't get it. There was no way they could see what I saw.

My mother would tell us "the blacker the berry, the sweeter the juice". I have always admired darker skinned people. Although I *am* gorgeous, Keith had dark skin, and I could remember sometimes wishing that my skin was more like Keith's. Maybe my father would've embraced me like he did my brother. Maybe not. My mother straightened out my thinking without words, but no less adamantly reinforcing that "that's his problem, not yours." I doubt she ever knew how I felt or how she helped me cope. Thank God for mothers.

One day while I was in the lunchroom eating some delicious and nutritious government-issue tater tots and fish sticks, Big Head Eddie materialized from out of nowhere.

"Hey, Eddie," I said while wondering to myself just how he balanced himself with a head that big. But little did I know, my peace with Eddie was about to be obliterated.

25

"Say it to my face, boy! Say it to my face!"

Oh God! Was I thinking aloud or what? Big ...I mean, *Mr.* Eddie couldn't possibly have read my mind. He couldn't read. But he could pummel me into recess. Prompt and evasive actions were required. Prompt like yesterday!

That instant seemed to be an appropriate time for me to get rid of my Paul Robeson vocals, as I tried to sound like one of the Olsen twins.

"I didn't say anything about you, Eddie." That was good, I thought. Maybe he believed me and was planning to call off the dogs of war.

"You did too." Eddie said. "And I'm gonna beat your ass after school, Kenny!" Maybe not. (Note to self: Why is it that every second grader can perfectly enunciate the word "ass"?) Mr. Eddie made a solidly clinched fist with his right hand and carefully put his fist to his own right eye, then to his own left eye, then to his nose, and finally, to his own mouth.

Now, for those of you who never experienced the second grade in the seventies, please take note. What Mr. Eddie was so graciously, and graphically, demonstrating for my benefit, were the forecasted, strategic placements of his fist when he commenced beating me up after school. And, as if that wasn't terrible enough, as Mr. Eddie paced away from my table, he looked back at me, grimaced, and then demonstrated how he wouldn't neglect to punch me in the stomach, too. No kid ever wanted to get punched in the gut. That was seen as the equivalent of a large man falling asleep inside of a tattoo parlor and having the name "Big Willie" emblazoned across his behind. If you were that man, no matter how you tried to rationalize that it wasn't as bad as it seemed, you knew it was worse. And your buddies were always there to remind you, just in case you forgot.

Growing up in Newark, my entire family was well versed in how we were to behave if a fight came our way. However, my mother never met Big Head Eddie. And my thoughts rang loudly inside of my trembling soul. That was when I began to truly doubt my mother's motives for telling us to fight. Maybe she had an insurance policy or something on me. Or maybe *she* used to get beat up in the second grade and thought it was just dandy. Maybe she wanted to pass butt-kickings down to her children, as if gut-punching were hereditary or something.

I could only fight one battle at a time. *The hell with my momma's credo. I'm running home and I'll deal with momma after I get away from Big Head.* That thought dominated my mind for the rest of the school day. Mr. Eddie was planning to pummel me for something about which I had no clue. I might have thought many things about Eddie's big head and the sub-intelligent substance that swirled inside his cranium, and I may have even laughed at what others said, but I didn't say it. And I felt justified in my thinking. Eddie was too dumb to reason with, and the "Jedi mind-trick" hadn't been created yet.

Moreover, that was the first time I noticed ol' Big Head had some really big hands, which meant that he had some really big fists! Right then, I did some "save-me-Jesus-help-me-Holy-Ghost- Memphis, Tennessee-Church of God of Christ-Bishop Mason"-type praying. *Oh God! Help me. I'm scared.* The same sun that moments earlier shown brilliantly through our classroom windows was suddenly draped by swollen clouds. Death's shadow was making a trial run, sizing me up.

I'm gonna die. Even my own thoughts were trying to escape that beating. And wouldn't you know it, the stress of it all multiplied because I still had the responsibility of trying to look cool. Being thought of as cool shouldn't have mattered at that point because, by then, every girl in school had at least heard that my voice went higher than Mickey Mouse's.

Then came the wait. The anticipation of my inevitably embarrassing beat-down was worse than anything that Mr. Eddie could have poured out on my little soul. My friends were all there, but not for my protection. In fact, they began sounding like some of Job's friends, the same friends that Job called "miserable comforters". Every few minutes, my "friends" enthusiastically took turns vividly refreshing my memory about all of ol' Big Head's past victims, in a sort of "where are they now" retrospective. *"I'm dead,"* was the new ruling constantly permeating my mind. And then came the Reaper, better known as the dismissal bell.

I passed my friend Rufus on the way down the stairs, who suggested I hit the ground running, and then keep running until I was old enough to join the Marines. Everybody who heard me sound like a Disney character was waiting for the slaughter to commence. I knew I was going to run away. I really wanted to run, but I couldn't, and it had nothing to do with being brave.

That's when it hit me, and the whole picture finally made sense. If I ran today, he was going to beat me up tomorrow. And, if I ran tomorrow, he'd do it the next day. I was stuck. I had to stay to fight Eddie, but I didn't want to get beat up. I wanted to run, but the fight would always be waiting for me, somewhere.

So I stood there, my shriveled feet frozen atop the weathered concrete sidewalk that ran along Hawthorne Avenue. The other kids were making such a commotion, some patting me on the back while others were saying how Big Head would beat me senseless. I was terrified. Confused. Lost. Then, in a hopeless and helpless panic, I tightly clinched both of my fists together, and I slammed the lids of my eyes shut. My small, insignificant fists, and my big, beautiful, brown eyes, were both clinched tightly. I held my breath and grinded my teeth together, forcing a vein to appear in the center of my forehead.

Suddenly, without warning, I involuntarily released an excruciating screech, for the fear of what was unbearable had overpowered my futile reasoning. It was a moment in time that lasted forever. And I would be forever grateful, for I later learned that *fear* wasn't my enemy, only my response to fear was.

That screech deceived me, as well as everyone with a ticket to my massacre. It was a deception greater than anything for which I could have wished. The sound of that deception wasn't in sync with my heart. Fear had already embraced my heart, but that sound was an angry growl. The same kind that accompanied those sick-and-tired of being sick-and-tired.

That sudden resonating of my own voice had shaken me, too. I was startled so much that I unsuccessfully tried to re-open my eyes and hysterically began blinking with both eyes still shut. Because they had been shut so tightly, I struggled to pry them apart. My vision wasn't immediately clear, but when I was able to focus, I was seduced by the altered landscape surrounding me.

It was then that I recognized two major events had occurred: First, Big Head had just come out of the school and his big hands weren't balled. They were open. Second, Eddie was dressed in passiveness. He wore an unmistakable look of defeat on his face, the same look I had anticipated wearing. The look of confidence he had carried when he viciously demonstrated how he would whoop me was a distant memory, as was the intense anger when he demanded... no, *dared* me to talk about him to his face.

Eddie's shame resembled the knowledge instinctively bestowed upon a fawn the instant her silhouette is painted on the frosty road by the headlights of an oncoming tractor-trailer traveling 75 mph. Fear had arrived at Eddie's house. But for Eddie, fear of somebody smaller than he was didn't resonate. Eddie was used to being afraid of somebody like his brother. But the notion of fearing his own prey was incomprehensible. Big Head looked up on me the way a timid boy named Eddie would look up on his meaner, older brother. Big Head was scared.

The Bible talks about the Prophet Elijah's servant fearing when seeing a host of warriors surrounding him, and asked the prophet "Alas, my master. How shall we do?" Elijah used his servant's fear to teach him a lesson. The servant's eyes were already open, but he couldn't see clearly. When the prophet prayed that God would open the servant's eyes, the servant was able to see there were angels in chariots of fire surrounding the prophet's enemies, with arrows pointed at the host.

My eyes had been open all day, but seeing blocked my sight. Like Elijah's servant, fear had truly opened my eyes, and the answer to the question "How shall we do?" was crystal clear. My teeth and fists were still clinched and Big Head wasn't walking towards me. Instead, he spoke gently to me from afar.

"Why were you talking about me?" Eddie's eyes danced as he stared at me.

"I didn't talk about you, Eddie." That's what I told him, but my voice, reborn from the screech, didn't sound like Mickey. Somehow, fear had made me not afraid.

"But they said you did…." He paused as he sighed. His eyes glanced at his filthy shoes with a broken lace, then back towards me. "Everybody keeps picking on me." Right then, Eddie was no longer Big Head. He was a second grader that watched social worker after social worker mutilate every home he ever cared about.

"They're lying to you, Eddie. I didn't talk about you."

Eddie paused and continued staring at me. He stood there, more hurt than angry, but I still remembered his reputation and that kept me in the reality-zone. The brief reprieve extended until I had no more use for it. I was able to stand alone, inhaling the comforting aroma of confidence.

"I don't want to fight." Eddie had said the words I had prayed for, right there in front of everyone. Thank you Bishop Mason!

I should have been glad, gloating over how he backed down, and relishing in my newfound status. But I felt sorry for Eddie. What he had said was half-right. Everybody had something nasty and mean to say about Eddie. And, even if I didn't say those things aloud, I laughed and encouraged others to make fun of him, which made me at least partially culpable for his pain. There was no justification for cruelty in any fashion, and I understood that words hurt.

"I don't want to fight, either." My statement wasn't based on fear and that made me feel tougher than Ali. Eddie turned and walked down the avenue, alone. Some of the other kids cheered me on, as if I had done something great. By the time I made it to school the next day, it was rumored that I had beaten up Eddie so bad that he went to the hospital. I guess you shouldn't believe everything you hear. Eventually, Eddie and I became good friends in the second grade and remained that way until my family moved from our Clinton Place apartment into our first house in the Vailsburg section of Newark.

A young fan of Bugs and Elmer J., I had proven the adage, *Everybody's having fun, until the rabbit gets the gun!* From the instant that we agreed not to fight until this day, I have refused to allow myself to ever be crippled by the fear of physical violence again.

THREE

The Hole in Alice's Wonderland

What a surprise! They told me I was fourth on the list to be hired at the Mountainview Youth Correctional Facility in Annadale, New Jersey, but there were only three vacancies. After six years in the Marine's, and a few bookkeeping positions, I found myself unemployed right at the time my wife was pregnant with our first daughter.

With my baby about three months old, a representative from Annadale's personnel office called me and asked if I wanted to start working as a Corrections Officer. My start date was Monday, July 25, 1994.

If the question was whether I wanted full-time employment under civil service rules, full benefits, and a means to provide for my three-month-old infant, then I considered the question to be rhetorical. I happily accepted.

Annadale. That's what they called the Mountainview Youth Correctional Facility. I showed up for work ready to begin a career that would expose me to the darker side of society and life. Frank Wiersky and Ginger Happe were also starting that day, and we all got along fine.

After about a month and a half of working in the jail, they

sent Frank and me to Skillman, the Correction Officer Training Academy for the State of New Jersey at that time. Ginger had been a county corrections officer prior to working for the state and was spared from the academy. The only additional training required of Ginger was qualifying with her handgun. It was only for one week and outdoors. Trust, Ginger to be a deadeye shot with a gun. Cute as hell, and skills to boot!

After graduating from the academy, I volunteered for the graveyard shift from 10:20 pm until 6:20 am. The veterans took all of the first shift work, so the only alternative was second or third shifts. Second shift was the "working" shift. They spent the relaxing portion of the day (2:20 pm until 10:20 pm) with inmates instead of with their families. I didn't mind working at night because it gave me the entire day to spend with my daughter.

For the most part, Corrections was not much different from other occupations when it came to seniority. Those with the most time received the best shifts and work areas. The early morning shift was preferred because you were in early and out by 2:20 pm. That meant that you had plenty of time to run errands or pick up children from school. A pure luxury for those that had it, and a distant fantasy for the new guys.

Third shift became my only option. I quickly got used to watching my daughter go to sleep right before I left for work. Eight hours later as I walked through the front door, I was the first thing that both her smile and her eyes beheld in the morning. From time to time, my hour-long drive home was graced by Eric Clapton singing what I had already dreamed for my child. "If I Could Change the World" seemed to stay on the smoothest radio station in the Tri-state Area, Smooth Jazz, CD 101.9. Those reminders gave me something to look forward to during those difficult nights, and made the hardship of working among felons seem rather bearable.

In the midst of all that was happening, my family felt extremely safe. My employment was secured by civil service laws, and the health benefits of government employees and their families were off the charts. My regular paychecks, alone, allowed me to quickly catch up on some debt without impacting our family recreation. Movies, dinner, vacations—you name it, we were able to comfortably swing them.

The Department of Corrections had flown under the radar of public scrutiny when it came to the quantity of overtime paid. Barber Shop scholars labeled New Jersey Corrections Officers' perks as the State's best kept secret.

Vacancies were everywhere in the system and officers received mandatory overtime. There were times when as many as ten officers would be ordered to work a double shift. With that abundance of overtime—all the overtime that a young family could handle—I viewed our household debt as foolish and was determined to get out from under weight that I had created during my years in the Marines. As for Priscilla, her debt resulted from those dreaded student loans and a few other things. The student loans followed her in everything that she tried to do, and they had to be dealt with before we could move on to home ownership.

I regularly put in 30 to 60 hours of overtime in a two-week period. My overtime checks were, at times, more than my regular checks. And, by the summer of 1995, Priscilla and I were debt free. Man, that was sweet!

I transferred to the "real deal" in September of 1995—Rahway State Prison, or the newer and politically correct name, the East Jersey State Prison. Yes, the most segregated prison in the world, yet the best prison in which to work. I initially noticed the separation when I first walked into the 6:20 am line-up. The white officers were standing on the right side and the black officers were on the left. Of course, there were a few sprinkles here and there, but I got the message.

Rahway's culture was nothing like that of Annadale. The Rahway staff was from all over the state, and the inmates were older and more knowledgeable when it came to coping with prison society or "jailin'". Annadale's staff was a family affair. Nearly all of the officers and clerical personnel seemed to live in or near Phillipsburg (P-Burg), NJ or Easton, PA, and those yahoos specialized in marrying each other's ex-wives. Literally. "Desperate Housewives" couldn't hold a torch to what went on at the jail. For example, "Apgar" was a familiar last name at Annadale. There were uncles, cousins, in-laws, ex-wives, puppies, asteroids; you name it, all with the same last name. When they called the name 'Apgar' in the morning line-up, a tribe of those yahoos would yelp "prey-sent".

You surmised that Annadale's officers loathed each other by the way they all would talk dirty about each other while inside the officers' dining room and during breaks. However, that was a trap set to snatch any outsiders who dared to comment. Unlike the majority of the Phillipsburg population, the yahoos had a peculiar Hatfield-mentality way of viewing anybody not from the "P-Burg" or Easton areas. Because they respected former heavyweight champion Larry Holmes so much, blacks from that area were partially accepted. The shame of it all was that Phillipsburg was, by all indications, a very nice town.

But those yahoos viewed the Grand Wizard of the KKK as nothing but a nigger with a sheet, because he wasn't from P-Burg or Easton. They didn't let any outsiders, including rednecks, forget that bit of reality. They were all family, and they stuck together tighter than the mob. Even after they married each other's wives.

But it was at Annadale that serendipity crept up and smiled on me. About a month or two after we started working, Frank, Ginger, and I were asked to write down our thoughts about the institution. Nothing serious, just our own personal observations, with the promise that only our training officer, Lieutenant Sandberg, would read it. And so, we all complied. The problem was that nothing in a jail remained private for very long. Once any kind of news or gossip made its way to the prison's Center Command, its spread was dispersed faster than Paul

Revere on a speedy horse. And to set the record straight, men gossip just as much, if not more, than women do.

I wrote something extremely mild, only because I didn't feel like talking to Lt. Sandberg about anything. He was a nice guy, but he had a way of extending a simple, two-second "hello" into a forty-page dissertation. So I wrote,

> *The institution doesn't seem to be that bad. A few*
> *of the senior officers are not that willing to assist you.*
> *However, those that are willing to assist you more than*
> *compensate for those that are not willing to assist. I*
> *have received plenty of direction and I like it here.*
> *(TTE)*

My thinking was that my lieutenant *would* read it, yawn, and go on to either Ginger's or Frank's insights for his thesis. Man, was I wrong. The very next day, I was the main attraction. I wondered if they thought I had moved to P-Burg and agreed to join their W.E.P. (Wife Exchange Program). However, the logic behind their elation became obvious.

My letter to the lieutenant was passed around the prison the way a group of high-school seniors passed around the Chronic. *Puff-puff-give.* My memo had been rolled into a giant marijuana cigarette and every one of those yahoos was stoned, fully enjoying the psychedelic trip they got from my comments.

One-by-one, the first-shift officers gleefully expressed to me how much they agreed with what I had written, and gave me kilos of unwelcome advice. One of the supervisors entered my cottage to allow inmates to present their version about pending institutional charges. It was almost a daily occurrence at Annadale.

"You're gonna have a long career in corrections. You've got to ignore them assholes." Sgt. Richardson's admonishment wasn't requested, but I accepted it anyhow.

"Thanks, Sarge. That's seems to be the general comment that I'm getting today." Sgt. Richardson laughed and shook his head.

"And I bet the biggest assholes are warning you to ignore every other asshole, right?" My expression was all that he needed to see. He signed my book and commenced listening to the inmates that lined up to complain about trivial matters.

"Something like that."

"No, Freeman. Exactly like that! If you don't remember anything else, remember this—whatever you write or say will be made public." I nodded. "Let me take care of this gentleman who thinks it's okay to disrespect one of my officers." Sgt. Richardson pulled his ink pen from his uniform shirt pocket and shuffled nearly seven disciplinary charges that were inside of his folder.

"Okay, dick-wad. What do you want to tell me before I find you guilty?" Needless to say, Sgt. Richardson didn't have much sympathy. I learned that whatever you wrote or said in the department would be made public.

As upset as I was over the breach of confidentiality, the situation provided its own silver lining. With all the talk of my memo filling every corner of the jail, I learned that listening to others was an under-appreciated art. Allowing a windbag to rant about with his self-serving advice usually ended with that windbag revealing valuable character information about himself and others.

From my years in the military, I knew that women missed the mark regarding how men stuck together, and about the impetus driving those they considered the strong, silent types. Guys kept information from everyone, even other guys, unless you caught them at their weakest moment. Moreover, the weakest moment had nothing to do with women. A man's weakest moment is when a group of men with a common purpose, a common enemy, or a common goal, find themselves in an area and atmosphere where they're comfortable. That same type of environment at Mountainview hatched some of the best gossip ever.

The guys couldn't help it. Gossip in Mountainview was the highlight of any day, and the best gossip depended on how many laughs, or grunts, were elicited. The white guys, with one exception, gossiped in groups about the deepest and most sensitive matters. That meant that if you stuck around a group of white men, one of them would eventually start talking about his penis size, without anybody asking. The black and Hispanic guys gossiped about other people, but only told on themselves when it came to bedroom conquests.

The exception was Italian guys, who never criticized themselves, but who were irritated by almost anybody and everything else. Everybody was either a jerk, a dick, or a moron to them. They were very entertaining, but they didn't provide much useful information, so I didn't waste my time probing Italians.

Sometimes, you have to go through a mental trough before you find that treasure. Generally, women didn't hang around through the trashy, and sometimes lengthy, filth of the gentlemen's group discussions. Maybe that's why the ladies always believed that men stuck together. Rest assured, nothing could be further from the truth.

I have both heard of and witnessed best friends hang each other with their diatribes, exposing very personal and intimate information time and time again. That kind of "dime-dropping" crossed racial, ethnic, and religious lines. My education at Mountainview would continue to mold my conversations, and alter my responses. I learned my lessons well as I watched how and why others failed, even if I didn't realize that I was being educated.

I requested a transfer to an institution closer to home, Rahway, and it was approved. My transfer to Rahway brought few tears, and an exaggerated sigh of relief. We were told in the academy that our true training would only come from time spent inside major institutions, and there wasn't any jail with the reputation Rahway possessed. I left Annadale expecting the unexpected. And, with that, my education began in earnest.

FOUR

The School of Hard Knocks

Rahway State Prison was renamed the East Jersey State Prison after some of the local residents complained because the city of Rahway was too closely identified with the prison. It may have been only an hour's drive away from Annadale, but their cultures were several millennia apart.

Both institutions dealt with the pendulums of racism, discrimination, and animosity, but Rahway had an X-factor. That factor poignantly epitomized how a prison had to operate—Captain "Cracker Rob" Robinson. If you crossed him, you quickly discovered that he was an Equal Opportunity S.O.B. However, if you pulled your own weight, he proved himself to be your greatest ally.

Cracker Rob made it clear that he was nobody's buddy. His major pet peeve was the mere *thought* that a Rahway cop didn't sprint faster than Carl Lewis to a prison disturbance. It didn't matter what kind of disturbance occurred. An inmate fight, an assault on another officer, or any other kind of an emergency required swift action. When the prison's siren sounded, which happened very often at Rahway, every cop was expected to run *towards* the problem, not from it. And Cracker Rob was right there alongside of you.

Rahway's prison had many different areas where inmates were permitted to enter. Certain areas in the institution were located far from the main rotunda of the prison. One such area, "Down-under", which was at the farthest corner of the prison, had its own Center Control and a mess hall. Unfortunately, the visit hall was also located in the Down-under section, and there was no more sensitive area then the visit hall.

The officers were forced to balance securing convicted felons while safeguarding private civilian visitors. The problems exploded when one of those civilian visitors and one of those inmates were involved in a "domestic" altercation. The problem usually began when the officers' attempt to separate an inmate's baby's-mama, girlfriend, wife, and/or *his* boyfriend (another example of the gay-for-the-stay philosophy) from that particular inmate. It was just a part of a precarious cycle in which the inmate beat the wife/girlfriend/baby's mama/boyfriend, the Officers beat the inmate, and the wife/girlfriend/baby's mama/boyfriend beat the officers who were beating their "misunderstood lover". What a crock! And a no-win situation.

But, there was another reason for our caution. Fights were sometimes staged in an effort to draw our attention away from drugs being passed through mules. The visit program allowed inmates to have physical contact with their visitors. Drug carriers, or mules, would hide drugs in their clothing, rectums, vaginas, you name it. Male mules tape drugs on that small piece of skin between the rectum and the testicles. It was a perfect hiding place because most male officers instinctively resisted touching another man's genitals. Therefore, if a male mule was thought to be homosexual, and who smiled erotically while being searched, success was almost guaranteed in carrying narcotics into the institution.

Nevertheless, our main concern was the safety of the other officers. "Watch their backs." Cracker Rob spoke adamantly about staying vigilant when chaos and violence entered the visit hall. "You've got to see what everybody else missed. That's how we all go home."

Most of the time, nobody was sure if a fight involved only inmates, or if an officer was in need of help. In the back of your mind, you considered that one officer might be responsible for an entire wing or unit, which may have 50 to 80 inmates, and that some areas were extremely secluded.

Response time was critical. It took just a few seconds for a distracted officer to get hit by a combination lock hidden inside of a sock or to be stabbed by a sharpened toothbrush. No matter the situation, whenever the siren sounded, everyone reacted. Every officer had better been en route. Failure to immediately respond resulted in a boisterous visit from Cracker Rob.

Rahway's inmates were, and possibly will always be, much more aggressive that Annadale's inmates. As such, the officers at Rahway were more dependent upon each other for survival. Petty differences melted through the black steel bars as reluctant officers conjured ways to unite against the common threats at the institution.

The officers held all of the keys. But in practice, it was understood that the inmates ran the prison, or at least allowed the officers to run it. At any time, a violent uprising threatened to overrun control of critical areas of the prison. The united culture of the officers at Rahway maintained the control of the institution. Cracker Robinson and Chief Maggi understood that bit of awkward reality better than most, which in turn made Rahway a pleasure to work.

However, with my transfer from Annadale to Rahway came an interesting dilemma. Like Annadale, the senior officers grabbed the best shifts, which meant that the best I could expect was second or third shift with Tuesday and Wednesday as my days off. I was also transferred a couple months prior to the end of my probationary period, which wasn't allowed. However, the only person who paid close attention to that was me, and I wasn't saying a word.

That oversight went unnoticed primarily because my move came in the midst of a mass lateral transfer the department had authorized, which provided some officers the opportunity to move to a prison that was closer to their homes. The group of officers with whom I was transferred had plenty of seniority. Rahway was only a 10 to 15 minute drive from my home, and since it was "assumed" that I had seniority just like the other officers, I was promised first shift! In writing, no less.

Not long after I had been working at Rahway, my lack of seniority and probation status were discovered. I should have been immediately reassigned to second shift, but there was something working in my favor. Neither Annadale's personnel department nor Rahway's personnel department wanted to take credit for such a screw-up. So, I kept my mouth shut and remained at Rahway—on first shift, of course.

That caused some animosity from a few of my disgruntled fellow officers. Corrections was knee-deep in cliques, with every group trying to best the next group. Officer Godown, pronounced "Go-Down" (yes, that really was his name) was angry because he had more seniority, but was stuck on second shift. Second shift was considered the working shift because the inmates were finished working around four o'clock in the afternoon. Back from their work sites, and not ready to get stuck inside and uncomfortable. In addition, it caused many problems for the second shift officers who were mostly new to the system.

All of the new-jacks were stuck on second shift, whether brand new officers or brand new supervisors. From 2:20pm until 10:20pm, during the time you were *supposed* to spend with your family, you were literally living with convicted felons. What a mind trip.

Officer Godown complained regularly to his buddies, or those that he thought were his buddies, that there was a new-jack with first shift hours. The fact that personnel couldn't (or wouldn't) do anything about it gave him hives. Godown was close to the assignment supervisor, Lt. Brown, who was in charge of Operations. She viewed herself as a god because operations assigned work areas as well as overtime. The games began.

Remember, I had no seniority, so I had no permanent spot, which meant I could be placed anywhere as long as it was on first shift. One day I would start at about 5:00 am, and the next day I wouldn't start until 11:30 am. I would be assigned to the kitchen one day and to special assignment the next. And, like clockwork, whenever there was an irritating assignment, Sgt. Tarsa would call me over the radio, "749 to Freeman...report to the star, ASAP!"

The star was the main entry gate inside the prison located outside the huge Center Control rotunda. The manpower supervisor's podium was decorated with a prominent star. As soon as I got there, I noticed his smirk.

"Freeman. I need you to inspect the tunnels." Jerk-off! As he handed me the tunnel keys, he rubbed in the idea of that hated inspection.

"Suit up, Freeman. Full gear! You never know what might be down there." The Star-sergeant and his brown-nosing cronies would giggle, as I had to put on full riot gear, including baton and helmet. The tunnels under the jail were dark, wet, dingy, hot, and had plenty of rats. Not regular rats, jail rats. Big ol' pack-rats that would put fear in the heart *The Lion King*'s Mufasa.

After returning the keys, the fun for him would just be starting.

"Hey, Freeman. Watch the thugs take out the trash." Another set of keys and more rats. Anywhere you found food inside a jail, you got rats for tenants. The garbage reeked something fierce, sour milk and all. But those kitchen rats were so well fed that they often just sat there and laughed at me as I tried to scare them. "Yah! Yah! Get out of here! Yah!"

After I returned from the kitchen trash area, I would have

to relieve the sergeant's friends from their posts so they could take care of "personal" things. All of that was seen as paying my dues. It pissed me off, but I refused to let anybody know that they were getting to me.

Things have a way of working themselves out, if you're patient. You see, Sgt. "T" knew that one of the hardest wings to work was Four-wing, and that's right where either he would stick me or where our Operations Unit would assign me. They got a kick out of it because senior officers never helped new-jacks learn the system. Old timers would delight in seeing new guys get suspended for failing at nearly anything. A suspended new officer meant more overtime. Sick as it was, it made sense. My first time on Four-wing started off as the ultimate di-saster. And somebody was going to get some overtime on me.

That morning, I reported directly to Four-wing to relieve the third-shift officer. He didn't speak to me, except to encour-age me. "You're toast." I shook my head at his prediction, and smiled as honestly and sincerely as a seasoned Jersey politician.

"Appreciate the pep-talk, friend. But if you hurry home, you might be able to catch the milkman climbing out your bed." I watched him as he stared back at me. His mind was revving, but it wasn't in gear.

"Well…" I shrugged my shoulders. "…that's what I heard." I wondered if I was successful in encouraging him as much as he encouraged me.

"Fuck you, rookie." My smile widened to display my teeth. Check and mate.

After our little verbal joust, I picked up my jail keys from the officer's desk and accurately counted all of the inmates on Four-wing. I was relieved that there were no inmates hang-ing from the top of their cells. Suicide by hanging, especially during the third-shift, always had a way of interrupting your morning coffee.

With my first count behind me, I now had to figure out which inmates were to leave at the first call. The morning kitchen workers left the earliest, followed by the shop workers. Inside the control box was a makeshift color-system identifying each. And that was where my problems began.

"Kitchen out, kitchen out." Center Control called for the A.M. kitchen workers before I could figure out which inmates were to be released or how to open their cells. Staring at the labyrinth of switches, I quickly surmised that I was lost. That was when I made a typical new-boot mistake—I listened to an inmate who knew that I was clueless.

The inmate's cell was close enough to my desk area that he could speak to me without yelling.

"Good morning, C-O" Nothing special, just an abbreviation for corrections officers. He was pleasant enough. "You need some help, sir?"

"No thanks." I had to be smooth. "I'm good, dawg." He laughed at me.

"I can tell. But you'd better get A.M. kitchen out, or Lt. Harris gonna be up your ass, Mr. Officer."

"I said I got this, a'ight?"

"Ay, man, I'm just tryin' to look out for a young brother like yourself. The top black switch, all the way to the right s'gonna open the kitchen workers' doors." By then, the kitchen workers were getting into it, taking turns with the insults and adding to the frantic scene.

"Yo man, you gonna make us late!"

"Open the doors, dumb ass."

"Open the gate, bitch!"

"Turn the switch, brain surgeon!"

"Hurry up, ass-wipe!"

With Four-wing right next to the main rotunda, everything I did drew the attention of Center Control as well as quite a few officers.

"Shut up, he's a brother trying to take care of his family." The inmate was working hard to earn my trust. "Relax, black man. I'm gonna take care of you. Go 'head turn it so those brothers could get to work."

I didn't trust inmates, and if I hadn't been in such a panic, I would have remembered my own advice regarding the term "brother". "Brother" usually corresponded with "screwed". But I had to do something. *Click.*

Oh no! *Clang!* Every cell on the entire wing flew open, and out of every cell came every inmate on the wing. Laughing and celebrating at my demise. "Ah, you dumb mother fucker. Didn't your mother tell you not to listen to strangers, bitch? Or was she too busy fucking the milkman, too?"

That's right. Inmates hear everything, and will use it against you at the clang of a cell door.

"Oh yeah! Junior, your ass is fired now!"

There I was, standing behind the gate yelling at them, "Get back in your cells! Now! Everybody! Back in your cells!" My voice was loud, authoritative, firm. And they took notice of me.

"Shut up, you stupid bitch! I'm callin' yo wife, tell her you'll be home early."

"Pack yo' shit, brother, and just walk!"

"Didn't Maggi tell you this a man's jail, boy?"

Now, I'm almost panicked. I was so nervous that I couldn't swallow. The inmates were bringing out clothes and heading to the sinks to start washing them. And although I managed to look confident and composed, I was powerless to stop them.

"Lock in! Right now!" And that's when it happened. Right then, in the midst of all of that turmoil, every inmate on the wing (MY wing)—except for the kitchen workers wearing all white uniforms—scrambled furiously, knocking each other over, fighting to get back into their cells.

I was finally getting the respect I deserved. Those extra push-ups had finally paid off. My command presence had done what most institutions failed to do. Order was restored and I was ready to take a bow.

While basking in the glow of my own omnipotence, I considered the possibility that maybe, just maybe, the glow wasn't coming from my slender pecks. A slight, warm breeze rose over my shoulder and gently passed under my nostrils. The breeze was tainted with the unique scent of somebody's breath who had just smoked an unfiltered cigarette. An undeniable voice, kind of crackling, but extremely authoritative said to me, "Kid, what the fuck are you doing?"

With an expressionless face, I turned to discover just why those inmates ran back into their cells. Cracker Rob had crept up behind me. All of the commotion could have been mistaken as a riot, but Cracker Rob knew there was a simpler explanation. A rookie.

"Good morning, Captain." Kill them with kindness, I was always taught, but Cracker Rob obviously didn't subscribe to that particular school of thought.

"Is this what you call a *good* morning?" If there was ever a question that didn't require an answer, that was it. "What *in* the fuck are you doin'!?" You know, I really hated having profanity directed at me, regardless of whether it was from an inmate or an officer. I also knew when to find a free space on the shelf to plant my pride. Kenny Rogers said it best, "*You've got to know when to hold 'em, and when to fold 'em.*" This was definitely one of those times that I had to swallow my pride and fold.

With a stoic face and a firm voice, I stared him directly in his eyes. "Captain, there's one thing that's for sure. Neither you nor I know what the hell I'm doing." We continued to stare at each other without smiling for a moment, the scowl on his continence unchanged. Unable to hold it any longer, Cracker Rob burst into laughter.

"You got that shit right, kid!" Cracker Rob stepped over to the controls. "Move over, kid." He looked at my nametag. "Freeman, huh?" And with that acknowledgement, he showed me what I had done wrong. He told me how he had worked Four-wing back when he was an officer and gave me a brief history lesson on the wing. It was easy to see that he had a special connection with the wing.

"Call out Jones-ie in 14 if you need anything. He's my people." Inmate Jones was an old timer at Rahway. Everybody called him Snowball. Snowball walked out of his cell with his bedroom slippers on, wiping his eyes.

"What's up Rob?"

"Hey Snowball, show this kid how to run the wing. If he needs anything, get it for him."

"A'ight! You got it, Rob." Just like that? That simple? Yes, just that simple. I just got screwed over by a bunch of inmates, and now, Cracker Rob expected me to let an inmate teach me how to run a wing? My pride took a serious hit.

"Hey Freeman, don't let them bitch-asses punk you." Snowball knew the control panel better than I was comfortable with, but being locked up as long as he had, he was bound to learn something. I couldn't ask more senior officers because they only wanted to see the new officers fail. An inmate explained the running of the jail to me, and forever changed my perception of right and wrong. It made me consider the reason why we do or don't trust. "You got that, Snowball."

FIVE

Rahway: The Real Deal

Profanity was the official dialect of prisons, but it never truly fit me. I didn't think I was better than anybody else because I chose not to use profanity. But I was exposed to a very good sophomore English literature teacher at Science High School, who planted certain philosophies in my consciousness.

Mr. Edward Cunningham, with his dry humor, never dulled his enthusiasm and respect for the power of words. Speaking and writing clearly was mandatory in his classroom. And, the best way to learn how to write and speak was to become an avid reader. It wasn't until I took his class that I developed an admiration for novels and writers, especially Shakespeare.

Reading helped me pay closer attention to my writing. Mr. Cunningham taught me that if your speaking or writing was unclear, then your thinking was unclear. He never accepted the excuse that you knew what you want to say, but you just couldn't put it into words.

Mr. Cunningham also taught me that people use profanity because they lack the ability to adequately express themselves. Profanity was, therefore, the result of a degree of frustration and a lack of self-confidence. Profanity masked a sort of intellectual incompetence. That thinking was strongly embedded in my young mind and I'm glad it remained there.

Rahway taught me many other useful lessons, and I enjoyed working in that environment. I met plenty of excellent officers of all nationalities. That was also where I met my brother, Curtis Cohen. The Bible says, "A friend sticks closer than a brother." It had to have been meant for Curtis and me. He was not very tall in stature, but his character was larger than Goliath. If he ever screwed up, he'd be the first to admit it. Because of that, he remained blameless in the eyes of others and retained his integrity, despite his errors.

Often referred to simply as "the minister", a near riot was averted by his mere presence. Another officer in the main yard was restraining an inmate. A mob of angry on-lookers thought the officer acted too aggressively and immediately surrounded the few officers.

"Minister, what the hell?"

"He made a mistake, a'ight? Walk away." And with that, the incident was over.

But, no matter how much I liked being an officer at Rahway, I knew that I wanted more. Ending my career at the same level at which I began it seemed like a waste. Plus, I had no intention of remaining in Corrections for twenty years. Nobody did. Somehow, the years kept passing, and the comfort level increased. And before they knew it, retirement was just around the corner.

"What the hell you looking at that for?" Kenneth Scott was an officer at Rahway and a friend of Curtis'. He approached me as I read a flier on the message board outside the personnel office. "That shit political. They've already got picked out who they want." The flier was for an opening in the department's Internal Affairs Unit (IA) for the entire state.

"What kind of hours they got? Bankers?" Their pay scale was much higher than ours. Many investigators were chosen for administrative positions, and even if I didn't stay in Corrections for long, it would be nice to have it on my resume.

"You'll never get in, brother." There was that word brother again.

"Shut up, Scott." Tony was an old timer and had advised me to look into IA whenever a position opened. He also knew that Scott had applied numerous times in the past and had been rejected every time, making him bitter. "Yo Freeman, you don't need to stay in this shit-hole. Get that promotion, baby!"

Tony didn't have to convince me much. My mind was already made up. "Yeah. I'm going to give it a shot."

"They don't take brothers." Scott was adamant, and so was Tony.

"What about J.R.?" Tony had a point. James Reynolds was an African American promoted to Principal Investigator in Jamesburg.

"I'm not talkin' 'bout weak punks." Scott turned to me. "You too strong." I shook my head as Scott laughed. "Just look at J.R. and Miggins. Hell, you ever see a dick-licker like Randolph."

"I thought Randolph was decent." Randolph didn't appear to be a brown-noser. But then again, he always grinned around his boss, Chris Hamner.

"Spineless. That's all. No pride." It was somewhat obvious that Scott didn't have a high opinion of Internal Affairs. But I wasn't trying to impress Scott. I wanted an opportunity to branch out and see all that I could see.

"Yeah. Well, I still want in." I copied down the information in my pocket calendar book. "You going to apply?" We both laughed. But our conversation would be revisited in the weeks to come.

In November of 1996, I was selected for the Internal Affairs Unit at Northern State Prison in Newark and nobody resented my promotion more than Scott.

About a week prior to the date I was scheduled to report to Northern State, and a few days before the Christmas holiday, I joined some of the other officers that were on break inside the jail's barbershop.

The cheers went up as I entered. "Watch out y'all! We've got a snitch in here!"

"There *you* go." I shook hands and laughed with them. "Now just tell me where's your stash and I'll be sure to screw you over. Real good!"

"Here it is. I hid mine up my ass! You ready to toss my salad for justice?" Tossed salad referred to Snowball's televised interview in which he described his lover licking maple syrup or grape jelly out of his rectum. Since he was the one who helped me figure out how to run Four-wing, the joke took on more insinuations than it should have. I could barely respond through my laughter.

"I guess I don't need a drug bust as bad as I thought."

"You sure, Free? I mean, we've got some jelly right over here. What'll it be, strawberry or grape?" Everybody wanted to show me how willing they were to hand me my first drug bust. Needless to say, I declined.

"You just look out for Scott." The mood immediately shifted.

"Fuck him." Officer Caruth abruptly curtailed my warning, his Caribbean accent emphasizing his sentiments. He was very upset about the way Scott treated another officer, a former friend, who was recently promoted to sergeant. "Scott good people, but he's got some serious issues. But that's his problem, man, not yours!"

The typical IA jokes resurfaced for a while. Good spirited well-wishing. Until Scott walked in. The mood rapidly evaporated. I had heard about some of the things Scott had said about my promotion, but since I didn't hear them directly from Scott, I ignored the rumors. Nevertheless, some rumors were true, and hurtful.

"What's up?" Scott nodded his head.

"What's up?" I responded in like fashion.

"So I hear you sold out?"

"Sold out? A promotion is selling out?"

"Shit..." Scott forced out a laugh. "...that ain't no promotion." He took a seat in the large chairs where officers would have their boots shined.

Scott's brain tried to jump-start itself with a quiz. "So what if you saw me and Curt doing something, you know." I knew what Scott was hinting, but I didn't want to let him off that easily.

"Something like what?"

"Like something."

"Like what?"

Scott snickered. "C'mon man, you know what the fuck I'm talking 'bout." He adjusted himself in his seat and stretched his shoulders. "You gonna turn me and Curt in?"

He purposely used Curtis' name to test the limits of my close relationship with Curtis, but I wasn't about to start toe tapping around any questions regarding my integrity.

"*Curt* wouldn't put me in that kind of position."

"But what if!" Scott's cool persona had finally cracked. He was angry with me. The idea that somebody else might excel threatened Scott and, therefore, caused him to feel inadequate.

I stared at him, and with an audience listening as if my broker was E.F. Hutton, I responded. "If you're wrong, you're just wrong."

"So, you would tell on your boy." Delighted, Scott's face illuminated with his own brand of self-righteousness, as though his barometer of justice trumped anything else.

"If anybody does dirt around me, I'm telling. No apologies." With those words, my tongue drew a line in the sand, a line that would characterize my entire career in Internal Affairs.

The false humor camouflaging Scott's disgust fell and, for the first time, I was exposed to his true feelings towards anybody that stepped outside of his circle. "You gonna fit in well. Real well." Scott grinned with contempt. "They only take house niggers who kiss their asses and won't bite them."

Scott, me, and other officers ate dinner together, went out together, and even went to Washington D.C. together. He had nothing but positive things to say about me prior to my acceptance into IA. How could my desire to improve myself have affected his perception of me to such a great degree, or was it something else?

"Did I just become a house nigger or was I one all the time?"

"You can't just turn a field nigger into a house nigger overnight. That's like turning a whore into a housewife." Scott's grin was cheaply plastered on his mug, but the laughter refused to echo.

"You wrong, Scott." The other officers chided Scott to no avail.

"Y'all know a Tom when you see one…" I interrupted Scott right there.

"Have you ever read the book, Scott?" I knew that anybody that ever read Uncle Tom's Cabin would have a different opinion of what defined an "Uncle Tom". Scott didn't answer as he strolled out of the barbershop and headed back to his wing. I was again reminded to be careful who I call "friend".

That December I transferred to Northern State Prison's Internal Affairs Unit along with two other investigators, Thaddeus Caldwell and John Antinoro. A pay raise, no more uniforms, and best of all, weekends off. Nice! I had known many of the officers who worked at Northern State either from Corrections' academy or from my youth in Newark, but IA was something completely different.

In Internal Affairs, I learned the true meaning of politics. Right away, I gasped and nearly choked at the way many of the investigators took "ass-kissing", or "A-K", to a whole new level. Most of the A-K's were groveling out of a fear that stemmed from a lack of self-esteem. Intimidation was the cornerstone of IA, and that usually forced compliance.

Some made it look enjoyable and maybe they did enjoy looking spineless. But it was during those times that supervisors were not present that you'd discover who was zooming who. More than 50% of the investigators had ties to Mountainview or P-Burg, and the gossip never ended. In short, IA was a true work of art.

I had no idea that every situation I had encountered thus far in my life would be called upon, and provide guidance for me during the hardship to come. Would I be ready?

SIX

The Riot That Never Was

Northern State's officers were revered across the state as fighters. Other jails would talk trash about Northern, but everyone knew all too well what I witnessed first hand. No inmate would dare to daydream about assaulting an officer at Northern State. If he did, he'd better not only apologize, but check into protective custody and request a transfer out of Northern.

I saw the officers there in a different light. The cops at Northern State rolled hard, but weren't fighters. They definitely had an aggressive mentality, but I could trace the escalation of most of the encounters I witnessed at that time.

Cell searches were normal and were conducted randomly during an officer's regular shift. At other jails, if an inmate refused to follow an order to come out of his cell during random searches, a supervisor would have pled with the inmate, making deals. That type of negotiating would allow the inmate, and all the other inmates who witnessed it, to feel as if he had a choice. Other inmates would copy that behavior and also refuse to exit their cells without some sort of concession from the supervisor.

At Northern State, cops told the inmate to do something one time. Non-compliance would denote that the inmate "got stu-

pid". If the inmate got stupid and refused to exit his cell voluntarily, the officers came in and involuntarily removed him from
the cell. The cops routinely left the inmate with a few *reminders* in order to "encourage" other inmates not to get stupid, too.

I commonly referred to any inmate who cried for Internal
Affairs' help after both acting tough and putting on a show
inside of his cell as a CPA (certified punk ass). Once Northern
State cops received the order to "suit up" with riot gear, negotiations were over. Pop open the cell and watch that CPA start
wailing and whining before the cops got a chance to slam a
shield into his face.

It may have seemed harsh, but they gave the CPA a chance
to come out and the idiot got stupid. So, the way I saw it was
that he'd signed a waiver of decent treatment and filed a request
to get slammed against the concrete.

The morning of May 1, 1997 changed my acceptance of
the way Northern did business. My wife had planned to take
me out to dinner at our favorite restaurant to celebrate my 31st
birthday. Sylvia's, a short ride across the George Washington
Bridge into Harlem. After dinner, we were going to take in a
show at the Beacon Theater in Manhattan.

When I worked an hour away in Annadale, I always arrived
early. Now I was rushing to get to work on time almost every
day. That struggle made no sense in that now I worked less
than five minutes from home. I thought about calling out sick
for the day. I figured that I could relax for a while and do a
little birthday shopping before our date. But, it was a Thursday
and I had planned to call out sick on Friday anyhow.

"I'm going to get my hair done this morning. So if you
call and I'm not here, you'll know where I am." My wife had
to drop off my daughter at Carol Jackson's house. Carol was
a godsend. She watched my daughter and would even counsel
the parents on just about any topic.

"Do you mind if I take out some money?" That was merely
a rhetorical question. I didn't care if she withdrew anything

from our bank account, but as a courtesy, we'd inform each other about any account transactions in order to keep track of our spending.

My wife worked, but I never saw her money and I never knew how much she made. I was making decent money and I didn't spend much on anything, so it didn't seem to matter that much. I was neither naïve nor ignorant. I both loved her and trusted her completely. And that was a beautiful, and foolish, mind-set to have had.

"I'm out of here. Peace." And, just like that, I was headed to work. I arrived at 7:32 am and immediately noticed something was wrong.

"What's up Freeman? You headed to the mess hall?" The officer at the front control booth was hurrying me through.

"What's wrong?" I reached under my jacket, searching, feeling, and trying to decipher what was happening.

"You better go straight through to the mess hall." The officer that controls entry was waving me through in a huge hurry. But I finally felt it. I was still wearing my service weapon, a fully loaded Smith & Wesson 4053 semi-automatic pistol. "Hold up. I gotta go lock up something."

"Well, you better hurry, man."

I sprinted upstairs where I noticed the Internal Affairs door was ajar and nobody was inside. *What in the world is going on?* I ran into the main compound and saw officers scurrying out of the mess hall with inmates in plastic flex-cuffs. A multitude of inmates had their faces against the walls, while even more were laying face down on the ground. Every inmate that I could see was either handcuffed or handcuffed *and* shackled, and bleeding.

There were two mess halls—the north compound and the south compound. I ran into the north compound mess hall and saw the remnants of what used to be order. Later, I discovered that the south compound mess hall mirrored the view inside the north compound. The floors were completely covered with garbage—food, fluids, serving trays, clothing, you name it.

Sgt. Frankie James was the only one not slipping on the refuse. He was walking through the mess hall holding two football-sized canisters of mace, pointing them at the inmates that were still in the mess hall, standing facing the walls. His sole mission was to protect the officers that were securing the area.

An officer went unnoticed as he staggered near the center of the mess hall. Rubbing his forehead, recalling how several inmates trapped him only moments earlier. *Thump!* An inmate hit the ground after a fierce punch from that same officer, retaliation and revenge, justified and wrong.

"Stand him up!" The handcuffed inmate's arm was suspended in the air as his face was glued to the concrete floor. "Cut that shit out, and get him out of here!" The supervisors knew their first responsibility was to restore order, which meant that certain activities received a mere wink of rebuke.

It was clear that there were going to be some real problems. Edwin Melendez, my supervisor, knew what everybody else knew—we had a mess on our hands. "Freeman, there's nobody down in Administrative-Segregation. Get down there, and don't leave for *any* reason. Reyes only had a busted lip. Watch him!" Reyes[2] was one of the main conspirators in the riot and would be identified by the officers as such. However, Edwin had another reason to worry about the extent of the chaos.

The day before, a couple of inmates were locked up for running their mouths off to some officers. One was ordered to turn around so that he could be handcuffed, but the inmate told the officers he was not going to be locked up in the segregation unit. But that wasn't the way it worked at Northern State. The officers body-slammed the inmate and carried him to the segregation unit. Some of the inmates thought that the officers should have tried negotiating with the inmate, and some of the inmate's friends wanted to get back at those particular officers.

---

2 The name has been changed.

The problem was that those officers had worked the second shift, and the first shift officers had no clue about what had happened the previous day. They were caught completely off guard, but Internal Affairs wasn't caught off guard.

The life and strength of Internal Affairs was our ability to gather information about events before they occurred, often from disreputable sources. We even had a telephone line, the "Rat Phone", specifically for those confidential informants, our snitches or "rats", to contact us directly and provide such information. The Rat Phone was located in the main area of Internal Affairs.

A snitch had called the Rat Phone soon after the first plans of the melee were set. He notified one of our investigators that the Latin Kings were planning to catch as many officers as they could during the morning mess movement.

The Kings were very organized, which also made them highly predictable. First, the observation: ensure that all targets are blocked from exiting the attack zone. Second, the distraction: ensure that all targets are preoccupied, thereby limiting their ability to respond to the attack. Third, the attack: ensure that the attack is swift, quick, and multi-directional, coming from many angles simultaneously.

We received many bogus tips from our snitches, but Robert "Bob" Karkoska always took them seriously. Bob was good people, but just a little too gung-ho for most folks. Once, Bob set up his own sting operation in the visitor's area. He was the only Caucasian visitor and wore dark Blues Brothers shades, tight Bruce Springsteen faded jeans, and a John Deere baseball cap, all the while peering through two eyeholes in his upside-down newspaper. The visit officers couldn't take any more after Bob forgot that his handcuff key was still on his key ring as he passed through the metal detector.

Nevertheless, Bob knew it was important to relay any information that threatened the safety of officers to Center Control so that they could check it out. Edwin didn't like Bob because

Bob made Edwin work, and because Bob did a lot of silly things, too. Edwin sat on that information and conveniently *forgot* to notify the prison's Center Control of the potential danger.

Sometimes, Edwin would disconnect the Rat Phone because he didn't like to hear it ring, or so he would say. Edwin's favorite reply to why the Rat Phone was turned off was "fuck em", regardless of what kind of information could have been learned or life saved. God forbid an informant dropped a "note" to IA. Edwin would take it from you and send it through the "inmate fax machine", a huge shredding machine he used to destroy critical evidence and other documents on a regular basis. It was so common that it almost became a daily joke with him. Edwin believed we were too busy doing other things, and that those notes and requests would only make more work for us.

"Them bitches shouldn't have got locked up!" Edwin destroyed a lot of vitally sensitive information and evidence, but we were IA and nobody dared question us. As for me, I was getting a crash course on just how Internal Affairs rolled and why the good officers, as well as the bad, despised us. With Edwin at the helm of our unit, their loathing was better than justified.

The first shift officers reported to their regular areas without a clue as to what awaited them. They didn't notice how Stage 1 was unfolding. Several inmates, cups in hand, casually strolled over to the milk dispenser near the center of the hall. The inmates discreetly positioned throughout the mess hall, effectively blocking any escape routes.

Then came Stage 2. A fight broke out in one of the corners of the north compound mess hall between two inmates. It appeared as if the altercation was the result of a dispute over positioning in the food line. Maybe somebody tried to cut in front of somebody else. The officers reacted as they were trained to, and focused on the fight. They charged towards that area in an effort to regain order.

Finally, it was time for Stage 3. While the officers' attention was elsewhere, the inmates unleashed their fury. The cops were significantly outnumbered, effectively out positioned, and betrayed by Internal Affairs. Officers were beaten unmercifully. Inmates wearing work boots stomped and kicked the officers that were down, and makeshift weapons materialized out of the inmates' pockets.

But you've got to remember that Northern State officers were, without a doubt, a cut above the rest when it came to heightened situations. One, Officer High, was in the south compound mess hall when the riot simultaneously broke out there.

Due to budget cuts, only a limited response team was available. That team ran to help the officers in the north compound, leaving Officer High to fend for himself among an angry mob of convicted felons. The videotape of Officer High as he defended himself against every inmate that charged him was something right out of a Wesley Snipes movie, except High had no stunt doubles.

With both fists clinched, he gave every inmate that tried to assault him a memento. As multiple inmates charged Officer High, he was skilled enough to thump them back. He never went down and he never tried to run out of the hall. With a constant stutter-step, Officer High stood his ground, and soon, the inmates backed off. Numbers meant nothing inside the south compound mess hall that morning.

However, the north compound was not as fortunate. The inmates charged the officers and beat them at will. Most of them never found out IA knew about the threat until much later, and Edwin's denial only created more unsubstantiated rumors.

I grabbed a video camera and sprinted towards the Segregation Unit, which was in the rear-portion of the entire prison complex. Reyes wasn't one of the main players in the Latin Kings, but he was about to be famous.

As ordered, I hurried, but I had to get through the sentry-controlled gate that stood between where I was and where I wanted to be. The officers controlling the gate were extra slow at *finding* the correct switch to open that gate to let me pass through. The delay was considerably prolonged, but I kind of expected that.

The switch was finally *discovered*, and I ran onto Three-wing, where inmate Reyes should have been held.

"Where's Reyes?" The officers were clearly irritated both by what the inmates had done to other officers and the fact that IA appeared to be more concerned about the welfare of a convicted felon than the welfare of another officer.

That perception had plenty of merit. I mean, I wasn't rushing to take any videotape of the injuries the officers sustained. I *was* rushing to protect a thug, who had just carried out a hit on several officers. In the eyes of the cops, I was lower than dirt.

Where's Reyes? was my first question, and there was no second question. I never asked how they were holding up during such a difficult time. Nor did I ask if they had any news regarding the injured officers. Reyes was my only concern.

"What's his number, Mister Freeman?" I knew what the officer was trying to do, but I didn't loose focus.

"Where's Reyes?"

Their stares got longer. Their movements were extremely deliberate. The three officers faced each other.

"Check the infirmary..." *The hospital! Why?* I guess I already knew why.

"Right." I ran from Three-wing over to the Ad-Seg infirmary, which was only about 80 to 100 feet away. Before I could get in the door, I spotted Reyes sitting on the ground, leaning against the red brick building. I was too late. Much too late.

Reyes was still handcuffed and his face was barely recognizable. Blood covered his skull, his face, and his neck. I was able to find minute spots of white on his T-shirt, but there weren't many of them. Blood was everywhere. His breathing was shallow, his eyes were unresponsive, and he was barely audible when answering my questions.

"Reyes! Reyes! Reyes!!" I really didn't have to interview the officers about what happened to him. I was sure they would tell me how hard he fell, or how much he "resisted", or how he "attacked" them, and that they were just "defending" themselves.

"Reyes!!! We're going to get you some help. Hang in there." I reassured him and, in effect, put the officers on notice.

The looks on the officers' faces were of total disgust as they watched me reassure that convicted felon. However, I really didn't care at that point. I despised what had happened to Reyes just as much as I despised what happened to those officers inside the mess halls. Wrong was still wrong. I didn't care what explanation or justification anybody gave.

I got Edwin on the telephone. "Hey Ed. Reyes is busted up something bad."

Edwin was hyper, always on edge, always worried about some ghost in his closet, and ready to explode at the slightest provocation.

"I knew them punk bitches would do that! Stay with him. I'm sending you some help now." While all of this was happening, inmates were still colliding into walls and falling facefirst onto the concrete, handcuffed and escorted. I wanted to say they deserved it. But that would make me worse than either the inmates or the officers.

Reyes' condition was too severe for the infirmary to treat. He had to be sent to a state trauma center. Two officers escorted Reyes to the University of Medicine and Dentistry of New Jersey (UMDNJ), located in downtown Newark. The medical center was renowned for having a state-of-the-art Intensive Care for trauma patients. I was ordered to stay with Reyes all the way, videotaping everything.

It was about that time that IA received a visit from Mr. Morton, a Director in the Department of Corrections. Renowned as the "decisive" Administrator at "The Big House" (Trenton State

Prison) for many years before being promoted to his director position, he was the Commissioner's right-hand man.

Mr. Morton, accompanied by other superintendents and department bigwigs, wanted to view the videotapes of the riot in preparation for a press conference scheduled to be held in the main lobby of the prison.

The suits assembled in Edwin's office at the rear of the IA unit to view the tape. One of the first things they watched was the way Officer High defended himself against insurmountable odds.

"Who's that?" Mr. Morton's face showed his pleasure in the cop's performance.

"These guys are fighters, sir." Edwin never let an A-K opportunity pass without puckering his crusty lips and aiming low. "That's Officer High, sir. He's one of our best."

The mood turned sullen, almost vengeful, echoing their dismay at how other officers were trampled at the will of angry convicts. The complete disregard for order had visibly infuriated the suits and would not be allowed to go unpunished.

But that wasn't all that they viewed. The tape continued to roll, and the evidence of officers' vengeance against the inmates came on screen. The suits watched as a handcuffed inmate, who was being escorted by two officers after order was regained, was sucker-punched by another officer. Another scene showed handcuffed inmates slammed face-first into cement walls.

"Turn it off!" Mr. Morton sat stoically. He had just witnessed inmates violating rules, regulations, and the law. He also witnessed officers violating rules, regulations, and the law. What a paradox. But not for Mr. Morton. Based on all of his accolades, he was surely an upright man. A man of integrity and conscience. Somebody not afraid to make the right decision, even when what was right was least popular. And that decision was clear. Black and white. Or, at least, that was what I was always lead to believe.

Morton rose from his seat, buttoning his jacket as he cleared his throat. "The officers were justified in all their actions." He brushed off his sleeve and turned to one of his assistants. "I didn't see anything that they did wrong." What videotape was he watching?

Integrity? Conscience? Clear? Crystal clear! In Corrections, nobody would dare cross the director and expect to remain employed. Corrections would not only fire you, but they would prevent you from working for anybody else through a campaign of degradation and slander.

The other suits didn't blink at his decision, and some voiced their agreement. "They had no choice, sir." They nodded like a half-dozen bobble-head dolls.

Word spread quickly throughout the prison and, of the many incidents regarding the officers' lack of restraint, not one officer was disciplined. Edwin made it clear that Chief Debbe Faunce didn't want any investigations regarding the officers' conduct. In the days that followed, all cases were closed before they had a chance to be opened. The inmate fax shredded yards of complaints regarding the aftermath of the riot as well as later incidents of retaliation.

The press conference was nothing more than a photo opportunity, producing more propaganda about the great job the State of New Jersey was doing. Because of the riot, nobody really asked any questions. The rule was trumpet how officers were harmed by convicts and embrace the public's sympathy.

There were essentially two riots that morning, but only one made the newspapers—a situation that would be repeated at other prisons. Bayside State Prison, headed by Debbe Faunce's husband, Scott, went one step further. The stabbing death of an officer by a lone inmate was the catalyst for ramped-up, indiscriminate beatings of inmates by the department's Special Operations Unit, which were taped. The beatings were so severe that an investigation had to be conducted in order to protect the state from litigation. Debbe headed the investigation of her husband.

The department claimed that no conflict of interest existed. Some of the tapes were edited, while others simply disappeared. Of course, the inmates' injuries were attributed to "resistance" and "furtive" movements made towards officers. Debbe never worried, especially considering the type of things that you can get away with when your defense counsel is the Attorney General's Office.

SEVEN

Take It Like a Man (Teth)

I was not in denial about Mr. Morton's politics. It kind of reminded me of what Gunnery Sergeant McCann told me when I was stationed at the Marine Command Air Station located in Cherry Point, North Carolina. Gunny Mac hated stupidity, and so did I. But there was a huge difference between the two of us. Gunny had all the stripes, so Gunny had all of the say. I was just a corporal at the time.

Gunny Mac made it clear that nobody was to discipline his Marines, except for Gunny himself. He was able to block a Colonel from disciplining one of us by "taking the hit" himself. That was just part of why Gunny commanded so much respect throughout our unit, and part of why you kept your mouth shut when Gunny spoke.

Gunny rarely got upset or yelled. It was also rare that Gunny got pissed at any of us. He may have seemed very serious, but after working with him for some time, you eventually figured out his peculiar sense of humor. When Gunny *was* pissed, he'd holler and yell until your ear wilted from the excess volume as occasional trickles of saliva encroached upon your brow, narrowly missing the corners of your mouth. As disgusting as that was, it was not the only reason to keep your mouth shut during a tongue-lashing.

I never had a problem with Gunny Mac, and he would talk to me from time to time about my goals. He'd tell me how to make the Marine Corps love you and how to make the Corps hate you.

"Free, the Corps is real proud of herself. She loves her image." Gunny thought of the Marine Corps as a hot woman with PMS-on-demand.

"Whatever you do wrong, never embarrass her." And it really was that simple. Many died in order to give the Marine Corps the reputation she had, and she wouldn't take too kindly to anybody tarnishing her name.

"I don't care who you kill, who you fuck, or where you shit. Just don't bring the Corps' name into it, and you'll have a great career."

I served for six years and watched a change in attitudes beginning with my first tour of duty. It started in Japan and my final tour of duty ended in West Germany.

When I started, they encouraged us to cause some trouble. "If you don't get drunk and raise a little hell," the old-timers would say, "then you ain't a Marine!" But by the time I was discharged, if you had a single beer in the Enlisted Men's Club, they would order you to go to Alcoholic's Anonymous. Nevertheless, no matter what she endured, the Corps' pride remained awesome.

I heeded Gunny's advice, and went out of my way not to embarrass the Marine Corps. But the Marine Corps had a lust for integrity that distinguished her from any other organization in the world. That lust was the catalyst that launched a hundred investigations into the exploits of Marines who may have violated Corps standards. The Marine Corps will always retain the grand title of "The Finest".

Gunny's message was clear. Like the Marine Corps, the Department of Corrections had high-ranking individuals that would face a firing squad before they would admit that their employer had the kind of flaws that force structural changes to be made. Minor embarrassments threatened to expose larger deficiencies.

Nevertheless, politics are politics, and every organization has its own brand, but what I was witnessing in Corrections was completely different because Corrections had no integrity. There was no conscience to limit or guide the actions of individuals within the department, only the arrogance associated with power, nepotism and political favors. Those individuals with the ability to facilitate change were not interested. Their smug "this is how we do things here" mentality, culture of intimidation, and lack of any uniformly enforced standards fostered helplessness among the rank-and-file.

Mr. Morton was dead wrong. And nobody wanted to even discuss what had happened. I spoke about the incident to Edwin on occasion, only to hear him joke about it.

"Them punks got what they deserved." Then he deployed a transparent defense tactic. Attack the dissenter. "What are you, a damn social worker?" This was my supervisor who was supposed to teach me how to be a true investigator.

Edwin hammered me with that type of hostility day-in and day-out partly because I spent so much time on the telephone. But that wasn't what he was really angry about. Edwin wanted to make me pay for having a conversation with "Chicky", his woman, and because she enjoyed our conversation more than he thought she should have.

Stop there. It really was just conversation. Well, maybe she and I acted as if it was more than just conversation, but Edwin was also upset because of a comment I made. Our secretary told me how small Edwin's dick was. Edwin had picked on me all morning, and I finally struck back. During a moment when Edwin was bragging about his sexual prowess, I informed him that a "confidential informant" had provided information that would differ significantly from what he claimed.

"Well Ed, an eye witness with a magnifying lens told me you're able to piss on your own balls." Edwin wasn't laughing, but I sure was. "But in your defense, my "informant" was only able to judge the evidence for about eleven seconds, eleven *tiny* seconds."

His eyes asked, *"Which one told you?"* But I didn't answer as I watched the blood rush to his face, and that single vein in the center of his forehead began to throb.

Well, Melendez didn't take my comments kindly, and I would pay the full price for that swipe. I wasn't upset by it all because I figured between the phone calls and the "small" remarks I made, it was reasonable to assume I'd bought my torture from Edwin.

I apologized for my remarks, but the culture of IA always punished and made examples of individuals that weren't A-K's. The only brown on my nose came from birth, and not another man's rectum.

Everything I did was harshly scrutinized and, during the summer and fall of 1997, I paid dearly. Thaddeus Caldwell and John Antinoro were both promoted to Investigator at the time I was promoted, but TC and John went to the academy in the class ahead of me. That left only seven investigators in our unit to carry the workload at Northern State, which was the busiest jail in New Jersey.

That September, I carried over fifty percent of the investigations that came into the office. The criticisms escalated to the point that Edwin would humiliate me in the presence of my peers. As I said before, I refused to say much because I knew what I was getting into before pissing him off. That was about to change.

Until then my reports were never questioned and nothing else Edwin had done appeared to outwardly faze me. I was affected, but I was determined not to let Edwin know the effect of his tactics. That's when he began hammering my reports.

Every report I submitted for his approval was rejected.

When it came to writing, I have always been my own worst critic. I hated for anyone to tell me about a mistake in anything I wrote. I hunted for my own mistakes because anything I wrote became my ambassador. Mr. Cunningham told us that words are power and they are permanent. Therefore, regardless of whether it was an investigation report, a statement, or my private poetry, I strove for perfection. Edwin quickly became my worst critic and I took his attacks on my written reports personally. Very personally.

One day after I returned from interviewing an inmate in the Segregation Unit, my secretary stopped me. "Don't get mad, Kenny."

I sighed heavily. "Oh boy, what did Ed do now?" I had become accustomed to him doing stupid things, trying to anger me. Everybody in our office was well aware of what was going on, but nobody excluding Pamela Trent said anything above a mumble. After reviewing my latest report, and Edwin's comments written in red, she confronted him.

"Now Ed, you know that's not right." Edwin would just laugh and go back into his office. "Keep your head up, Kenny."

"I'm good, Pam. Thanks." I shrugged it off, but the game had passed irritating.

She handed my latest report to me, wincing. She knew my writing was fine, but she also knew how devious Edwin could be. His comments were not only unprofessional, but mean spirited. At least they were to me. I marched directly into his office without knocking.

"Ed, what's wrong with this [report]?" He was sitting at his desk reading another report I had submitted.

"That shit is sloppy." He grinned and kept his head down.

"What's sloppy about it?"

"All of that shit is sloppy."

I was composed and searching for a way to put him on the spot. "Could you be more specific, Ed." Edwin looked up at me and laughed.

"I'm serious. Show me exactly what's wrong with it." I knew he couldn't. Edwin was just using phrases without any particular meaning behind them. That's how people criticize when they don't have anything real to say. They use buzzwords to avoid providing a basis for the criticism.

"I don't have time for babysitting your ass. Ask Mike to help you. Both of y'all can go cry together."

Edwin was angry with Michael Chando because Mike was getting a transfer out of Northern State to work with the Fugitive Squad. Mike was an avid reader, and his writing showed. I liked talking to Mike about books and writing. It was Mike and Pam who I looked to for advice on investigations and reports when I joined IA. But this was different. As I walked out of Edwin's office, I handed the report to Pam.

"Kenny, nothing's wrong with this report."

"I know."

Mike came out of his office and walked into the general area of the unit. "What? Ed again?"

Pam nodded and responded. "Jerk!"

Mike was done with Edwin. "What's his problem now? You said 'hello' to *Chicky* or something? I told you, Kenny, just fuck her and get it over. Ed's little Johnson probably couldn't make it past her lips!" Mike laughed, but I didn't. And neither did Pam.

"Mike, you're not helping!"

"Oops! My bad, Pam!"

"This is so messed up." Pam was more disgusted than I was.

"No shit." Mike reflected on his own predicament. "That's why I'm getting the fuck out of here!"

I listened to both Pam's and Mike's analysis of my dilemma, and answered with my trademark response.

"No problem." Typical to Corrections, and especially IA, Edwin was so arrogant that he was like a thoroughbred with blinders. It wasn't that he was stupid, but his anger overruled his intelligence every single time. I walked to the file cabinet and started searching.

Pam got a bit nervous. "Kenny, don't do anything stupid. Kenny! What are you doing?"

"Just sit back, and watch the show." I smiled at Pam to try to calm her. She was good people and in the awkward position of trying to account for the money that Edwin stole from the evidence locker—a move that eventually got Edwin transferred from Northern State to the Equal Employment Division months later.

Mike knew something good was in the works. "Oh God! I got to see this." He laughed and ran to one of the open seats.

"Not yet, Mike." I closed the file cabinet and returned to my desk. "I'll tell you when it's time. You won't miss a thing. I promise."

The type of investigation report Edwin had marked up was a typical protective custody report. Nothing stood out in this report and there was nothing peculiar about the inmate. Investigators had completed these types of reports for years and that was exactly what I was counting on.

Edwin had been an investigator at Northern State before being promoted to Principal Investigator. He had worked under William "Bill" Blake and was rewarded with the position partly because of some malicious politics against Blake, who was a very nice guy. Some say a little too nice for his own good.

Chief Faunce hated Blake because when he initially formed our union, he prevented Faunce from joining. A chief and her subordinates in the same union? Unheard of anywhere, and Blake was correct in blocking her. However, that wasn't how Faunce saw it, and she took Blake's stance against her sovereignty as a personal attack.

Ironic that when Blake needed the membership of the union he had formed to stand beside him, the membership demonstrated why one is the loneliest number. Between the cowardly, the incompetent, and the outright corrupt investigators in I.A.,

Debbe had her own handpicked lynch mob, ready to carry out a campaign against him.

Edwin didn't need any additional motivation to hang Blake. Blake attempted to discipline Melendez for conducting "desk interviews" with inmates in the Segregation Unit. Actually, Edwin would disappear during the workday for an hour or more with Chicky. They would go to the Holiday Inn, which was located within a rock's throw of the prison. When he returned, Edwin would write an official report, documenting the "interviews" of inmates and officers he never saw. Edwin normally indicated a conclusion of "no finding", claiming that the inmates either refused to provide a written statement or outright declined to be interviewed.

So it was no strange thing when Faunce had Edwin and the other investigators gather incriminating evidence against Blake. She boldly held a meeting and informed them that the goal was to terminate Blake, even if the evidence was false. Faunce wasn't stupid, but her arrogance made her bold. Out of nine investigators, only two opposed the chief; John "Jack" Dale and Lawrence Sapp. The other investigators, especially Edwin, agreed whole-heartedly to the setup.

I was certain that one of Edwin's desk interviews involved a protective custody investigation. However, just finding a PC report from Edwin wasn't enough. I had to get one where he lied about interviewing cops and I found one signed by Senior Investigator Edwin Melendez. It was written a year and a half before he was promoted to Principal Investigator.

"Perfect." I glanced up at Pam.

"You are bad." Not bad meaning bad, but bad meaning good.

I copied his report verbatim, only replacing his name for mine, his inmate for my inmate, and his dates for my dates. Everything else was exactly the same. By the time I finished writing the report, the area was full of activity, and Mike was smiling.

I walked into Edwin's office. "Ed, here's that report, again." I shook my head as if I were exhausted from the task of re-writing the report.

"If you find something wrong with it, let me know, alright?" As I turned to walk out of his office, Edwin immediately put down the other reports, picked up a red pen, and started slashing mine.

"What happened?" Pam was whispering to me as she normally did.

I softly put my finger to my lips. "Shhhh." Now Mike was really grinning. Waiting. Anticipating. The other investigators were still talking and really had no idea what was happening. And, like Ol' Faithful, Edwin erupted!

He stomped towards my work area and slammed the report on my desk. Barrels of bright red ink were bleeding through my report, full of critical comments. The word "shit" was written across the top of my report—his professional evaluation of my competence.

I lifted the paper high as I leaned back in my swivel chair. "What's the problem, Ed?"

"That's the worst fuckin' report that I ever read." If you give an idiot a noose, he'll put it on his own neck and hang himself.

"Could you please be a bit more specific?" I figured since Edwin was describing himself, why not allow him to elaborate.

"That report is shit! Is that specific enough?" I sat quietly and just waited for a pause in his tirade.

"None of your sentences make any sense. It sounds like a retarded first-grader wrote this."

I snickered slightly, then quickly regained my composure. "A first-grader, Ed?"

"Retarded first-grader."

"Well, you're the boss. Any advice about what should I do?"

"Quit!"

"Quit?"

"Fuck yeah! You should quit and just go home! Anybody who writes like that shouldn't have a fuckin' job, especially not in IA."

It was time to tighten the noose. I removed my template from my desk drawer and handed it to him in the presence of the same crowd in front of which he just finished undressing me.

"That's not my report, Ed. That's your report. I just copied it...verbatim."

Edwin looked like Scott Peterson when he learned that Amber Frey would testify against him. After a brief pause, he picked up the report and starred at the report with a more compassionate disposition. Edwin looked around the room and noticed Mike's head about to explode. At that point, words weren't necessary. Edwin slowly walked back into his office, with me following. This was my chance to really rub it in his face. However, I knew I would still have to work under him and I only wanted the nonsense to end.

"Get off my back, Ed. I said I was sorry. I've been doing my work, staying off the phone, and I don't even say 'hello' to Chicky." I never complained about my workload, which was much larger than the other investigators, and he knew it. "Leave my reports alone."

Edwin handed back my report. "It's good." His red-ink evaluation of my report was scratched out. "Go ahead and send it out."

Later that day, he justified himself by claiming that my case load was heavy because investigator Karkoska was under investigation by Central Office for comments he made about an officer arrested in a drug sting, Pam and Mike were busy trying to account for the unit's evidence, Cicale was extremely lazy, and Scott Russo, although an accomplished A-K, was incompetent in every other area and couldn't be trusted to tie his own shoes. It would be nice to say that Edwin and I got along fine after that, but years later, I found out that you can't teach an old dog new tricks. A hound is a hound. In the meantime, Edwin never questioned my investigations unfairly.

EIGHT

No Good Deed Goes Unpunished

In one of the many investigations I conducted, a name appeared on my protective custody reports in the summer of 1997, which caused a great stir at our headquarters and with the Federal Bureau of Investigations. That inmate's name would never be anonymous again. Muhammad Aburami was Northern State Prison Internal Affairs' most productive confidential informant, or "snitch". We had a lot of practice learning how to manipulate informants without ourselves being manipulated, or "worked", by the informant. I had never worked Aburami, but Bob did. He worked Aburami well in many cases. The proof of Bob's work was evidenced by all the recorded hits, two huge files of drug confiscations and other references, filed in our office.

Aburami was extremely apt at getting close to other inmates, then finding out when, where, and how drugs would enter the prison. On those occasions when Edwin did not unplug the Rat Phone, Bob would get a hit from Aburami informing him of where to find a stash.

Bob was awkward, a bit unpolished, and kind of unconventional, but he worked extremely hard. He suffered from what

IA considered a dangerous, and sometimes fatal, disease—not being a Team player. Bob was honest, and that type of defect would draw deceitful accusations against him.

I was assigned Aburami in August of 1997. I looked up his name in the case file and immediately saw Bob's name on previous records. Bob had recently finished a protective custody case on Aburami, also. Bob concluded that protective custody wasn't necessary for Aburami, but he gave little explanation as to why.

I went to Bob to get as much information on Aburami as I could before I interviewed the snitch in the Segregation unit. Bob was sitting in an office he shared with John Antinoro. Together, that odd-couple spelled drama in four different languages.

"Hey, Bob, what's up with this guy?" I handed Bob the letter from Aburami. "He dropped a note, claiming that he's our snitch."

Bob was sitting in his chair, searching incoming inmate mail for contraband. He had brought his own personal chair into the office because he thought it was more majestic and it played into his self-anointed stardom. He had ordained himself "his royal fly-ness". Bob leaned back in his chair and started laughing, never looking up.

"Claimed?" Bob spoke slowly, trying to add bass to his soprano voice. "He was my main bitch!" There was nothing worse than a Catholic schoolboy trying to be a thug. He reminded me of Jamie Kennedy in *Malibu's Most Wanted*.

"Speak English, dumb-ass." Antinoro shook his head, having continually endured Bob's tirades. I laughed at them and their often-hostile interactions, but Antinoro was definitely irritated. "You ain't no brother."

Bob was a constant reminder that it was better to be silent and to be thought of as a fool then to open your mouth and remove all doubt. "Double negatives, dick-wad. Don't use no double negatives."

"Shut up and help the man." Antinoro shook his head and continued searching mail headed to the inmates in the Gang Unit.

Bob swiveled his chair around to me and sprung to his feet. "Come here, junior. Look at how the pros do things."

His royal fly-ness opened himself up to ruthless jokes because of his many flops. And Antinoro was normally waiting in the wings. "If that's how the pros do it, how did you find out?"

"I schooled you, didn't I?"

"Schooled me on what!"

"I schooled you and Thaddeus down there at your first autopsy! Both y'all asses were lost!"

"Oh yeah!" Antinoro could barely keep from laughing. "That's when you coughed up your guts as soon as they started cutting."

Antinoro and Bob were put into the same office because of Edwin's crude humor, sort of a way to chastise both of them. They were the quintessential boiling oil and ice water; they just didn't get along.

"Bob, the files?" The files were the last thing on his mind, keeping his attention on John.

"What about Ad-Seg?"

"What *about* Ad-Seg?"

"Don't play dumb, bitch. The cops called us and told us about how you tried to videotape an inmate fight without a battery or a videotape!"

"They exaggerated!"

"Exaggerated? Then where's the tape?" Antinoro returned to the mail without a whimper. "The fuckin' cop had to ask you why the red light wasn't on, you stupid bitch!"

"Stupid?" Antinoro dropped the nude photos somebody sent to an inmate and returned to the battle. "What about your solo-sting operation?"

For the next few minutes, Bob and Antinoro argued like a bitter married couple.

"If you ladies are through, maybe royalty wouldn't mind giving me the pro's perspective?"

Bob pulled himself from the banter. "C'mon, junior. Check out my skills."

But Antinoro wasn't done. "Skills! What skills, you ..."

"John, give it a rest." I really wanted to get out of there as soon as possible. They would argue all night or at least until four o'clock if I didn't stop them.

Bob handed me the first of two very large files. Dates, times, names, everything. Aburami had been assigned a confidential informant's number so we could monitor his activities. There was ample documentation of every hit for which Aburami supplied information. The second file just got better.

"He wants a transfer, junior. He's a pain in the ass." Bob was only one or two years older, but he insisted on calling me junior because I looked so much younger.

I took his files to my desk and poured through them. I also checked Aburami's information on the NCIC (National Crime Information Center) printout. NCIC was the NJ State Police computer system used to research a person's federal and state criminal history, driver's license, you name it. I also checked Aburami's prison history, which detailed transfers, disciplines, aliases, felony charges, maximum sentence, etc.

Aburami had a checkered past, and when I met him, I understood why. Aburami was more than happy to talk to me about what was happening on Three Wing in the Segregation Unit.

"Mr. Freeman, d'ese inmates know I worked fo' you, and, and, and now d'ey wanna kill me." Aburami was nervous, looking around, trying to see if anybody was listening.

"Pump your brakes, you NEVER worked for me!"

"No, no, no! I mean IA. You know, Karkoska? I worked a lot fo' him. Ask him. He tell you." Aburami's English wasn't clear, but I could understand what he was saying.

"Do you want a transfer?"

Without hesitation, Aburami chimed in. "Hell yeah, I wanna transfer. D'ey know I ratted 'em out, and d'ey sayin' d'ey gonna cut my throat."

He'd just confirmed that he was shooting for a transfer, using every trick in the book. I acknowledged that. But there was something else going on in his eyes, something that made me reconsider whether his desire for a transfer was because his life was, in fact, in jeopardy.

"How did they find out you worked for us?"

"I tell'd 'em." Aburami's answer was straight, nothing wavering.

"You told them? What do you mean you told them?"

He shrugged his shoulders and fiddled with his hands. "It kind of slipped out when I talkin'."

"How does *that* just kind of slip out?"

He began nodding his head and getting more excited. "I told d'em d'at I was police, you know, and d'at I worked fo' you." A braggart. Plain and simple. That idiot thought that he could impress other inmates by bragging about his relationship with IA. However, that type of mistake could win an inmate a trip to the Coroner's office.

"How many people did you tell?"

"I don't know…maybe…"

"How many!"

"I said I don't know!" This guy was both aggravating and irritating. His face simultaneously grimaced and smiled with every question, clearly disgusted, but he knew I was the closest thing he had to a friend. Yet, I was the furthest thing from a friend to Aburami. What's more, that nut had no clue how many inmates heard him bragging, so I moved on to cover other areas.

"Alright then, *who* did you tell?"

"You know, some of d'ose Ricans."

I hated racist and demeaning comments. Moreover, if I've ever learned anything about derogatory characterizations, it was that they're all connected. In other words, the bigot you laugh at today will be talking about *you* tomorrow.

"I don't have all day. If you don't want to talk, I'll just go back and say that you. . ."

"Kings."

I paused. My eyes blinked quickly as my jaw slowly dropped open. "Kings?"

"Yeah, Kings."

"You told some Latin Kings that you were 5-0?"

"D'ey real pussies, you know?" I was wrong about Aburami. He wasn't the idiot I had suspected, he was a moron! Why would any inmate brag to the Latin Kings about being a snitch? At that time, the Kings and their rivals, the Nétas, were the two largest gangs inside Northern State. I didn't like any of the jail gangs, but I respected the Latin Kings for their organizational structure. That made me think, "*Maybe he really just wanted a transfer.*"

"Why didn't you tell Karkoska about this?"

"I did. He said 'fuck you'. They no let me into da library an' I got to make som' calls. Karkoska won't even take my phone calls now."

"Why do you have to go to the library to call Karkoska?"

"No. I got to make ot'er calls. Cops startin' to search my mail again."

"From the library?" Aburami never answered my question, and I didn't think much of it at the time, expecting he was about to complain about his mail being searched, which was standard. Boy was I wrong, and it would be years before I found out why. Bob's report lacked the details I needed, so, I decided to interview as many other inmates on Three Wing as possible.

But, there was a problem. Inmates didn't voluntarily talk to IA in view of other inmates. I wasn't about to pull 70 inmates out of their cells, individually, and expect them to confess to conspiring to kill Aburami. That's when I got the surprise of my life.

As I moved along the tier, an inmate yelled to me, "Hey, Freeman." I was in a hurry to talk with Bob and find out why he didn't mention any of the details in his report, so I headed for the door.

"What's up, baby. I'm in a bit of a ..."

"You better get that fucking snitch out of here before his ass gets carried out!" I stopped dead in my tracks. The inmate was in the cell next to another inmate who remembered me from Cottage Four at Mountainview Correctional Facility. He said it loud enough for not only me to hear him, but for most of the tier to hear also.

He had to be pretty pissed off to scream something that I thought was close to a threat in any investigator's eyes.

"Come again?" I doubted he would repeat himself.

"You heard me. Take his ass out of here." As I approached his cell, he walked back towards his bed in the rear of his cell, and sat on top of the green blanket.

"I need to talk to you." He completely ignored me. "I'm talking to you. Come over here."

He glared at me and slowly rose to an upright position. He glided towards me and stopped at the stainless steel commode in his cell.

I moved my face close to the thin, rectangular pane of glass in the cell door, attempting to be discreet. "Explain yourself. Who's gonna get him?"

Facing me with a devious smirk, he reached inside his pants with his hand, pulled out his penis, and began urinating in the direction of the toilet without ever taking his eyes off me. Urine hit the floor near the door where I was standing, completely missing the toilet.

"If that piss hits me, you're going to have more than a crooked dick to worry about."

His smirk never flinched. "So you like looking at grown men's dicks, huh, Mr. Freeman?"

Before I could think of a good rhetorical comeback, the

inmate in the cell adjacent to him interrupted our battle of wits. "That mother-fucker's dead-man-walking!"

I looked over to the other cell. "Who's gonna kill him, you?" I moved from crooked-dick's cell, upset at myself for not getting in the last word. Being outsmarted publicly inside a jail was extremely humiliating. I was already planning how to later justify tossing his cell.

"C'mon, black man."

"Come on? Where we going?"

"What the fuck, Freeman? You know how this shit works. We see him talking to Karkoska's white ass by the gym. He even got Feds on his list."

"What Feds?"

"Ay. That punk-bitch working for you, he's gotta die!"

"Says who? You?"

The inmate's eyes dropped down to my toes. He scanned me as if I had a wire, and then his eyes returned quickly to my face.

"Fuck you, bitch! You don't want to know shit, I won't say shit." With that, he walked to his bed, and sat down. My focus should have been gathering as much information as possible, but I was preoccupied by an off-color comment and how it affected my pride. It's all business, even the personal stuff. I tried to work him a bit to get some information, but he wasn't talking.

I began the arduous task of interviewing many of the inmates on Three Wing. It was clear that nobody was going to admit they were conspiring to murder Aburami. However, as I interviewed the other inmates, it became obvious that Aburami had no friends and even fewer well-wishers. Most inmates were extremely angry with Aburami, and even the officers hinted that he needed to get off their tier while he was still breathing.

But, like I said, the Latin Kings were very organized at Northern State. So, I knew I had to go to the top of the organization in order to get real answers. Ramos[3] was the second in command at the prison. The top man had no personality and would often assert "no hablo englese" when he didn't want to talk.

Ramos was different. He was a master at manipulating staff by seeming to cooperate with our many requests. I was aware of that, but I had to find out where the threat was coming from and Ramos would know about any plans for a hit on Aburami.

I initially met Ramos when I was allowed to sit in and observe one of Edwin's interviews as part of my Internal Affairs orientation. Edwin was investigating a separate matter and let me come along as an observer.

There was no need to beat around the bush. "What can you tell me about Aburami?"

Ramos sat at the other end of the table and smiled. "Who's Aburami?"

I knew he was only feeling me out. The direct approach hit a bump in the road. Ramos wasn't an amateur. He wasn't about to cough up anything without gaining something in exchange. So, we talked nonsense for a minute. He tried to see what kind of deals I would offer, which was pretty common, but I was prepared. The standard IA practice was to promise the inmate being interviewed anything they wanted. After we got the information we needed, we'd add the infamous disclaimer "...but I have to run this by my boss first". That way, you could always turn down the request and save face.

"Do you think that maybe we could talk about Aburami?" My patience was running short, but I didn't want Ramos to see me getting aggravated. My patience and focus during our session had impressed him, so much so that he abandoned his attempts at intimidation, which were common during Latin Kings

---

3 The name has been changed.

interviews. Since I had won Ramos over, I knew that even if I didn't get what I wanted now, maintaining a good rapport with him was like having a pair of aces in my pocket.

"What do you want, Freeman? A confession?" Ramos normally smiled when he spoke, but it wasn't because anything was funny nor because he was nervous. It was simply the way he spoke and I was sure not to read anything more into it.

"You want me to say that I put a TOS on a man?" He paused and let his fingers glide through his short, cropped hair. A TOS was a hit denoting "Terminate-On-Spot." That hand through the hair gesture was unplanned and a sign of trouble. Ramos had flinched, and he knew it. His mannerisms revealed that Aburami's time was short.

"I got no problem with him. None of the Kings do, you know? We about peace."

I researched the origins of the Latin Kings, Nétas, Five Percenters, and other groups in the prison. The Kings were a unique organization. Their mission statements and intentions, as well as some of the others, outside of prison appeared to have been above board, even admirable. However, in prison, protection and order became their goal. Not being perceived as soft or weak took precedence and was critical to their survival.

An ordered TOS directed any Latin King to kill a person on sight. Failure to carry out orders resulted harsh and, many times, brutal repercussions.

But like I said, Ramos had flinched and I knew there was something he wanted to get off his chest. So, I tried to help him out.

"Ever since I was a kid, I liked hearing stories."

Ramos sat forward and leaned on the table. "What you talking about, Mr. Freeman?"

"Well, maybe you can tell me a story."

"A story?" Ramos understood exactly what I was asking, but he was still feeling me out. He wanted to be sure I didn't have anything on him, and I knew I had to make him relax. His broken English was not an indication of his intelligence. In fact, I believed that his broken English was part of his act.

"Yeah, one of those hypothetical stories."

"About what?" He felt like playing and I was calm enough to seem entertaining.

"Oh, I don't know. Maybe somebody like you and somebody like Aburami." The pleasant look never diminished. "That kind of story's not real. It's not like you can be tied to anything, right?"

Ramos had a peculiar stare, tempered by his childish smirk. "How old are you, Freeman?"

"Old? What, you want to date me or something?"

We both burst out laughing. "J'ou make me laugh. J'ou a funny guy, j'ou know?" The broken English had suddenly returned and his playfulness was not calculated.

"The story, please." A basic rule of interviewing, never allow your subject to change your focus. There was no more information that I could get from him outside of the story. I allowed crooked-dick to literally "piss" me off, and I wasn't going to make that same mistake twice.

Out of respect, we both laughed at his attempt. "Of course this is only a story, right Freeman? What j'ou call 'em? A hypo-critical story, right?" Ramos was a jailer, and he knew the game well. Nothing could be held against him if he was making up a story at the investigator's request.

"Something like that."

"Something like that, or exactly like that?"

If I agreed with him by using the word "exactly", he'd bury me if his name was ever mentioned in connection with Aburami. I knew I had to show patience and that my patience was about to pay off. "Yeah. Something *exactly* like that."

Ramos told his story with a rare candor. "Somebody like Aburami, but not him, may have worked for j'ou and told j'ou when we were supposed to get something, j'ou know, something interesting inside of the lock-up, right?

"Bad enough 5-0, they grab my stash, then fuckin' rag-head start braggin' 'bout how he was police, and how we got fucked because we juicy pussies." Broken English aside, Ramos was getting hot at what Aburami had done.

"I no like getting fucked in here. J'ou know? So, hypo-critically, j'ou might find a man like that with a new necktie pretty soon, j'ou know? Of course, that's all hypo-critically, right, Mr. Freeman?"

Ramos made a cutting motion using his finger, slowly moving from one ear, across his neck, ending at the other ear. He grinded a crackling sound with his mouth, simulating the noise of the blade splitting Aburami's skin should make. Ramos was referring to a "Columbian Necktie". It was made by cutting a person's throat and then pulling their tongue from inside their mouth out through the incision in their neck. That type of punishment would signify that Aburami was a snitch, and discourage others from snitching.

Information in hand, I immediately headed back to see Bob. I wanted to know what story Aburami had told him that could possibly have persuaded Bob to dismiss any threat against Aburami.

Before I got to Bob, I saw Randy.

"Kenny, come in here for a minute." Randy was in charge whenever Edwin was out of the office. His office was directly across from Bob's.

"What's up, Ran? I need to talk to Bob." Randy gave me some distractive instructions Edwin left for me.

Randy was cool, but a bit nosey. "What up with his fly-ness?" Randy laughed until tears danced on his face. Images of Bob vomiting through his surgeon's mask gave Randy stomach cramps from the laughter.

"I've got one of Bob's rats."

"Give it back to Bob." Randy paused. "Or, did Ed give it

to you?"

"Yeah."

Randy whispered. "Ed can be a jerk. Just stay away from Chicky." There went Randy with that laugh. "You can tell me. Did you get some of dat or what! You know, I heard Ed got an itsy-bitsy…"

"Ran, I really need to talk to Bob." Talking about who's screwing who was Corrections' general pastime, but I had other things on my mind. "I don't think Bob's going to be too happy when he reads my report."

Randy's silliness ended. He leaned back in his chair and pointed to a quote he kept on his wall. "Young'n, you can't do things because they're popular or because they're easy. You do them because they're right." Randy had dirt in his closet, but he had a conscience and a desire not to make those mistakes again.

"Thanks, man."

"Anytime." Such poetic and powerful words should not have trailers attached to them. However, this was Randy.

"Young'n. You never denied banging Chicky." Randy's silliness was renewed and his laughter echoed as I walked into Bob's office.

After telling Bob what I discovered, he sprung into a self-serving tirade. "Fuck him. He's more trouble than he's worth. If he's got a hit for me, then I'm his man. If not, he's a fucking inmate. Let his ass rot."

I was floored. I heard Bob's voice, but not Bob's mind. "Did you interview anybody else?"

"What for? You see how much work I've got?" I stood there with my feet cemented to the floor, and my judgment in question, as I watched one of the few honest investigators in the state atypically ignore what was staring him right in the face.

"Bob!"

"He fucking brags about being my bitch? Fuck him! He should've stayed his ass in Iran or something." Bob's cheeks were flushed, his eyes holding an uncertainty about the decision to which he had reluctantly signed his name.

I knew Aburami bragged, but it didn't change the fact that he still worked for Internal Affairs. Furthermore, the threat against him was real.

"Well, I'm going to recommend that he gets PC." For some reason, I felt I owed Bob an explanation for doing what was right. "Those Kings are going to slit his throat if he goes back to G.P." General Population was the logical place for a hit to go down. Aburami needed protective custody.

"Knock yourself out, junior." Bob rubbed his head as he expelled a huge sigh. I saved his conscience by sticking to my guns and I should have been applauded. Instead, Bob focused on the obvious nature of how Corrections dealt with adverse situations.

"That punk mother-fucker won't come out of his cell anyhow, and they're going to charge him and leave him in there anyway." He paused and looked across the hallway at Randy who sat inside his own office. Bob whispered a tentative caution to me. "You might piss some other people off. But me, I don't give a shit."

Bob laughed at me, and himself, because he really didn't care if my report contradicted his earlier conclusion. We both knew that after protective custody investigations, inmates who refused to come out of their cells when ordered to were routinely charged with "Refusing to Obey a Direct Order". Afterwards, the stubborn inmate was simply left in that particular cell for months. The inmates didn't mind because they were able remain in a solitary cell in the Segregation Unit, away from the general population.

In the midst of his self-righteous babbling, Bob's warning did not go unheeded. I had already spoken to Randy about going against Bob's report and Randy had, for the most part, given me his blessings. In addition, since protective custody reports were the bulk of our work, there seemed to be no reason why my report would have been noticed. Who could have predicted that mine would garner the attention it did?

NINE

But, I Don't Play Ball

Within the law enforcement community, contradictory investigations were taboo. The "Us vs. Them" mentality pervaded all of Corrections, but was especially apparent inside Internal Affairs. You were viewed as not being a "team-player" if you voiced any disagreement with another investigator's findings. Right or wrong, we were expected to stand behind each other with no regard for error.

I completed my report, and Edwin approved it without much fanfare. Of course, he first asked me if I had copied one of his old reports. My findings were typed and forwarded to Central Office as part of the normal report distribution.

A few days later, I received a telephone call from James "Jimbo" Willie, an assistant chief in IA.

"Kenny? This is Willie." Jimbo was a blow-hard. He tried to intimidate people because he had a massive, elephant-man shaped head and a loud, obnoxious voice. His face was always flushed-red, as if he were suffering from oxygen depravation and could pass out at any moment. His hair was thinning on the top, and his comb-over hardly went unnoticed.

Jimbo was not particularly intelligent. But since 98% of

the unit imbedded their noses firmly up his hairy sphincter, he didn't have to be that smart.

Until that telephone call, I really hadn't had too much conversation with him.

"Hey, Chief. How's it going?" Jimbo hurriedly cut in. "I got your report on Aburami."

My mind immediately focused on whether the report had a time limit assigned, which was often the case with a Commissioner's Referral, but the investigation I completed was sent to us from Chief Faunce's office. I began my investigation on the same date that Edwin assigned it to me. So, I wasn't worried about the time.

"Oh, good. Celeste sent it out just a couple days ago and…"

Again, Willie interrupted me. "Do you know who this bastard is?"

"Yeah, Aburami." After giving my answer, it became clear Willie was talking about something altogether different, but he never explained what.

"Did you read Bob's report before writing this shit?" I paused, giving no answer. "Bob agreed that this mother-fucker is trying to get a transfer."

I thought, "*Agreed with whom?*," but left that question alone. "I read that, Chief, but I also interviewed some of these Kings, and I believe they're gonna cut this guy up pretty soon."

"You believe, huh?" It didn't sound as though Jimbo was waiting for me to justify my beliefs, however, it did sound as though I was about to get my marching orders.

"Well, your report makes us look like we're liable for this asshole. He bragged, so it's his problem. Right?" I didn't answer right away. "Kenny, you still there?"

"Yeah, Chief. No, Chief."

"You're not there…"

"I'm here. I just meant…" I paused slightly as I considered what I was about to say. "…I'm not sure if it's his problem alone. I mean, he did work for us, right? And these Kings up here are not too pleased about that."

Jimbo didn't cut me off this time. Maybe, I thought, his sense of reasoning had been pricked. I continued with logic, hoping for reason at Headquarters. "A cut throat is still a cut throat, even if he bragged, right?"

Willie's voice went up a notch. "We ain't fucking liable for him, and that's it! I'm tearing this shit up and you're going to write me another report. Your *real* report *will* say that he's a braggart, it's his fault, and that he don't need PC. You got me?"

I sat motionless. "Hey, Chief…"

"What's your fucking problem, Kenny?" Oh, besides having an idiot tell me to lie on my report? I didn't say that, but it was an excellent and accurate response. That was, until he came up with a better one.

"You like IA, right Kenny? Or do you want to go into social work? It's not like you've been to the academy already, right?" The insinuation was obvious. The department hadn't put much of an investment into me and I was easily replace-able. Social workers were the reproach of Corrections because they often went overboard in helping inmates.

"Write the fuckin' report!" *Slam!*

The sound of him hanging up the telephone reverberated inside my ear. Suddenly, I heard Edwin's telephone ring. My desk was positioned perfectly to eavesdrop on Edwin whenever he left his door open. After he answered his telephone, Edwin greeted the person on the other end of the telephone by address-ing them as "Chief".

I reminded myself that I was still on probation with Internal Affairs. So, I sat there, at my desk, still holding the telephone receiver in my hand, not having a clue about what to do. I had heard that Jimbo called other investigators and told them what the conclusion of their investigations would be prior to assign-ing it to them, but it had never happened to me.

Soon, Pam entered the office and saw me sitting there still

holding the telephone.

"Kenny, you forgot a number?" Pam, like Bob, suffered from that honesty ailment. She was definitely a straight-shooter, which meant promotion would be difficult for her. But, unlike Bob, she was extremely low-keyed, intelligent, and exceptionally observant.

Her jovial spirit left as she recognized something was amiss. "What's up, Ken?"

"Willie just told me how he wanted *my* investigation to end." Pam's face transformed from concerned to studious, without blinking an eye. There was no hesitation in her instructions. She spoke from a personal experience that she never disclosed to anyone, including myself.

"Whatever he ordered you to do, you do it." Pam stepped behind her desk and opened her drawer. "Then get yourself a journal and write everything down. Not in general terms, specifics and details. Dates, times, places, people, and note *exactly* what he told you to do."

She pulled out *her* journal and began flipping through the pages. "When they come after you, this will be the only thing that saves your hinny." She smiled as she reviewed her entries.

"Sooner or later, they will come." Pam smiled. "Kid, you don't seem to be very good at kissing their hinnies."

She struggled to laugh. "C.Y.A, Kenny, C.Y.A." (C.Y.A. stood for "Cover Your Ass.") Her voice softened considerably to that of a whisper. "Don't be swimming up crap's creek like Debbie Davies and Tom. They're going to hang her, too. And Jimbo liked Debbie."

Pam was referring to the Principal Investigator in charge of the Albert Wagner Correctional Facility in Bordentown. Debbie Davies-Kopp was involved in a reverse sexual harassment lawsuit against another investigator named Tom Ferrer. Tom made some lewd remarks about Debbie's body that had explicit sexual overtones. What he didn't realize was that Debbie wouldn't shy away from shooting back her own demeaning insults. Debbie worked in major jails and had proven herself among the male inmate population, which meant that anything Tom said to her was merely par for the course. He didn't expect Debbie to come back as hard as she did, leaving Tom's ego injured. That was when he physically attacked Debbie.

But Debbie was no slouch. She opened up an unused barrel of whup-ass just for Tom, further injuring his manhood. Tom complained to Chief Faunce who, instead of investigating, applied her own brand of justice on Tom.

That was where the Chief made her mistake. The lawsuit should have been dismissed, but the way Faunce handled Tom's complaint was malicious and vindictive. The Chief was angry because she viewed Tom's complaint as betrayal, kind of biting the hand that fed you.

Chief Faunce transferred Tom to another institution, conjured up ridiculous disciplinary charges and other blatantly discriminatory things against him. However, Tom made copies of everything they sent him along with the extensive notes he kept inside his own journal.

Debbie's problems exploded when she refused to lie during her deposition, and agreed that his complaint should have been investigated thoroughly. The state settled the case to the tune of $459,000.00 because of the Chief's screw up, which angered Faunce. She blamed everything on Debbie Kopp-Davies' "inability to supervise".

Tom would retire with a fat paycheck, compliments of Internal Affairs. With Tom gone, all of the Chief's henchmen at Central Office and throughout the state sank their fangs deep into the aorta of Debbie's life and career. Debbie stood her ground as best she could, but no court cares about a white woman claiming retaliation. This was still an old-boy's game, and white women were the wrong minority for complaints.

Having observed the events surrounding Debbie and Tom, I had no intention of being the only one without a chair after the music stopped. But Pam knew Headquarters wasn't my only danger. Most times, the danger came from those closest to you.

"And you'd better watch everything that you say around Mike." Mike and I spoke often about different books we read, and he was the one that taught me the most about investigations and how to conduct interviews. But Pam knew Mike better.

Pam's smile reappeared. "Just make sure that you document everything, Kenny. Everything."

I already knew that Mike and Charles Muller were close friends, and that they both worshipped the other Assistant Chief, William O'Brien. O'Brien had campaigned for Mueller to take over as Assistant Chief after either he or Jimbo retired, which was expected in the next few years. I couldn't understand Mike's bowing to them the way he did, especially since Mike was so much more intelligent than both Muller and O'Brien put together.

Heeding Pam's counsel, I documented everything about my conversation with Jimbo, including hearing Edwin's telephone ring and hearing him address the person on the other end of the line with "Hey, Chief." I wrote the names of the inmates that I spoke to, including Ramos. The officers on duty that day were also noted, just in case.

After documenting everything, I relaxed, knowing I wouldn't be the fall guy if anything suddenly happened to Aburami. Finally, I re-wrote my report according to Willie's specifications and concluded that Aburami was a braggart and not in need of protective custody. My job here was done, or so I thought.

Aburami proved to be more persistent than any of us could have guessed. And for good reason. Not even a month passed, and I was greeted with a Commissioner's Referral that was sent directly from our Commissioner, Jack Terhune, a political hire from Bergen County. The referral was for Muhammad Aburami, and had a highlighted due date that indicated when my completed investigation was required to be returned to the Commissioner's Office.

Although Debbie didn't document everything, I wished I had stood my ground like she had. I had to face the man that I lied about in order to save my job. He refused to return to the General Population, and was charged for refusing to obey an order, but my actions could have caused his death and I couldn't blame it on Pam's advice. Her advice was extremely rational and reasonable. It was still my choice. I placed my desire to remain inside of Internal Affairs above the life of a human being. I did that. Not Willie. Not the system. I made that choice.

Yet, there I was, with a gift handed to me that others may never have—a second chance to make right what I had done wrong. I was determined that the threat of losing my job would never scare me into such a shameful position again.

I immediately set up another interview with Aburami. He was still in the Segregation Unit, but placed on lock-down because of his refusal.

"What's up, Freeman? You lie on me!" It was clear that he had heard about my conclusion. "You know d'ey after me! Why you lie!" I put my hands up as if looking down the barrel of a moral shotgun, motioning towards Aburami, attempting to calm him a bit so I could talk.

"I messed up." No excuses or prolonged explanations. I just told him, "I'm sorry." There was no reason for me not to deal with this convicted felon as anything other that a human being. I was wrong for allowing my self-interest to weigh so heavily in my decision-making.

"Do I get out now?" Aburami was only interested in his transfer. The threat in his mind only existed at Northern State Prison. But I knew that he would be found no matter which prison he was transferred to in New Jersey.

"No. Not just yet." If I were going to go against what I knew the Chief would want, I had to be prepared. "Let's start from the beginning. Tell me everything that you believe justifies your request for protection, and I want to know who's letting you make calls from the library, who you're calling, and why your mail hasn't been searched."

"What?" Aburami attempted to get amnesia, but I had the cure.

"You don't remember? You'll be double bunked in Ad Seg with an old friend of yours."

Aburami hesitatingly told me about drug packages and illegal overseas phone calls, but I was missing the centerpiece of the puzzle, and didn't understand why. He was a little puzzled about why he had to tell every detail of his story again, but he did. I made sure that my notes were immaculate. I covered everything I had covered just a couple months ago, as well as minute details that seemed irrelevant.

Our secretary normally typed the reports, but I typed this one. Standard procedures permitting, the report was reviewed and then cleared by Edwin without much fanfare. It was then forwarded simultaneously to both Chief Faunce and the Commissioner. I filed copies of that report and my notes with some of the other cases scheduled to be taken over to the storage trailer. That way, just in case my files disappeared, I'd know how to find copies.

A week passed, and I hadn't heard anything about Aburami. I prayed that the report went unnoticed. Normally, the report wouldn't raise "red flags" because it was well written, without typos or errors. Moreover, Edwin cleared it. But, I wasn't that lucky.

The secretary's telephone rang. "Hold on, Chief." Her eyes lit brightly as she covered the receiver and screamed in a whisper to me. "Kenny, it's Willie. You want me to say you're not here?"

Man, I knew this would happen if Jimbo saw the report. "Naw. Send it to my desk." I walked back to my desk and tightly closed my eyes, waiting for the torrential rains to begin.

The phone rang. I picked up the receiver and put together my most pleasant phone voice. "Good afternoon, Chief."

"Who sent this shit to the Commissioner?" Yep! He saw the report.

"It's the normal chain. He got a copy and Debbe got a copy. That response didn't exactly address what he asked me and I think it pissed him off just a bit.

"You a fuckin' comedian now?" You'll be a fuckin' out-of-work comedian in a minute!" Without hesitation, I knew it was time to change my strategy.

"Chief, this guy's making overseas calls, getting packages without being searched…"

"Says who?"

"He told me, and he said he could prove it."

"Fuck him!"

"What?"

"He's a god dam liar! He didn't make those fuckin' calls! Get your head out of your ass. He's trying to get a transfer. That's it! Stick his ass in population."

"They're gonna cut his throat if he stays, Chief. Bob showed me his files. He's our snitch." I thought the rational approach would work on anybody, but I didn't realize that only an elephant tranquilizer worked on an irrational, raving idiot like Jimbo.

"If he gets his throat slashed, it's his fuckin' blood and his fuckin' problem, not yours!" I wished that someone who used any word so frequently would at least take the time to pronounce it correctly. And for the record, it's "*fucking*", with a "g" at the end.

"That fuckin' asshole got a big mouth. How else they know—they think he's working for IA. Debbe said write it over, same conclusion like the one Bob had. No fuckin' protective custody!"

I remembered Pam's advice, but without a public record of what had transpired, it would have been my word versus an assistant chief's denial. Thinking about big head Jimbo reminded me of Big Head Eddie. Eddie was a greater threat than Jimbo could ever be. So, my plan was to give full credit for the investigation to whom credit was due.

"No problem, Chief. I'll change the report. No problem." Jimbo said nothing during my pause. "But I'm going to write in the report that you ordered me to change it to match Bob's conclusion. And, I'll note how much I disagree with Bob's findings and that I believe that this man's life is in danger. No problem, Chief. I'll start working on it now."

It seemed like a brief pause, but there really was no pause at all in our conversation. "What!" Jimbo wasn't that sharp, so it took him a little extra time to decipher what I said. He figured he needed to speak to somebody that was afraid of him. "Put Ed on the phone!" He was forceful and his voice dropped two octaves.

I transferred the telephone to Edwin and just waited for the punch line. Edwin continued the day without mentioning anything to me about his conversation with Jimbo. He left the office to go home at the end of the day before I did, and I refused to worry about if I would have a job the following day.

The next morning, however, Jimbo called back and told me that I could keep the conclusion unchanged, but said I had to remove all of the specifics regarding Aburami from my report. His justification was that my report was "too long" and the details were "unnecessary". I believed that the specifics were very necessary, because they formed the foundation for my conclusion. But, I saw it as that a small victory and that was enough for the day.

TEN

The Road to Perdition (Teth)

During this time, my professional life was soaring. I developed excellent contacts within other law enforcement agencies such as the Newark Police Department, the F.B.I., and the Essex County Prosecutor's Office. And, as a byproduct of my work, I gained valuable experience by writing every day. Short stories were my favorite, but I still enjoyed putting together sonnets. I perfected my art, and researched many obscure legal aspects of my profession in the process.

My professional development was formalized through the endless training classes with the Division of Criminal Justice. I studied areas regarding the policies and procedures of Internal Affairs not practiced in our department, to the dismay of Jimbo. The Aburami matter should have been a distant memory, but his grudge from the case was unyielding. Unfortunately for Jimbo, his anger was outweighed by my performance, so much so that top brass labeled me the Rising Star of the department.

I was only getting better at learning the subtle nuances of my new vocation, celebrating every milestone, no matter how minute. I stood up to an assistant chief, withstood his threatening wrath with style, and had survived unblemished and stronger than ever. I was making excellent money, had a beautiful home (which had just been renovated) a nice car, and a beautiful daughter who was seemingly joined to my hip.

With all of these areas of my life prospering, I slowly began to forget God. I put on the proper face when required, but my heart was too preoccupied with my own desires, and that left me little time to sincerely search out what He thought of my personal life. I prayed to God for the sake of tradition, recalling how in times past, my faith was bolstered from the clear moving hand of the Almighty. But, I failed to cultivate two of the three most crucial relationships in my life—my relationships with God and with my wife. Four years earlier, I stood before God and vowed that I would forsake all others for my wife, and my wife promised that same devotion to me. For my part, that was a lie, to both God and to myself, a lie that I never paused long enough to consider any consequences regarding.

Less than a year after our nuptials, I began ignoring signs that would have been obvious to any man outside of a relationship, but invisible to love. To her credit, I never had any solid proof that she was being unfaithful. Instead, I was left to implode with the guilt of my own actions, and no response to her assertion that the only reason that I would suspect her was if I was doing something that a married man shouldn't.

My precious child and I were inseparable, perfectly complementary and joyously content with ourselves, as we lived in our own Barney-type world. My wife could have entertained another family, considering the way my daughter and I ignored her, leaving her to her burgeoning anger, tiredness, and selfishness. In every respect, I was the father of whom fairytales were made, yet I was a husband of nightmarish proportions.

In February 1998, I was assigned to the New Jersey Division of Criminal Justice Academy in Sea Girt for training. It was the location of the state mandated Basic Course for Investigators, alongside the State Police Academy. All of the state's investigators trained there, whether they were from a county internal affairs unit, county prosecutors' office, or the Division of Criminal Justice. I was formally introduced to the woman whose inner strength and toughness I tried to emulate, Debbie Davies-Kopp, and we soon became each other's confidants. The course was nearly four months long, and I rarely stayed overnight at the Academy. I rented an apartment during the time I was training, which further complicated things at home.

I excelled in the course, and put my years in the Marines to the challenge as I called cadence for our class during the early morning runs. As the course ended, my wife asked me to give up my apartment so that we could attempt to reconcile and I agreed. However, something wasn't right about the way we interacted with each other. After a short time, it became clear that my wife wasn't so eager to see me. We talked regularly, but her conversation was different. They say absence makes the heart grow fonder. Well, I found out at the onset that absence also made the heart go wander.

The joke was turned around and it wasn't all that fun any longer. The Bible says, "So a man sows, that shall he also reap." It was harvest time for me and I didn't know how to farm. Now it was me wondering where the hell my wife had gone, with whom she was spending time, what she was doing, and what she was thinking. The questions were merely rhetorical in that I already knew the answers.

It forced me to consider what she must have had to endure during my absences. Now, I was the one left alone at home with my daughter, just waiting until my wife walked through the door to ask the same questions she used to ask me. There was no humor when confronted with the hard reality that the joke's not funny unless it's on somebody else. I was feeling the same pain that I put her through, but that hurt was nothing compared to what was just over the horizon.

Knowing what was going on wasn't enough for me. I followed her everywhere, determined to catch her in the very act because I was convinced that would provide me with some kind of closure. And, as much as I wanted to leave, I wanted her to want to stay.

Her job kept her out of the house until after midnight. Waiting up for her didn't bother me at all because I was used to staying up late to write. The nights were serene and my poetry embodied my private thoughts, my own personal Shan Gri La. It haunted me, as it reflected my aspirations of a perfect marriage, blotting out every indiscretion, making whole the vows that we made before God, and withholding nothing from each other. As my writing increased, my need for sleep dissipated and I began taking three doses of sleeping pills at a time. Normally, those three doses, nine pills, allowed me to rest for a few hours. Soon, five doses only granted me maybe five hours of uninterrupted sleep, if I was lucky.

I was desperate for tranquility, the kind that seemed to exist only in fantasy. That desire exposed my own hypocrisy, for I was still involved in what I suspected of my wife. There I stood, seeking sympathy for myself while I was totally unsympathetic. Any suffering I endured almost seemed fair.

My hypocrisy should have forced my conscience to remain a safe distance from begging for pity, especially since I had so utterly annihilated my marriage. I could have asked for God's forgiveness, and I believed that He would have forgiven me, but I understood that praying selfishly was just as bad as not praying at all.

So, I asked God for the only two things I could pray for in my situation. The first prayer was for God to forgive me for all I had done wrong. The list of my errors and mistakes were extensive. The more I recalled, the more I realized how low I had been. I stood off at a distance and saw myself in a way that I never could have imagined. My faults were relived, one after the other, like a documentary crafted in my honor but to my horror. It was at that time that I was formally introduced to Guilt, and he made a home in the midst of my consciousness.

The second prayer was more difficult for me because,

although I had bowed to the power and dominion of my guilt, something inside of me refused to be sorry for the pain that I had caused her. What I was doing, no matter how deplorable, seemed, in some incomprehensible way, acceptable. However, when faced with the thought of anybody else doing the same thing, it was surely unacceptable. Therefore, I looked at my deeds as if watching a movie, seeing a character not connected to my soul. I prayed, *"Father, not my will, but let Your will be done in my life."* (*Teth.*) Realizing that God wasn't pleased with my distorted reckoning made me fear His reaction. Never have I been so terrified in all of my life. My behavior would reveal an unrepentant heart. Nevertheless, God had a way of bringing a man to his knees.

The next day was Sunday. I went through my ceremonial preparations for church, sure to keep up all of the appearances expected for a happy family. But my facade was shattered when I stumbled across correspondence that had fallen out of my wife's work jacket. It should have made me jump for joy. My wife was pregnant and I was on my way to having the family of which I'd dreamed.

But something nagged at the back of my mind. I immediately ran downstairs to confront the calendar that hung on the kitchen wall. With my pointer finger gliding swiftly across the months, I discovered a few unpleasant facts about the pregnancy. The most likely time of conception coincided with a trip of Priscilla's, which I later discovered was with her lover. A less likely date corresponded with her disappearances for hours at a time when she claimed she was getting her hair done three or four times a week.

Oh, God! Not again! Nearly a decade earlier, I had survived a soul-shattering false paternity, and those wounds never healed. A hollow rage erupted inside the abyss that was my heart. I repeatedly reviewed the probable dates of conception, and realized the likelihood that the child was mine rested somewhere between slim and none. I stood aimlessly before the calendar of misfortune, reduced to only a frame of a man. All of my inner organs had been ripped out of my body through my nose. A monsoon of tears rained down my flushed cheeks until my entire face was swollen.

In a haze, I drove to Northern State Prison, thinking that Thaddeus was working some overtime during the inmate visits program that operated on the weekends. A lively group of officers was busily working at a registration desk in the lobby a short distance from the front entrance. They weren't taking any particular notice of me. It was close to their break time, and they normally tried to wrap up all of their paperwork early. I walked hastily towards the stairs, not giving any attention to one particular officer who slyly observed me entering the building.

"Well, hello Mr. Freeman." Although I had always greeted her as well as those other officers, I continued walking without as much as a glance.

"Mr. Freeman?" Without hesitation, I walked past her and the other officers and proceeded up the staircase.

When I got upstairs to the Internal Affairs Unit, I almost vomited when I discovered that Thaddeus wasn't working, but Charles "Chuck" Walters was. Chuck was new to the unit and always on the prowl for a friend. He was goofy and spineless, and that was a perfect fit for Jimbo and company. But, I was already there and I could no longer focus my tear-filled eyes to drive.

I had to talk to Thaddeus. Not only did we start Internal Affairs at the same time, we had developed a solid rapport over the past year. T.C. had gone through a tough divorce years earlier and emerged unscathed.

"Where's T.C.? Get him on the line." Chuck was shocked to see me in such a raggedy condition.

"Hey, Kenny. Thaddeus ain't working today." The obvious never dissuaded Chuck from verbalizing it, no matter how irritating. So, I repeated myself.

"Call him! I need to talk to him." Chuck's eyes were blinking, but I understood that it took a bit of time for my words to register. "Call him, Chuck!" The monsoon continued to wash over my face, never relenting. My thinking was gravely distorted, so much so that calling Thaddeus myself never entered my mind. My voice was clear, but the tears showed no mercy.

"Alright. Just sit down." Nervously, Chuck picked up the telephone and paged Thaddeus. I stood for what seemed to be hours, leaning against the interior wall, watching Chuck as he watched me.

"What's wrong?" Chuck was trying to appear accommodating, but I knew that the less I said to Chuck, the less everybody in the department would find out when Chuck got on the telephone to gossip.

"Did you call T.C.?"

"I paged him, brother." Once again, that word brother made me leery, and I knew that bad things were in the works. But before I could reply, the secretary's telephone rang. When I heard that it was Thaddeus, I sat on the edge of my desk, waiting for Chuck to transfer the call to me.

Chuck sighed in relief, and poured himself out to Thaddeus. "Hey T.C., you'd better get in here quick." Chuck paused. "I don't know man, but Kenny's in a bad way." Chuck hung up the telephone.

He turned to me. "T.C. said he'd be here in about five minutes." Thaddeus lived in the area, barely five minutes away.

At that moment, the officer who was working at the visit desk downstairs entered the office. She was concerned and wanted to make sure I was alright.

"Kenny!" She pushed her forearms against me as I sat on the corner of my desk, and firmly held my face between her hands. Her fingers separated as they tenderly sank into my swollen cheeks, her thumbs coming to rest on my lips. Her eyes rapidly shifted as they searched my face.

"Why are you doing this?" Tears immediately poured from

her eyes as she simultaneously tried to wipe my tears and hold me securely in her arms. The secret of our romance revealed, her heart broke into infinitesimal pieces as she watched me implode.

"Stop." Her command for me to regain my senses fell on deaf ears. "Kenny. Talk to me." No response. "Please?" I never looked at her directly and my shame refused her comforting embrace.

"Leave me alone!" I struck out with the precision of a viper. Her mouth dropped and face vibrated, but she wasn't giving up so easily. She continued her efforts until the final straw was dropped on her overworked back. "Get out!" Her heart fell further and faster than the expression on her face after my vicious rejection. The poison of my strikes had worked their way to her heart, wounding her, driving her away. Her mouth moved frantically as she extended her arms, but made no sound. The thumbs that only moments earlier caressed my lips now bitterly covered her own.

She reluctantly left my side and backed out of the office, staring at me the entire time. Her eyes were immobilized, glued to the dream that never would be reality. She headed back to her post, contemplating her folly, trying to forget the investment that she had placed in a relationship with her married lover.

Thaddeus finally arrived at the unit. I stood up to greet him. "Kenny, what's going on with you?" he asked. His voice was uncertain, but remained conversational.

My voice had started to crack by then. "She's pregnant, man, and the baby might not be mine." I repeated that statement two or three times under my breath as the tears continued to flow.

I was oblivious to my own embarrassment. Chuck stood an exaggerated distance away from us, but he was taking notes. I tried to remember to keep my voice low, but considering the drama that was going on, I could have cared less what Chuck heard. My pride was as shattered as my heart.

But Thaddeus knew what Chuck heard mattered. He moved closer to me and firmly held me by my shoulders, peering into my eyes, ensuring he had my attention. Quietly, Thaddeus seared into my consciousness words that struck a cord in my psyche. "That's real fucked up what she did." He glanced slightly over his shoulder locating Chuck. "Now straighten up! Shut your mouth and just listen."

Thaddeus told me to sit down because he said I looked like I was about to fall. "She's fucked up for that, I know. But you can't let these bitches see you like this. Especially the one behind me." He tried to adjust my disheveled shirt.

"Get yourself together and I'll tell you what you're going to do. You're going to wait until the baby's born, and then you can find out who's the father, alright?" Thaddeus brushed off lint on my shirt's sleeve.

"Until then, you're just going to have to suck that shit up and be a man." He moved closer to me and whispered. "And don't ever say that shit out loud again, especially not to any of these back-stabbing bitches. And, if they bring this shit up, you'll just tell them that you had a problem but you've taken care of it. You got me?"

Thaddeus walked over to Chuck and told him that I was fine, that I just had some marital problems that I was taking care of. But, we both knew that with Chuck, there was no such thing as an un-rung bell. Thaddeus turned his attention back to me.

"What's your brother's phone number?" Thaddeus called my brother, Keith. He also called our supervisor, Terry, just to cover himself, but not to harm me. Thaddeus worked quickly to get me out of there. I was tore up from the floor up. My descent into pity was so severe that I stayed home for about a week just to cry and feel sorry for myself. Unfortunately, I didn't know Corrections used personal tragedies as leverage should the need arise.

After a few days of calling out sick and speaking to nobody, my boss decided I should talk to him about my problems. Terry loved gossip, and he craved every detail, no matter how minute. I was still in bed Thursday morning when I called to let him know I wouldn't be in for the remainder of the week.

"Bullshit, Kenny. What the fuck happened last weekend?" Terry never claimed to be subtle. In my wounded state, I maintained a superficial defense.

"No problem, Terry. I'm cool." I swallowed the thickened saliva that built up inside of my mouth. "I won't be coming in for a while."

"Hell no, man. I need to see you now! What the hell happened to you?" Terry's purported assistance was as desirable as a used sanitary napkin. He was desperate for some gossip, which he could spread around during his Sunday morning brunches with Chief Faunce, our union president, and the Chief's other confidents. Talk about conflict of interest. Terry's persistence had a sobering, yet calming, effect on me.

"I'm fine."

"No! Get in here now! You hear me, man! Right now!" Terry paused briefly, waiting for me to respond. "You need T.C. to come get you or what?" I really wasn't feeling Terry that morning. I wanted to stay at home, basking in my own unwashed funk, but I had enough sense to know that when I received an order from a supervisor, I had to follow the order.

"I'm on my way. Half an hour. I'm coming."

But obeying Terry's order was a terrible mistake. I returned to work too soon, and paid dearly for it. I looked awful. I didn't bother ironing my clothes, brushing my hair, or even checking the mirror before I walked out my door. I couldn't focus on the larger picture about my situation and the nature of the department. I rambled to anybody with whom I was cool. My rambling caught the ever-open ears of Randy Cicale.

Randy enjoyed the nectar of gossip even more than Terry, but he was much more sophisticated and intelligent. Had I had more time to recover at home, I may have been more alert and kept my mouth shut. But, I was pitiful. Extremely pitiful. I hunted for anyone who would affirm how terribly I had been treated. Seeking sympathy was dangerous, especially among vipers, and I was in the bosom of their lair.

Randy shared my trouble with Terry, who in turn informed the Chief. That's when Terry summoned me to his office for the news.

"Kenny, I just talked to Debbe, and she's concerned about you." That was the bait, and the trap was coming. "Hand over your weapon and your key to the gun-locker." I was angry that they were taking away my handgun and it showed, but I reluctantly complied with his demand. I removed the magazine from the weapon, cleared the chamber, and placed it on his desk.

"This ain't right!" I walked out of his office and started to leave the unit, but Terry followed me to the front of the unit.

"Wait, I'm not finished." Pointing at Randy's office, Terry tilted his head. "Come on in here, man." Randy's office was near the front of the unit, and that was where Round Two went down.

I sat down and listened to Terry. "Debbe wants you to go see Dr. Kahn. He's a psychiatrist. Don't worry, brother, Jimbo said nobody will know."

Brother? I knew I was screwed. I sat near the door of Randy's office completely disheveled, shirt wrinkled, mismatched socks, thick eye-boogers, and badly in need of a haircut.

"Willie?"

"Yeah. He suggested it."

Jimbo's grudge had found an opening. "I'm not going to see a psych." I had always thought of the state-employed psychiatrists as buffoons, and I never heard of a state-psych going against what Internal Affairs believed. In other words, if we called one of our psychiatrists regarding an officer's ability to function in law enforcement, they'd first ask our opinion, and then provide us with their official findings, which normally mirrored our opinion. Cut and dry. No questions asked.

"That's not a request." My consent was not requested, and Chief Faunce was used to getting her way. "T.C.'s gonna drive you there."

"I'm not going."

"You go or you're fired." Terry was unrelenting. "You look fucked up, man. Just go see the doc, alright brother?" I was done.

Randy chimed in on the conversation. "Kenny. You look a mess, man." Well, at least Randy didn't call me brother. "Don't get in a pissing match with Debbe. Just go see the doc. You don't have to talk…"

"Hell yeah, he do!" Terry was emphatic about the extent of my participation. He called for Thaddeus and told him to take me to see Dr. Kahn, whose office was in South Orange, NJ.

Apparently, he was there waiting for both of us to arrive. Both? Why would he be waiting for Thaddeus and me? My suspicions displaced a huge portion of my pain. Thaddeus was the only other African American in the unit and everyone assumed I trusted him completely. They wanted to identify Chuck as African American, but he bragged about being a mixture of Caucasian and Japanese. Faunce's reason for sending Thaddeus had more to it than just our common backgrounds.

Dr. Michael Kahn was the head of the state's Employee Advisory Service, commonly referred to as E.A.S. At Dr. Kahn's office, Thaddeus was asked to remain in the waiting room while Dr. Kahn *evaluated* me in a small room down the hall. Oh yes, this was an evaluation, and it was mandatory. I grew extremely impatient and deliberately withdrawn as the evaluation proceeded.

"Kenny, you don't mind if I called you Kenny, right?"

"Actually I do."

"Great! Kenny. Let's begin." I guess the ability to hear wasn't a prerequisite at Dr. Kahn's former employer—Dewey, Cheatum, and Howe.

"So how are you feeling today?"

Ordinarily, I would agree that he asked an innocent question, but the circumstances surrounding my mandatory visit strained any possibility of a cordial exchange. Dr. Kahn was a man impressed with himself, and he wanted everybody else to be just as impressed.

I had prayed that God would allow his will to be done in my life, but I couldn't fathom how Mini-Me could be a part of God's plan. Whatever answers I gave the psychiatrist would determine my fate with Internal Affairs and with Corrections. I knew that I had to smile through my adversity, so I set my face like a flint.

"I'm fine." That became my battle cry. I knew that in order to survive, the weak had to say that they were strong. I was hurting, but I was also a fighter, a kid from Newark that stood up to Ol' Big Head, and lived to tell about it.

With a smug expression, and a sense of superiority, Dr. Kahn continued his evaluation. "Well, is there anything that you would like to tell me?"

"No."

"There has to be something, right?"

"I'm fine."

"Well, Chief Faunce seems to think that you're having marital problems…"

Another dramatic pause. There was no question, so I gave no response. "Well…" Still no question, and, of course, no response. "Are you having marital problems?"

I shrugged my shoulders and let the corners of my mouth drop. "I think all marriages have problems."

Dr. Kahn's self-exalted shell began to show a few cracks of impatience. "Is your wife pregnant with another man's child?"

I began speaking to myself with calming words, reassuring

myself that this quack wasn't worth choking. His questioning was way out of bounds, to which he may have expected an out of bounds response. But I refused to give him the satisfaction. My answer had to be brief and direct.

"You'd have to ask her." Another victory, especially considering the fact that I hadn't leapt out of my chair to choke the living crap out of that miniature quack.

Dr. Kahn backed off his rude questioning for a while, and instead asked me a barrage of background questions—religion, parents, children, siblings. But, he'd lost ground in our first exchange, and he wasn't going to let me leave his office without a rematch.

"You don't seem to want to be here. Am I correct?"

"I'm fine."

"But you don't like our counseling?"

"I'm fine." Dr. Kahn sighed heavily as he continued taking notes using the faint light emanating from the small lamp on an adjacent end table.

"Then how do you handle these marital problems?"

"I told you. I'm fine."

"You mean you never had marital problems?"

"That wasn't your question." He quickly glanced at me, and then returned his attention back to his pad.

"Do you have marital problems?"

"Sometimes." He waited in vain for me to elaborate.

"Well, in general, how do you like to handle them?"

"I like to pray about them."

I don't believe that was the proper response. Dr. Kahn looked up from his notepad and stopped writing. "That obviously doesn't work, right?" That quack was entering dangerous territory, and although he took the time to enunciate each word perfectly, I couldn't believe that he said what he said.

"Excuse me?"

"I said it's obvious that your method doesn't work. Right?" Without realizing it, Mini-Me's question had placed me in charge of our conversation.

"You don't believe that God answers prayers, sir?"

"Well if prayer worked, you wouldn't be here now, would you?"

I knew that answering him directly was ill-advised, not because I didn't know the answer, but because either he was very clever at finding a way to elicit a genuine response from me, or he was an imbecile with a degree of authority attached to marching orders from Faunce. But I just couldn't just let him get off that easily, as an inner strength began to swell inside of me.

"Are you telling me that you're greater than God, Dr. Kahn?" Dr. Kahn began his answer by leaning back in his chair and grinning. With his elbows balanced on the arms of his chair, he maneuvered his pencil with the tips of both his thumbs and pointer fingers, deliberating in his mind, as if a profound lesson was just waiting to pour from his thin, crusty lips.

"Well, God does a part of the work. As for the other areas, there's me."

He rambled on for a while about the "necessity" of his profession and his greatness. I chose not to stop him, especially since I was the one asking all of the questions and this quack was figuratively laying on his own couch. He violated the first rule of an investigatory interview, which mandated that the investigator controlled the questioning. I couldn't help but grin just a bit as that pompous moron shamelessly bathed in his own conceit.

I couldn't tell you most of what he said because all I could think about was how thin the line between doctor and patient had become. I couldn't help staring at the Quack, his eyes rolling as he gestured with his hands, profoundly, ostentatiously, magnanimously. Good, Lord! I was experiencing the long-term effects of what happened when the patients ran the asylum.

Before I knew it, my grin grew into a gloat, with an uncontrollable snicker to boot. The Quack quickly stopped ranting, as reality extinguished his glow. He was angry, and I knew that I was in for a ride.

"You must first admit that you have a problem before I can help you."

"I'm fine, sir."

Dr. Kahn leaned forward towards me and attempted to give me an illustration as to why he thought it was important for me to "confess" my problems to him. "If you and your daughter fall off of a ship and are drowning, who do you put the life vest on first? You or your daughter?"

The answer for me was simple. "My daughter."

"No, you put it on yourself first." Having handed me an example of his superior wisdom, his glow returned. "You save yourself, then you'll be able to help your daughter, Can you understand that, Kenny?"

He was taunting me from his elevated perch. That may have been the way psychiatrists are taught to view life, but I didn't see it that way. I didn't respond to his prompting, and there was dull silence in the room.

"Kenny? Do you agree?"

"No, sir. I don't agree." The Quack gave the same example all over again, as if I didn't understand him the first time.

"I understood your example. I just don't agree with your decision to save myself first."

Frustrated, Dr. Kahn attacked my explanation. "Do you love your daughter, Kenny?"

"Very much so. And that's why I'd save her first." He didn't ask a follow up question, but I decided to explain anyhow. "You see, sir, I can swim, but not very well. If I have time to place the life jacket on at least one person, I want to be sure that my child lives. Even if that meant I'd probably drown. You know, even with a life jacket on, I'm not so sure I'd be *able* to save my baby if she went under. So, no. I wouldn't save myself first. She's my priority."

Clearly irritated, Dr. Kahn exposed to me all that his doctorate had hidden. "You say that you love your daughter, right?"

"Of course." *What's his angle?* His question had been asked and answered.

"How much do you love her?"

"Very much."

"Yeah, but how much is very much?" I wasn't sure where that quack was heading, but it couldn't be anything good.

"I don't understand your question." There was no way I was going to guess at what he wanted, so I waited. It wasn't long before he ripped out the pin and dropped a psychological grenade into my lap.

"Do you ever think about having sex with her…you know, like when you and your wife aren't having sex?" The connection between mental restraint and Einstein's Theory of Relativity finally made sense. Not strangling that piece of hippopotamus excrement until *my* biceps withered made those few moments seem like three consecutive eternities. "Kenny? Do you want to get it on with your daughter?"

Son-of-a-BITCH! (Sorry, Mr. Cunningham.) To this day, I'm not sure what kept my firm, butter-almond gluteus maximus glued to that wooden seat. I stretched my neck from one side to the other, never breaking eye contact with the pervert who was protected by both his MD and the State of New Jersey.

"Kenny. Did you understand the question or do you need me to repeat it?" I was depleted of reasons for not attacking the pervert, and I needed to quickly justify my non-violence. So, I instantly convinced myself that if that Quack had no reverence for God, how could I expect him to have any for my child. And it worked.

"No." My answer was not loud, not forceful, barely audible.

"No to which question?"

"Both." The pervert sat back in his chair, switched his crossed legs from right over left to left over right, squirming, grinning, relishing within the borders of his own majesty, shamefully allowing his disgusting imagination to flourish in my presence and without my consent.

"Do you enjoy washing your daughter in the bathtub? And maybe sometimes your hand might slip, causing you to *mistakenly* fondle her?" The Quack rubbed the center of his bottom lip with his forefinger while he gazed at my poker face, his hands gesturing his own thoughts, desires, inclinations. "Kenny? Maybe?"

I felt numb. I finally appreciated Terry having taken my weapon from me, but I wouldn't have shot that perverted quack. I would have removed the magazine from the gun and pistol-whipped that scrawny mental-molester. I knew that no matter how provoked, the department would conjure a pardon for his actions and condemn mine. My answer managed to choke itself past my *true* desire to rip out his throat, and became a permanent record of my behavior for all involved to scrutinize.

"No."

His questions lingered unmercifully for the remainder of the hour as I stubbornly stood my ground. My demeanor became my weapon, hands stuck glued to my lap, my eyes rarely blinking, and a perfected deep breathing exercise were all used to hold back my wrath.

The Quack abandoned his unprofessional jeering at that point, deciding, instead, to attack me from what he believed would be a more friendly perspective. That was when he told Thaddeus to come into his office and to join us, where he asked Thaddeus questions about me, in my presence. I had never heard of a mental evaluation like that, and my anger was escalating to a fevered pitch. He answered all of Dr. Kahn's questions and never wavered, including Dr. Kahn's request that Thaddeus give his own opinion of my mental status.

"Well, I'm not a psychiatrist."

"But what do you think about his mental state?"

"I think the man had a marital problem that he's working through, and that we should allow him to do that without everybody getting involved. I had marital problems, too, and I worked through it. Let Kenny work through his."

What kind of evaluation required the questioning of a co-worker, seeking the co-worker's opinion of mental state? I fully expected Thaddeus not to answer, but he had nothing to gain from not answering and he also had nothing to hide.

After speaking with Thaddeus, Dr. Kahn telephoned Chief Faunce. The duo decided that I had to undergo further mandatory psychological evaluations with a psychologist that Dr. Kahn handpicked.

We exited the Quack's office and got into Thaddeus' car. I immediately unleashed the riot act on Thaddeus. True or not, I felt Thaddeus should have refused to speak about me to that quack. Although his comments and responses to Dr. Kahn were fair and accurate, I thought he'd betrayed my trust. Thaddeus wasn't moved by my tirade and, after I was done, he very calmly reacted by turning my assault into a full retreat.

"Before you get too bold, let me tell you what I *could* have said to that psych, and technically, I would have *still* been telling the truth."

His double-dosage of reality was like having a cup of iced water thrown into your face. Needless to say, I quickly regained my composure as well as my humility. "My bad" was the only response that I could muster, and wisely so.

He didn't hold my words against me, maybe because he saw in me the helplessness that he had endured. So, we took the scenic route back to the office. That gave us enough time for Thaddeus to recount the unabridged version of his own divorce. At the end of his story, he passed on to me what an older friend had passed on to him.

"The only way that you're going to get back on your feet is to figure out what you can live with, and what you can't live with. No excuses and no apologies."

"If you can't live with what she did or what you did, then fuck her. Walk away and don't bother explaining why. If you *can* deal with it, and if you're fine with it, then fuck everybody else. Stay with your wife and tell the whole world to kiss your ass. Take your time, though. As much time as you need to figure shit out."

I shook my head in dismay, wondering if his advice would work for me the way it worked for him. Thaddeus watched my doubt as he opened the car door and turned off the ignition. "Come on. Let's go inside."

We headed for the front of the prison and I didn't say a word. We walked up the stairs and towards the office door. Before we entered, I shook my head and grinned at him. "I screwed up, huh?"

Refocusing my mind on his speech, Thaddeus ignored my sentiment. "Don't worry. It'll come to you."

That advice bridged my expectations to my realities, and reassured me that I would be fine. During a quiet time in the days that followed, I made Thaddeus a promise. "We're going to have this conversation again real soon, and I'm going to be straight." Shamefully, I never again discussed our words with him, ever. I would've liked to thank him for his advice right after then. But, I guess right now will have to suffice. Thank you, T.C.

ELEVEN

Less Than Zero (Teth)

As soon as I returned to the office, I lamented to both Randy and Terry about the type of questioning that the Quack unloaded on me. Terry appeared shocked and suggested that I go back and "handle my business." But Randy had a different take on the situation.

"Who knows. Maybe in some goofy-ass kind of way he was trying to piss you off enough to open up." I stared at Randy, the corners of my mouth dropped. "Or maybe not. He's a fucking quack! What did you expect?"

I felt no pain, only anger. Dr. Kahn had verbally violated me, and for what? I still had the same problems I went there with, and now I had to live with that quack's gruesome comments. I couldn't "repay" Dr. Quack the way I wanted to and, worst of all, I knew I eventually had to forgive him.

Terry informed me that hour-long psychological sessions were scheduled for me with a Dr. Daniel Williams, PhD., whose office was located in East Orange. I had never heard of Dr. Williams, but anybody that Dr. Quack Kahn and Chief Faunce recommended were, by definition, suspicious.

The evaluations began immediately, and I was charged sick

time for those mandatory counseling sessions. I expected the worst trap to be set for me once I arrived at Dr. Williams' office. But words cannot describe how relieved I was about being wrong about Dr. Williams, who had an extremely low-keyed attitude. He took the time to inform me about everything told to him by Dr. Kahn, which provided a slanted history of me. He asked me about my marriage, my wife, and my life in general, just as Dr. Kahn had, but he was decent in his approach. He respected my privacy and didn't exploit my predicament.

I wanted to speak frankly to him about everything I was feeling, but my defenses were sharp, and with good cause. With the lashing that I'd received from Quack Kahn, I despised all quacks. After only a short time, I saw there was something different about Dr. Williams and hated that he was rapidly disproving my perception of psychs. However, I refused to let down my guard during that counseling session. My answers to him were consistently "yes, sir", "no, sir", and "three bags full". I answered him honestly and succinctly. No elaboration. No details.

I met with Dr. Williams four or five times during the summer of 1998. And somewhere around the second or third meeting, Dr. Williams, with his raspy voice, proposed a scenario to me.

"Kenneth, we can continue to meet like this and waste both of our time, or you can give me your take on what occurred." He remained straight-faced as he looked me in my eyes while he spoke, a sure sign of respect. "Who knows, maybe I could give you the help that you're asking for."

I pondered his words for a moment and then I asked him about his choice of words. "Why would you say *asking for* when I'm forced to see you?"

The doctor sat back slightly in his chair. "What do you mean *forced*?"

"I had no choice. Either I come here, talk to you, and watch what I say, or I get fired. To me, that means forced." I didn't believe Dr. Williams was an actor, so I accepted his troubled look as being sincere.

"Who forced you?"

"They didn't tell you that I objected to seeing a psych?"

Dr. Williams quickly responded, "No." Dr. Williams exhaled confusion out of his lungs, and scratched his head rearwards. He nodded his head as he flipped over his pad to a new page and spoke to me. "Forget what they said. Tell me about your marriage, Kenneth."

He had his own suspicions about their version of my problems, especially regarding why somebody so enthusiastic about counseling only offered one-word answers and kept asking if the session was over. He was misled by Faunce and Dr. Quack, so I decided to take a chance with him. I lowered my guard and told him that my marriage had problems, but I that I thought I could best address those problems if the department stayed out of it.

"Did they say that my work was affected?" I asked.

"No, they didn't." The doctor was beginning to see my point. "If your work isn't affected and you didn't volunteer, I'm not sure they have the authority to force you to undergo these sessions. Have you spoken about this to your boss?"

"She was the one behind this." Dr. Williams paused, seeming to reflect on my predicament.

"I want you to understand that I am being employed by your supervisors, and I have to decide if you are a danger."

"Yeah, I can understand that. It's my weapon, right?" I carried a weapon both on duty and off duty, and it was reasonable for Dr. Williams to be cautious about clearing me.

"Exactly."

"I've got no problem with that, sir."

"Well, lets finish these sessions, and I'll let you give me your story, okay?" This guy seemed okay. And, by the end of the summer, I had developed a level of mutual trust with him. I respected Dr. Williams and the profession of psychology, and saw Dr. Quack for what he was—a misprint.

Between my sessions with Dr. Williams, I was ordered
to see Dr. Quack as well. My sessions with the Quack were
extremely brief—"yes, sir", "no, sir", "three-bags-full". Plus,
I made certain that I informed Dr. Williams about anything the
Quack said or asked. Routinely, the Quack would tell me about
how great a doctor Dr. Williams was and how I should listen to
Dr. Williams' advice. He then sang his own praises, waiting for
me to say Amen. Yeah, right. Like that was ever going to happen. I didn't open my mouth around Dr. Kahn, so much so that
I didn't even respond when he said hello, unless he put in in
the form of a question. That coward had insulted me and now
pretended as if we were best friends.

From time to time, he would ask me either what I said to
Dr. Williams or what he said to me. Respectfully, I informed
him that my conversations with Dr. Williams were between
Dr. Williams and myself. But, you know I couldn't wait to run
back to Dr. Williams and tell him what the Quack asked about
Dr. Williams. As expected, Dr. Williams was perturbed that
another doctor would question one of his patients about his sessions. Although he never verbalized his disgust, you wouldn't
have to be an astrophysicist to understand a real doctor's ratio-
nale.

I continued working without my firearm, which had become
a significant part of me. It's easy to get attached to having nine
hollow-points riding on your hip every day. It was almost like
a security blanket, and I didn't want anybody else to touch it.
But it was taken from me, and there was nothing that I could do
about it.

"Kenny, get in here for a minute." Terry wanted me to fax
some pages from our unit's official log to another Internal Affairs unit regarding an officer who had been arrested in Newark
the night before.

"Make a copy of this page for me. Hold on a sec…" My
recollection of my conversation with Terry the week prior was

as vivid as if it were happening at that moment. So, I really wasn't feeling him. I looked away and weighed Terry's hand in the status of my private situation, especially to Chief Faunce. I glanced over at his desk and noticed something wickedly foul.

I stared down at Terry and stepped closer to his desk, as he busied himself. Terry's ink pen was working frantically, when I asked him a forbidden question, which wasn't a question at all.

"What are you doing?"

Terry looked up at my frowned face, my mouth slightly open. He was in complete confusion. "What?"

"The logbook. What are you doing?"

"What the hell are you talking about?" Terry erased two lines out of the logbook that noted the officer's wife had notified Internal Affairs that her husband had assaulted her. Terry never followed up on the wife's warnings about that officer, who we knew was problematic. Now that this guy had been arrested for domestic violence, the wife was complaining that she reported her husband to Internal Affairs and nobody had listened to her warnings. Of course, it would look terribly negligent for Internal Affairs to admit that we took no action. So, Terry was simply "adjusting" our official history.

"You use *erasable* ink in an *official* log?"

Terry looked at me as if I had used profanity at noonday mass at St. John's Cathedral. "Hell yeah!" My mouth dropped open. "What's your problem, brother?" I stood speechless as Terry grew impatient with my ignorance. "What the fuck you staring at me for...you gay or something?" He laughed. The copies were made because if the original logbook was turned in, an examiner would see the changes. If a copy of the pages was faxed, there would be no way of telling if it were tampered with. And who would think to question Internal Affairs. "We ain't got to worry about it. Debbe gave us the fucking pens."

Somehow, I didn't see the humor that amused him. And I didn't try to hide my feelings. "You go ahead and copy it yourself." His smile corrected itself as I walked towards the doorway. "That's illegal."

Terry didn't understand my opinion of what had long been standard procedure for Internal Affairs in the southern region of the state.

"What the fuck you talking about?" Terry trusted Faunce with his life, especially considering everything that the Chief had done for him and his alcohol problems at work.

"That's illegal, Terry." But there was no way that Terry would take my word over a well-established Internal Affairs practice.

"No, it's not...never mind. Is Scott out there?" Terry was finished justifying himself to me.

"He's up there in the front." I saw Scott near the secretary's desk at her computer.

"Tell him to get in here. Geez, brother." Scott was not the kind of person to say no to a supervisor. Any supervisor. About anything. But that was Scott's problem, not mine. My problem was that I had just witnessed an atrocity.

I approached Pam and told her what Terry was doing. She smiled. "Nothing surprises me any more."

Pam chuckled, but stopped when she saw that I wasn't laughing with her. "Kid, I told you before. Keep your own journal about this place, and note everything that you witness. The log? That's just the tip of the iceberg. Just keep your eyes open, and you'll see a whole lot more."

My personal journal was full of dates and times, but until now, my descriptions were vague. Now, I made a point to list details. Very specific details about everything I heard or saw.

Terry's revelation added to my chaos. I was lost in a fog that kept getting thicker with each breath and nothing made sense to me. I was angry with everyone and everything, completely ignoring that there was an enormous quantity of pain that went unresolved for almost a month. All of the warning signs were there, but I allowed them to be shrouded in my fog of anger. I had fallen down Alice's rabbit hole and was about to discover that I had reached the bottom of my abyss, and the end of my charade.

For months, I had been the ultimate professional at work and anywhere there were people. But, when I got home, I would retreat to my favorite couch in the family room down in the finished basement. That was my sanctuary—the only place where I didn't have to be strong, where I could cry in blissful harmony, and then try to get a bit of sleep. I was extremely exhausted that summer, not sleeping for days at a time, and afraid to sleep because of recurring dreams about my plight. I had mastered the art of camouflage to the point that I'd even fooled myself into believing I was indeed fine.

But, I was far from fine, and my masquerade came to an end that same summer on a warm, Saturday afternoon. With tears resting on my cheeks, I finally dosed off to sleep on the couch in the family room. I had taken a few days off from work, implying to my coworkers that I was headed out of town to spend some time with my wife. Instead, I hid myself downstairs, away from everybody, to officially kickoff my invitation only pity-party. I didn't hear my wife return home with my daughter. She was in love with her daddy, and right away, without an invitation, she came looking for me in my sanctuary as she always had.

As I regained consciousness, I slowly opened my eyes, focusing on the image weeping before me. I was shocked to behold my baby's face less than inches away from mine. She had kneeled on the floor near my face, and was resting her chin on the sofa's flower print cushion next to my cheek. She had been crying softly, trying not to wake me, and using her doll-sized hand to wipe the tears off my face.

"Hey, sweetie. What's wrong?" I asked as if I didn't know any better. I discreetly tried to sit up, but my entire left side was recovering from the thousands of needles that accompany lying on a limb too long. It took a moment to gather myself and to recover from my shock without having her notice.

She spoke to me in a soft, clear voice, "You going to die, Daddy?" She paused briefly, her face so close to mine that I tasted her fear as I felt her short breaths. I focused on her perfectly placed small teeth, the way they looked right before she lost that first front tooth. "Please don't die, Daddy."

There is a movie entitled "Less Than Zero" in which Robert Downy, Jr. is a dope-fiend in an extremely upper-class community. Drugs made him betray his friends, steal from his family, and work off his debt to his dealer by prostituting himself to the highest bidder. He allowed his addiction to drag him so low, less than zero, that the only thing that was able to get him over his addiction was death. In the final scene, you realized he didn't kill himself; he killed everybody that cared for him.

What was I thinking?! I was attempting to place that quack's lifejacket on myself and not my daughter. What I should've done was follow my own advice and place the life jacket on my daughter first. If I had, I would have seen that not dealing with my pain was drowning both of us. Her safety had to come before my self-pitying. There was a child, who, if I didn't get myself together, would be just another statistic. My pains and hurts were important, but they could no longer take precedence in my life.

"No, sweetie. Daddy's not going to die." I sat up and smiled, possibly the first time in recent memory that I wasn't putting on a front. I rubbed her neatly braided hair. "C'mon." I firmly gathered her petite, tear-moistened hand. "Walk your daddy upstairs."

In the Book of Daniel, God cursed King Nebuchadnezzar to crawl around like an animal until the king acknowledged that God was truly God. When that happened, God immediately returned to the king the two things that a man most needs: the capacity to understand and the ability to reason.

Nietzsche once wrote,

When a man stares into the abyss and sees nothing

*but darkness, this is the time that he finds his character.
And it is his character that keeps him from falling into
the abyss.*

I understood the King's plight as well as the scope of
Nietzsche's warning. I never would have truly appreciated the
significance of maintaining both the abilities to reason *and* to
understand until I found that zero point in my misery. An encounter with my child, who I would save even if it meant sacrificing myself, accomplished what a summer of psychological
counseling from two, rather, one and a half professionals never
could. The memory of her tears won't ever let me forget that.
My masquerade ended immediately, and I was better for it.

I entered the bathroom and turned on the lights. As I stood
there, I stared at the stranger whose frightening image appeared in my bathroom mirror, thirty-four pounds lighter than
I had been several months prior. He hadn't showered, brushed,
shaved, or smiled in nearly three days, and he had unwittingly
terrified a four year-old girl who genuinely loved him.

It didn't take long for me to accept my run-down state. My
daughter saw me through rose-colored glasses, and cared too
deeply for my feelings to mention the obvious. I never wanted
my child to make excuses for me, so I decided to help her out.

"Daddy looks bad, huh, sweetie?" She smiled just enough
to see my reaction, ensuring that she didn't hurt my feelings.
That's when I made an animated yuck face. She laughed until
her cheeks hid her brown eyes. That laughter was a long overdue release of all of the fears and inhibitions I had created in
her tiny, little world.

"Your breath stinks, too!" Oh, yeah. She had jokes, even
at four years of age, to accompany an honesty she wielded with
the precision of a wrecking ball. I was also reduced to giggles,
but my laughter quickly ended after my tongue ruthlessly delivered a full whiff of my hardened breath as it painfully chiseled
against my collapsing nostrils. I immediately tried to mask the

stench of my breath with the delicate aroma of one of my farts. (Just kidding about the flatulence, but you get the idea.) My teeth celebrated the triumphant return of Colgate™ with Baking Soda, along with his trusted sidekick, Listerine™.

The anger I had embraced for so long had partially dissipated and my appetite ravenously returned. I anxiously anticipated reestablishing the everyday closeness with my daughter, moment by moment, that had been displaced by my anger. The time we spent together convinced me that I was blessed beyond measure, and that my child was a gift from above, a gift that must be cherished at all times and in all situations.

She wanted me to be well and I desired the same thing for her. Much of her well-being was locked inside her yearning for my wellness. And it was our mutual love and connection that ended my need for sleeping pills in order to rest. My daughter and I would fall asleep on a Futon next to the radiator in our den while we watched television. My back sometimes ached from reclining on that Futon, but my daughter's presence made that lumpy pad more comfortable than my Simmons BeautyRest™.

Having returned from beyond zero, I also had a chance to reflect on several aspects of my marriage. Thaddeus' words had struck a powerful cord in my mind. Also, my return from the black hole brought with it a newfound ideology, one that confirmed there was no rush for me to decide how I felt or what I wanted. Whether I made my decision that day or that year was totally up to me, and to me alone. Furthermore, I owed nobody any apologies, excuses, or explanations for my choices or my feelings.

It was an amazing comfort to know that my decisions about my feelings didn't have to make sense to anybody other than myself. And, I had no intentions of altering that ideology for some quack in South Orange.

TWELVE

Once I Was Blind

I endured a few more sessions with Dr. Quack-Kahn, as well as with Dr. Williams, after the Masquerade had ended. At work, I continued being productive and carrying out my daily tasks. I opened up more to Dr. Williams during those last sessions after he reviewed some positive information regarding our meetings. Unfortunately, I had to continue listening to Dr. Quack-Kahn impress himself, elaborating on how much he loved himself as well as why I was so fortunate to have met him in this life. Needless to say, I was not impressed.

On August 19, 1998, I had my final session with Dr. Williams. I returned to Dr. Williams' East Orange office a few weeks later to pick up a sealed copy of my Fitness for Duty Evaluation, with instructions to hand deliver it to Quack-Kahn in Trenton.

After handing Quack-Kahn the envelope, I sat motionless while the perpetually grinning doctor opened the envelope and reviewed the evaluation. Large, dreary wrinkles crept along the Quack's countenance with every line of the report. He quickly turned in his chair and unsuccessfully searched for a telephone number. He then swiveled only his head towards me.

"Do you remember Dr. Williams' number?" I gave the wrinkled Quack the telephone number, and his corpse-like fingers fiercely fired away at the telephone buttons.

"Hey, Dr. Williams. This is Dr. Kahn." He leaned back in his chair, stroking his receding hair. "I just got this evaluation and it seems like you are saying nothing was wrong with Investigator Freeman." He nodded at the response that came from the other end of the line. It became obvious that the Quack wanted something Dr. Williams wasn't offering in the evaluation.

"But did you know that his wife is. . . Yeah, but his Chief said. . ." There was an extremely elongated pause in their meeting of the minds, when the Quack finally broke his silence.

"Okay. Whatever!"

The Quack was pissed. And he soon let me know just how pissed. "Well that's what you get when you *only* have a PhD." He dropped the evaluation in the center of his cluttered desk and pulled out a form from his overflowing in-basket. "*Your* doctor seems to believe that there was no reason to send you for counseling. As if nothing is wrong with you."

That snotty-nosed punk was asking for what he used to get in junior high. But I composed myself long enough to use logic on an idiot, which by the way, never worked.

"But what if he's right, Dr. Kahn? What if, just by chance, there's nothing wrong with me?" I sat forward, leaning towards the Quack, closing the distance between our knees.

"Would you admit that you're wrong, doctor?" No answer. Only a faint smirk. He reluctantly dialed the telephone again, this time speaking much easier, yet exhausted.

"Hi Debbe, it's me. He's cleared to go back to full duty." Whatever her response was, Quack-Kahn wasn't too pleased. "Yeah, you can give him his gun back. I'll explain later."

Disappointment oozed through his grin as he reached his hand towards me holding that form letter. But I wasn't finished with my questions, and after a summer of listening to him, I deserved something more than what I was getting.

"Dr. Kahn, but what if I am fine?" He responded, but not the way that I wanted him to.

"Hand this to Chief Faunce so you can get your weapon back. You're done with your evaluations." He turned back in his chair, not even bothering to attempt to offer his customary handshake. *So rude!* That was when I decided to get one last jab in before I left.

"Hey doc?" The Quack looked over his right shoulder, barely lifting his pen from his pad. "How many people has psychology actually cured, you know, from depression and stuff?" What a stare! *So, that's what teeth grinding looks like.* Oh well. I had my "get-out-of-jail-free" card in hand, so I really didn't care.

I stopped by Central Office and headed straight for that Xerox machine near the secretary's area. After making a copy for myself, I proceeded to the Chief's office where I handed the original to Debbe and then walked to the Special Operations Unit to retrieve my firearm as ordered. I left headquarters in a great haste.

After the long drive back to Northern, I ran into Kevin Bolden, a senior investigator who worked at Rahway. I filled in the gaps about what had happened to me over the summer, and about Quack-Kahn. His response was simply one word, "What!" He repeated that synopsis frequently, until I included the part about being forced to see both psychiatrists.

"Something ain't right about that, Kenny. You got a lawyer?" Kevin had been around Internal Affairs a while and didn't like what he was hearing.

"For what?" Although I didn't like what happened to me, I didn't think I needed a lawyer.

"I don't know. But something just doesn't seem right about that shit." I shook my head at his analysis and said nothing. Kevin sighed as we shook hands. "I know that you're still hurting from your shit, but don't go back in there if you're not ready to handle your business."

"Yeah, you're right."

"I'm serious, man. Keep your eyes open and watch for everything. Something don't seem right, Kenny."

As I walked up the staircase and went in the office, I started thinking about some of the things that had happened over the summer. Not necessarily about the psychiatrists, but everything. And one thing stood out from everything else. The official logbook.

I asked Terry about the logbook incident, but he just shrugged off the question. He claimed that the erasable ink helps to keep the logbook "clean" looking. In other words, Debbe considered a logbook, with scratched out lines or other visible corrections, to be unprofessional. I believed that those visible corrections bolstered credibility because they demonstrated that you weren't trying to hide anything.

But regardless of Terry's contentions, nothing could reasonably explain why there was no record of that woman's telephone call to IA. I wondered, *"Is this truly law enforcement?"* And if so, what a shame.

More and more, questionable things began to re-surface. My reasoning had returned with a vengeance, and although my understanding lagged behind, it was gaining fast. I re-learned the art of sitting still, and taking specific notes of critical details in my surroundings. And who better to learn from than a pompous buffoon. Every department had one, but we had the biggest one of all. He was the one Deborah Kopp called "M.B.M." (Muscle-Bound Moron), a play on Will Smith's *Men In Black*.

Charles Mueller embodied everything that was wrong with Al Bundy and Homer Simpson. Don't get me wrong, I liked Al and Homer, but "Chuck" was Al Bundy's alter ego and the prototype for Homer's logic. Chuck was an ex-jock who was a legend in his own mind. When wearing a coat, you'd think he still had the physique of a football player, but one touch of his flab proved he was made of more Twinkies than push-ups. His stories of scoring four touchdowns in a single game changed daily, depending on which details he could remember. M.B.M. was truly a M.B.M. in the purest sense.

Chief Faunce liked him because ignorance bred loyalty. Chuck didn't have to worry about scoring high on the department's promotional exams because Central Office got the tests and the answers nearly a week prior to administering the exams. That was why everybody assigned to Central Office routinely scored the highest on the personnel exams.

Debbe ensured that IA was protected from any outside eyes when it came to favors for certain investigators she wanted to protect. Nobody in Internal Affairs failed the annual firearms qualifications exams because our instructors were (you guessed it) other IA investigators and the answers to the exams were openly passed around during the tests. And who was going to investigate Internal Affairs?

Chuck was a perfect complement for Debbe. All she had to do was promote him to a position for which she knew he was not qualified. That way, the threat of being forced to simply "do your job" was enough to keep him in line. It worked like a charm because Chuck never questioned anything when it came to Debbe. He was an extremely loyal idiot. But, he was also a loyal idiot who loved to brag anytime he had an audience. And I learned the advantage of remaining silent during group discussions at Mountainview.

Chuck headed Internal Affairs' Fugitive Squad, a group of investigators that hunted for inmates who escaped either from prison or from a halfway house. Only loyal investigators were permanently assigned to the Fugitive Squad, those that would never question anything Chuck said or did. There were other investigators who would work with the Squad from time to time, like Kevin, Thaddeus, and Duane Grade, but their loyalty was always questionable because that trio was too intelligent to be trusted.

The three of them were voluntary victims of paychecks and benefits, robbing society of their greatness for the security of a civil service position. A mere thirty minute conversation with Duane had an unrelenting effect on his hearers, causing one to imagine the "What if's" of strong fathers in our homes. The way Duane would reflect on the masculine discipline he and his brothers received revealed how his father delicately draped love and compassion over iron fists. Thaddeus would inadvertently smile whenever he spoke of the many lessons taught by his late father, experiences that created a profound respect for authority and forged a man's integrity. Moreover, no matter how angry Kevin became about a situation, some portion of the Bible would drip from his tongue, evidence of an inescapably Godly home and a solid foundation for his children. But the greatness of these truly exceptional men would soon be consumed by the promise of guaranteed pensions.

One afternoon, Chuck and his squad returned to Northern State after an unproductive search for an escapee in Newark. They came in the office to relax and brag about their latest triumph. Sergeant Slattery, a NJ State Trooper assigned to the Fugitive Squad, sat quietly as the Squad squawked.

"You wouldn't believe what happened this morning!" Chuck was excited and had regressed to his Annadale-mindedness. Every detail was about to be revealed about the Fugitive Squad. But, first, Chuck boosted his own ego about how great an athlete he was way, way, way back in college. *Did you know that he scored four touchdowns in one game at Polk High, along with Al Bundy?*

They were searching for an inmate who had escaped from the Kintock House, a halfway house located in Newark. The first place they visited was his home address in a downtown Newark housing project. It was acceptable practice to check out the home of record because most escapees seemed to return to local hangouts or familiar places and few ever left the state. But, what happened at that apartment was anything but acceptable.

"We knew he had been there because we got a tip. But, he slipped us. His grandmother and his girlfriend were still sleeping when we got there." Chuck saw it as a game and was excited by the chase, no matter how many laws were broken. In fact, that's how the entire Squad referred to apprehending escapees.

"That old-ass lady didn't want to open the door, but Slat got her with his badge!" Slattery looked up at Chuck as he carelessly tossed the Trooper's name around.

"Fuck, yeah!" chimed in Ellis Allen. "She was scared shitless. Slat told her that he would lock her ass up and get DYFS to take her ugly-ass grand kids." Ellis could barely speak through the laughter, his eyes almost in tears from the memory of the grandmother's terror. Ellis was just the kind of person that Chuck needed—A moron, loyal to the end, and the poster child for America's dissatisfaction with Affirmative Action.

They all cheered with laughter at Trooper Slattery's manipulation of the woman, begging the Trooper to join in.

"Don't pin that shit on me." Slattery smiled, but he wasn't laughing as he walked out of the area, towards the front of the unit. Slattery may not have added anything to the mayhem, but Chuck couldn't resist the opportunity to boast.

"Slat had her scared to move in her own house. We couldn't find shit!" Chuck lamented about how their search for a 200-pound man escalated into an abuse of authority.

"We looked in her dresser drawers, shoe boxes. Ellis was in her refrigerator. Damn! We looked everywhere and we couldn't find any drugs or nothing!" I was mentally storing the information they provided and struggled to keep an expressionless face at hearing their crimes. They had confessed to illegally searching for drugs with an escape warrant. That is, unless they could prove that a six-foot man could reasonably hide in either a dresser drawer or a shoebox.

"But his girl was fine as shit." Allen rambled with the

145

shrewdness of an undersexed adolescent clamoring for another glimpse at his drunken, perverted daddy's Penthouse collection. "She had this little, tight shirt on."

Affirmative Action Allen was truly a moron, no discretion, acting on as much brainpower as abandoned plankton, but he had Chuck in his corner and Debbe at his back. "I was trying to ask her out, but dat bitch was still pissed off… because we tossed her shit."

"What the fuck's wrong with you, El." Chuck's bewilderment was not at Ellis' lack of ethics, but rather at the boldness in which he flaunted his perverse nature. "She was young as shit." Chuck laughed incessantly at Ellis' practice of going after what Ellis considered the easy catches, the ones without much baggage or intelligence. They were young girls—clearly too young for him, but Ellis never allowed something as ridiculously simple as morality to get in the way of his hyper-libido. Hyper exploits that earned Ellis the dubious distinction and reputation amongst his juvenile conquests as the best three and a half seconds of their life.

"But you could see her nipples, Chuck!" Ellis figured that young girls should welcome his "minute-man" disability since most of them had only recently graduated from high school, and in some cases, were preparing to graduate from high school. His tender, inexperienced mates shouldn't see anything peculiar about his prowess, or significant lack thereof. To Ellis, any conquest was a conquest to brag about and he offered no apologies.

Ellis also had a habit of relentlessly pursuing the wives, girlfriends, and female family members of the incarcerated men, angering many inmates who had no recourse outside of IA. Chuck winked at his wayward pursuits and, in turn, richly dumped the "attaboys" upon Ellis' brow, dismissing the many complaints made against Ellis as nothing more than "convicts being convicts".

Once the laughter ended about the harsh treatment un-

leashed upon the grandmother, Chuck's bravado switched
to more exploitive encounters regarding other fugitives and
institutional incidents, focusing on one particular matter that
was being thoroughly sanitized by the Chief of Internal Affairs
herself. That incident involved an investigation that Debbe had
completed about a year ago involving the department's Special
Operations Group as well as many of the officers and supervisors assigned to a southern New Jersey prison run by Debbe's
husband, Scott Faunce.

Chuck quickly ran through incidents under investigation
by inmates' lawyers like an auctioneer selling a warehouse of
valuables. Eventually, Chuck slowed down enough for me to
understand what was behind his suddenly irritable attitude,
and the details about every conceivable departmental violation Chuck could recollect rapidly drooled passed his lips. I
held my peace during Chuck's tirade, absorbing everything that
dripped onto my mind's barren dessert, mentally compiling
notes I would later copy into my personal journal for safekeeping.

His lecture about Debbe's merits sparked a memory for
me that had been meaningless earlier, a puzzle without enough
pieces to gather a glimpse of reason. However, within those
brief moments, a multitude of pieces emerged, adding meaning,
color, and focus.

I revisited in my mind a conversation I had with an inmate
named Steven Beverly in the Segregation Unit at Northern
State after he mercilessly, and without reasonable provocation,
slew Officer Fred Baker during the summer of 1997. Initially,
we were informed that Beverly wasn't Officer Baker's murder-
er. Instead, we were directed to Beverly's lover, a flamboyantly
promiscuous manipulator, and told he had stabbed the officer
to death because he and Beverly wouldn't be allowed to openly
engage in their sexual exploits. There were also hints that the
inmate I interviewed at Northern wasn't even Beverly, but some
other inmate whose identity was concealed. Maybe the charade

was intended to prevent anybody, staff or management, from retaliating against Beverly, who some groups portrayed as the poor, misunderstood victim trapped in his lover's web of deception. But I was pretty sure that Beverly was the culprit, and solely responsible for the officer's slaying.

A few inmates were transferred from Bayside State Prison to Northern State later that year, each one having documented his own complaints, graphically detailing the horrible atrocities that occurred under the hand of Scott Faunce's staff. They forwarded them to anyone who would listen—from an over-worked, under-compensated social worker, to some stressed out family members, to the United States Justice Department, to the Federal Bureau of Investigations, who swore to look into their complaints.

Chuck gloried in how easy and simple it was for Debbe to alter the videotapes of the beatings, dragging, and torture that those inmates suffered for Beverly's sake, those same smoking guns for which defense attorneys had begged the judiciary, but were denied. He flaunted the details of how Debbe sent other damning documents through the large, crosscut inmate fax, permanently shredding all traces of that evidence into minute checker-like confetti.

"We told Debbe, we support you, Chief. Those fucking inmates deserve whatever they got." Chuck sought more nods from his followers, and they didn't fail to deliver their unequivocal allegiance to the Chief. Even questioning the lone investigator who, after briefly championing what was right and lawful, reluctantly conceded to her conspiracy.

"I couldn't believe Ron tried to do that to the Chief." Chuck's anger resonated within his voice, his bottom lip disappearing under the pressure of his teeth. "As many times as she looked out for us," their heads kept nodding, cheering on their feared hero, "for all of us, and he's going to try to hang *her*?"

Ellis couldn't resist echoing Chuck's sentiments, a sidekick to the end. With lower morals than road-kill as his conscience, never passing up an opportunity to practice sucking up, he declared, "That shit be unacceptable. Debbe should fire his ass."

Ronald Randall was a senior investigator, heavily involved in the Bayside Prison beatings, and a lightning rod for the pending litigation that would follow for years and never seem to end. With the Attorney General's Office being apprised of every step of her investigation by both Debbe and the Commissioner, the trio decided that certain portions of the tapes couldn't be turned over to anybody, shielding Scott Faunce and the State of New Jersey. If Scott was to hang, he had enough blackmail to entangle quite a few other heavy Brass within and outside of the Department of Corrections.

At the discretion of the Attorney General's Office, all of those discoverable "smoking gun-type" documents were unethically classified as "work product", and, therefore, deemed privileged by the state. Internal Affairs often abused the "work product" privilege when dealing with undesirable matters. The Superior Court ignored the abuse for fear of retribution from attorney generals who were regularly appointed to New Jersey State Supreme Court positions as due compensation for their fidelity. Sensitive reports from some of the inmate advocates at Bayside supported many of the inmates' charges of being beaten and tortured at the hands of an angry uniformed mob, hell-bent on revenge, attacking any convict within their domain.

Scott was, once again, in the middle of the department's controversy and headed for another round of civil litigation. He smiled for the cameras, refused to give interviews, and tried to dodge the stigma of having been the focus of the federally mandated Holland Consent Decree. The decree was supposed to correct a wayward system, but it stopped millimeters shy of condemning Scott for his treachery in managing the officers that worked at the Adult Diagnostic and Treatment Center. As such, that decree served honorably as the lining of choice in countless birdcages throughout the state.

After Debbe erased a significant portion of the videotape

that supported many of the inmates' claims, she expected Randall to support her treachery by stating that the lapses in taped action were due to some type of unanticipated mechanical error. Randall was not too enthused about Debbe's explanation that the camera's battery simply died out. It was mandated that investigators verbally record that we were about to change batteries whenever the indicator light on the camera began blinking. Failure to note such a critical event would almost certainly result in disciplinary actions against the investigator.

That was when Debbe sprang into her furious damage control. With the backing of Commissioner Terhune, she threatened Randall with something that forced Randall to eventually check his integrity at the unemployment office—a tactic she used repeatedly against the unwilling and stubborn. Debbe threatened to send him back into uniform as an officer. Randall would've effectively been thrown into Internal Affair's own lion's den— working in the same jail he investigated for so many years, tainted with what could only be described as administrative leprosy—an honor granted only to IA investigators that had fallen from grace.

I listened intently to all the Fugitive Squad revealed, anxious to add it to my journal of life. And at the conclusion of Chuck's moron-fest, I noted everything that could be recorded with the utmost attention to detail. Oh, yes. Every date, every time, every place, every name—in short, everything!

I had a weighted measure of protection against Jimbo and his all-out, full-court presses. I thought I would be protected from anything Central Office could conjure against me, but I had no idea what raged around the eye of the political storm in whose path I blindly stood.

THIRTEEN

The Dawn of a New Day Glares

The holidays were approaching, and I expected much more joy in the year to come. But, right before Christmas, I received a hint that my troubles were only beginning in the form of a letter that I never anticipated. It was an invoice for $800.00 worth of services from Dr. Daniel Williams.

Obviously, I thought, it was an oversight. So, I took it to work and showed it to my supervisor so he could take care of it. "Hey, Terry. They sent me the bill from those psych sessions." Terry laughed and told me to give it to John Mulholland, who was in charge of personnel at Northern State Prison at the time.

"Kenny. What's up?"

"I got an invoice from last summer." Mulholland looked at it and grinned. "Don't worry, Darla will take care of this. Those Central Office asses are about as incompetent as the Keystone Cops." We both laughed as Mulholland date-stamped the invoice.

Terry suggested I also submit copies to my insurance carrier "just in case" for CYA. My carrier declined to pay the bill because the sessions weren't established through their company and they hadn't pre-approved them, which was required with any mental health assistance. Neither Terry nor I thought they would pay it, but we figured why not try.

As time passed, more invoices periodically came my way. Extra mail and only a slight nuisance, I simply forwarded them to Mulholland and thought nothing more about them until I received a final notice in May 1999. That particular invoice was different from the other slight nuisances that appeared in my mail because it included a special incentive to pay more attention to the outstanding debt. That invoice also served as official notification that my wages would be garnished in the immediate future if I, personally, refused to pay that bill.

With the doctor's ultimatum in hand, I spoke face to face with Mulholland, who told me that he couldn't understand why it wasn't paid, but that maybe I should submit a copy of it to EAS, who had expedited the evaluations in the first place. Seemed like good advice at the time, but simple things with Corrections were rarely what they appeared. And talk about bad timing, Murphy's Law was about to drastically alter my list of priorities. Topping that revamped list was Steven Tessenholtz.

Tessenholtz was a lieutenant at Northern State who had an Internal Affairs fetish, a curious wannabe, ever desiring to be with those whom he thought would propel his career even further. He was never in his own office, daily relating tales about how his chief supervisor, William Rogers, was hopelessly dependent upon Tessenholtz for the prison's survival. That was comical enough for brief entertainment, but Tessenholtz had a reputation for making inappropriate comments towards other officers under his command without ever suffering any tangible repercussions. For the most part this was because of his brother, who was also a lieutenant with many close, high-ranking associates throughout the department, including one powerful assistant commissioner. Without as much, Tessenholtz would have never exposed himself the way he did right there in the Internal Affairs' office.

With the Memorial Day weekend approaching, work in our office was normal. But on that particular morning, there was something quietly brewing that nobody noticed. All of the investigators ordered lunch as a group, as was common for us, and we ate together in the common area of the unit. Normally, I would volunteer to pick up the lunch, not so much because I was a team player, but because I knew no one would track my whereabouts as long as I made it back around noon. My home was approximately five minutes away from the prison, which meant that I regularly stopped by my house for a few minutes, visited with my daughter at her daycare, or ran errands during my lunch break. I'd tell Terry I planned to make a couple stops while I was out, but the only thing the other investigators were interested in was eating. My desire to remain mobile made that arrangement a fair exchange in my eyes, even if I sometimes returned a bit late.

Earlier that day upon arriving to work and parking my car, I saw Tessenholtz smoking a cigarette as he stood near the front entrance of the prison. As I approached him, his eyes gazed past my right shoulder. He tossed his newly lit cigarette in the opposite direction, and scurried into the building. Two other officers immediately followed his hasty example. I had taken a bath the night before and my teeth were brushed, which meant I was clueless as to what was happening. However, the clue made itself known as he drove up in a blue, Toyota pickup truck. Chief William Joseph Rogers had arrived, and the mere mention of his name struck more fear Northern State Prison officers and supervisors than a McGreevy re-election campaign.

Chuckling to myself, I entered the building and climbed the stairs to my office. Later that morning, Tessenholtz entered Internal Affairs and continued his tirade on his administrative, take-no-prisoner toughness. The full complement of investigators was yet to arrive in the common area, partly because lunch hadn't been ordered. As Tessenholtz continued, I chortled. Thaddeus, Duane, and our secretary continued with their daily tasks, barely noticing my outburst.

Tessenholtz turned to me and started up with a few of his crude jokes. "You laugh, Freeman, but I'd bet you never ran the jail in Rahway!" The insinuation that Tessenholtz was responsible for the critical operation of an entire institution was incredulous if not absurd. I was often chided, enviously, because I did my time at Rahway, which I considered a real prison to the grinding disdain of quite a few perturbed old timers at Northern State.

Tessenholtz had an irritating laugh that sounded like an old Phillip Morris litigant with chronic emphysema. "C'mon, Mr. Real-Jail. What you laughing at?"

Tessenholtz wasn't worth the time and effort of a response, but the morning's scene played in my mind's eye. I couldn't resist tossing my hat into the ring, especially if it could shut him up for a little while. "Say what you will, but I saw you."

Tessenholtz already-wrinkled forehead looked more like a deepened maze. "What?" Ideas were pouring through his mind, but he wasn't sure what I was talking about.

"You heard me. I saw you." My smile extended past my earlobes, as I continued writing at my desk, peeking upwards under my lashes to hide my sinister expression.

Moments seemed like hours as he fought to glean understanding from what should have been declared a passing comment. Suddenly, his demeanor shifted, his eyeglasses performing a glissade toward the edge of his pimply schnauzer. The expression on Tessenholtz' face testified that what had occurred that morning was beginning to solidify within his head, and he despised the mere mentioning of his true grit.

"You—you don't know shit, Kenny!"

"Maybe I don't." The corners of my mouth tilted sarcastically. "But I know what I saw, and you know what I saw." My smile reduced itself to a smirk as we began to draw the attention of others in the office. I shared my observations as Duane giggled, never pausing from his writing. "At least I don't tremble whenever Joe Rogers shows his face."

Our secretary gave a patented schoolyard ogle as a kind of "Well, I heard that, man!" observation while Thaddeus shook his head.

"I don't run from nobody!" Tessenholtz' defensive posture hit the ground faster than his ego. "You don't know what the hell you're talking about!" His eyes danced rapidly while he repeatedly tried to shove his hands inside front pants pockets, where they no longer fit no matter how hard he tried. The nerve that I hit must have been extremely sore.

"I saw you this morning. You ran right after Rogers drove up." My head tilted slightly to the side as I anticipated his patented denial. "Now, say that you didn't, lieutenant?" There was no denial in his stare, only a ginger smile that eluded the question laid before him. "You talk an awful lot of crap, but now you're speechless. How does something like that happen?"

Our secretary laughed quietly as she sat working at the only operating computer in our office.

"Tell us what happened. Say you didn't scatter when *your* Chief drove up." I returned my attention back to my work, and began writing.

"I didn't run from him. I was just..."

"Yeah, you scattered. All of that tough talk, and you scattered. We can't call you a runner, just a scatter-er."

Considering all of the bragging he'd done, the proper response for Tessenholtz would have been to merely walk away. But Tessenholtz wasn't used to defeat or humiliation at the hands of second-class citizens. Rather, he'd been accustomed to saying practically anything he wanted to *those* people. Nothing made this situation any different from any of those other situations. He opened his mouth and lashed out.

"Hey, Sambo! Why don't you go get my lunch!"

Everything, and I do mean everything, came to a screeching halt. There was a single question that hovered above Internal Affairs like a hungry vulture. Did he say *Sambo*? Thaddeus froze with the document he was reading congealed in his grasp. Our secretary looked me in the eye, quickly gathered her papers, and shuffled out of the area. Duane's pencil levitated from the tablet it was writing upon and hung in mid-air. His left eyebrow perked as he surveyed the reactions of me, the secretary, and Thaddeus, all stunned, all caught off-guard, all taking mental notes to be summoned later.

"What did you call me?!" Inflamed, I stood up and started around the desk towards Tessenholtz when I noticed Thaddeus simultaneously defrost as he stood. He wasn't charging towards Tessenholtz. He was moving away from him, deliberately, walking down the hallway towards his private office. I stopped in my tracks. "What did you call me?" My voice calmed and I began thinking to myself, "*start writing.*" As incensed as I was, I realized that if I were to strike him, no matter how much the situation called for such a response, he would get the benefit of the doubt.

"Hey, Kenny...let me explain..."

"Conversation over." I heard that professionalism was restraint from choking the living dog crap out of some butt-hole that truly deserved it. My professionalism radiated brighter than the sun, ready to extinguish itself at the sound of his voice. "Don't speak to me, Tess."

I returned to my seat and began noting the time, the comment, the witnesses. Anything I could think of, I noted it. Beating him up would've felt good, but I would have been the one fired, not him. I had been introduced to 'zero' just a year ago, and knew that I made my own choices when confronted with adverse situations. So, I chose to act, and not to react.

I won. I didn't polish his yellow teeth with the pair of leather Stacey Adams wing-tip shoes I was wearing. Instead, I put some distance between the two of us, ending up in T.C.'s office. It wouldn't take us long to begin talking about Sambo, to which T.C. had only one question: "Do you think Tess would cut you a break?"

Enough said. Tessenholtz would hang me if I had made such a comment about a Jewish person. I would have borne the stigma of being anti-Semitic for the rest of my career and throughout my life. And rightfully so. There can be no justification for that type of comment, especially in law enforcement. And there was no way I would accept being called "Sambo" by Tessenholtz.

So, I did the right thing by filing a complaint with the department's Equal Employment Division. But sometimes the right thing depends upon the side on which you are standing. My first hint that my complaint may have been a mistake came in the form of a telephone call from Chief Faunce.

"Kenny?"

I had spoken to her on other occasions, but only enough to be cordial and to transfer her telephone call to somebody else or to forward something to her office. I had no reason to believe this telephone call would be any different. "Good afternoon, Chief. How are you?"

"What's going on with you and Steven?" She was extremely blunt and direct, and I knew that she couldn't accept any officer speaking to one of *her* investigators in such a manner.

"Yeah, can you believe that?"

There was a slight change in the tone of her voice, one that I couldn't recognize, but would come to expect. "You know, Terry just started fixing some of the mess that Ed royally screwed up at Northern. Both Barbo and Terry have great things to say about you and your rapport with the staff there. They've even cleaned up that thing with Covin and those cops. Now, we're ready for you to take on some better assignments."

"Okay." That was the only response that I could choke out, not being sure if that was a compliment or if I was being softened up.

"Why don't you let Barbo and Terry handle Steven, you know, so we can keep this thing in-house." What in the world was going on? My facial expression must have carried through the silence. "We've got big plans for you. Don't worry, we know how Steven is, and we'll take care of him, okay?" That was when she dropped her atomic bomb. "We're going to withdraw your complaint, okay, and let Terry handle it."

I was definitely being patronized, and I hated it. Dropping my complaint would have implied that I, in some way, thought of myself as less than Tess. No way!

"Only if I'm ordered to," my voice as resolute as ever, "then I'm gonna file a complaint about that."

There was a slight pause. "File a complaint about what?"

"About being ordered, by you, to withdraw my complaint."

"Don't you think you're being a little too sensitive about this thing?"

Too sensitive? That man called me Sambo, and personally, I didn't see much difference between Sambo and Nigger. "Too sensitive?" Oops! My thoughts slipped passed my lips and were now heading into the telephone line. I knew that Chief Faunce wouldn't enjoy my response, and it didn't take long for her to respond.

"Where is Terry?"

Too sensitive? The entire situation was clearly not going well and I knew she hadn't changed the subject by asking for Terry. I would find out shortly where all of this was heading. "He's in his office."

"Transfer me!"

All the cordial conversation vanished, and I wondered what had just happened? I only got a whiff of what awaited me, and it was more stale than rotted pita-bread. I had assumed I would be applauded for following protocol and not resorting to a physical confrontation. I filed a complaint the way Corrections outlined in their policies, but nothing in those policies indicated there were exemptions for certain clans within its ranks. I found myself re-enrolled in the honors class of the Academy of Hard Knocks. My first course was a pre-requisite for all of the others I would be required to take—Murphy's Law 101.

With everything that was happening between me and Tessenholtz and Chief Faunce, I had almost forgotten about that $800.00 invoice, and the very real possibility that my wages would soon be garnished.

I followed Mullholland's lead and contacted the department responsible for setting up the evaluations in the first place. I telephoned department's Employee Advisory Service and asked the young lady who answered the telephone about the bill. I firmly explained to her how my wages were about to be garnished for not paying that invoice, and reminded her how many times I had submitted the bill to the department for payment to no avail. But for some reason, she wasn't at all interested in my plight.

"The department will not pay your bill, sir, because *you* voluntarily requested treatment."

She must have been thinking of a different Kenneth Freeman, not me. So I repeated the only line that seemed to cause her to take a breath.

"No, my evaluations were mandatory. The department hand-picked a doctor, and I was told that I had no choice in the matter, except for being fired."

She then quickly ended our verbal joust. "You don't know me, and I don't know you, right?"

"What are you talking about?" That was no way to respond to my inquiry, but she didn't relent.

"You don't know me, right?"

"Right."

"And I don't know you, right?" It started to become clear to me that she had a reason for asking me those questions.

"Right. You don't know me. Now what?"

"Get yourself a lawyer." Her advice didn't immediately register because I was still focused on getting this $800.00 bill out of my name.

"What are you talking…"

She abruptly interrupted me with her piercing words, un-mistakably clairvoyant, and eternally resonating within the hollow corridors of my conscience. "Under the circumstances that you just described, they can't *make* you get that kind treat-ment." She paused for a moment. "Do yourself a favor, get an attorney. And, you don't know me." *Click!*

There was an uncomfortably warm, empty cavity in the midst of my gut. That churned feeling didn't hurt, but it defi-nitely wasn't good, as I allowed that unwelcome feeling to usher me to my chair. A certain vindication emerged, knowing that my initial thoughts about the whole evaluation incident were valid. But, that wasn't good enough. I mean, I believed that they couldn't legally force me to go to a psychiatrist in order to keep my job the way that they had, and then stick me with the bill. The telephone call convinced me that I was cor-rect, and I should have gloated inside of my self-righteousness, away from prying eyes. But, I wanted that bill to get paid by somebody other than me. And I wanted an apology or, at the very least, a reasonable explanation for the royal screw-up that had fouled up my summer.

Apologies from Internal Affairs were tough to come by, even if the circumstances were ridiculous. I thought that hav-ing the bill paid would be a step in the right direction. After they agreed to pay the invoice, I would turn my attention to securing an explanation for the screw-up and finally, that ex-planation would lead to a half-hearted apology. That, in turn, would get the stain off my otherwise unblemished record in the department.

But at what cost? With my plan of action already in mind, I knew that the only question that remained for me was whether or not I would accept being wronged in order to stay in the "good-graces" of the department's top-brass. The many pos-sible responses and justifications continued to grow, even until the Day of Judgment. And let's face it, Chief Faunce didn't have many "good-graces" for me after I complained about Tessenholtz, no less a complaint that was made in writing. In the department, one dirty hand cleansed the other filthy hand better than hyssop.

As intelligent and knowledgeable as I thought I was, I was very ignorant to the politics involved. Because of my ignorance, my answer was simple and there was no great question to be answered. I had to blow the whistle on what had happened to me. How could I ever look myself in the mirror if I didn't stand up for myself?

My career was taking off and I was being groomed through those training classes and many inter-agency interactions for an elevated position in the department, and possibly, in the state. I had just returned from a two-week course at the Division of Criminal Justice, and was certified as an instructor. I received accolades from both my peers and instructors for doing an outstanding job. But knowing that my rights had been violated wore heavily on my conscience. The question of would I allow myself to be quietly wronged was displaced by whether I "could" accept that type of treatment. I've never felt any shame in not knowing something, as long as it was recognized that I needed help. And, I knew I needed advice from somebody more experienced in dealing with the department than I. That was where Jack fit in.

John "Jack" Dale had earned the reputation of being a maverick in Corrections. He was honest and known as a fighter, both with his fists and with paperwork. And, he had been around since the birth of Jesus. Jack was the one who told IA to go to hell, then *he* threatened to return to uniform after Internal Affairs pushed a couple of his buttons on a Monday. They knew what they would lose if they didn't keep Jack, and his pros far out-weighed his cons.

Jack listened intently to my story and chuckled as only Jack could. "Nothing that this department does surprises me."

"But how do I get them to pay the $800?"

"Call her and ask to meet with her."

I smiled as I stared at Jack. "Just like that?" I asked.

"Just like that, kid!" Jack said. "But you'd better watch your ass, kid. Debbe goes from belle to bitch in less than a blink!" Jack continued his emphysemic jeering. "Then she'll switch back from bitch to belle and wonder why you can't stand her ass."

"She's that bad?"

"Worse! You heard what she did to Blake? Well, I saw it first hand. But you're smarter than him, so just be careful."

I'm glad that Jack was serious because that was how I received his advice. So, I called Debbe, and after I told her that I would like to talk to her, she shocked me when she invited me to come to Central Office, which was about an hour-long drive away in Trenton, New Jersey.

"Hey Colleen, I'm here to see Debbe." Colleen was Debbe's secretary.

"Oh, you can go right in Kenny."

Debbe's office door was open and Debbe motioned to me as she hung up the telephone. "Kenny, how are things at Northern?"

"Well, Chief, Northern is still Northern. And how are you?"

"I need another vacation. So, what's up?"

I didn't waste any time. "I got this notice that my paycheck is about to be garnished because of that psyche bill from last summer."

"What bill? EAS?"

"Yeah, chief. Now, they're coming after me for payment and I don't think that I should have to pay it."

"Of course not. That's silly. They're always screwing up something. I'll have Don get this thing paid." Donald Doherty was the head of the Employee Relations department, and he was known as the department's hit man, a real "get-it-done" person. He was very smart and extremely shrewd, a deadly combination. No matter what it was, legal, ethical, moral—it didn't matter. Don got things done and was able to sanitize himself in the process; he was the *real* Teflon Don.

Debbe took the copy of the invoice. "Try to relax. Nobody's going to bother your check."

Debbe was so accommodating about the department's responsibility concerning that invoice, almost comforting with her voice as well as in her smile. But Jack's warning loomed large in my cautiousness.

"There's one other thing that I wanted to ask you about, Chief."

"Sure. What's up?" The delight in her eyes was mesmerizing as she sat near the edge of her seat.

"Last summer, when I was sent to those psych evaluation sessions, did I have to go?"

Her forehead wrinkled slightly. "I don't understand your question, Kenny. What are you asking me?"

"I guess I'm asking why I was forced to go?"

Debbe got up from her seat and called out to Colleen. "Pull Kenny's file for me." She waited in the doorway until Colleen returned with a slender brown folder that had my name printed at the top. She opened the folder as she returned to her desk, shaking her head and holding up one of the two single-sheet memos that were enclosed.

"The only paperwork I have on that is what EAS sent us." She quickly scanned both documents, holding the first one up higher than the folder. "This is our request for an evaluation and the other is Human Resources' confirmation [of the appointment]."

"Thank you, chief. But, did I have the right to refuse the counseling, or is there a policy somewhere that I've overlooked?"

Debbe's facial muscles contracted violently, marking the abrupt, rather explosive, end of our joyful journey to corporate Shangri La.

"I don't appreciate you bursting into my office and barking at me. Who in the hell do you think you are?" *Where did that come from?* My jaw bounced off the newly carpeted floor, and slowly returned to its original position on my face. I felt like Mike Tyson when he sat before Barbara Walters. *Ludicrous, I tell ya, thimply Ludicrous.*

I managed to retain my composure as she stood up from behind her desk, no longer the comforting, compassionate figure that was present only moments earlier. I remembered Jack's warning of belle to bitch in a blink, and I remembered Sun Tsu's teaching regarding an adversary that was more powerful than you. And so, I regrouped myself as I backed away from the impending battle.

"Hold on, Debbe..." I put my hands out in front of me, motioning for her to stop. "...I was just asking a question. I mean, if I offended you or something..."

"You're darn right, you offended me. Who the hell do you think you are?"

"My bad, Chief. I just thought that maybe if I mentioned it to you, that maybe I'd understand it better. There's no harm in asking, right?"

Her expression of rage renewed itself, and she was going to make sure that I didn't forget the proper way to approach her regarding matters with which she was unable to deal.

"If you got a complaint, you write it down and send it to me. You don't come barging into my office like this."

Debbe was heated. "No problem, Chief. Again, I'm sorry if I've offended you." I extended my right hand towards her as I stood. We shook hands, but it was clear from her cold grasp that I was not shaking hands with a happy camper. "Have a good day, Chief."

"Close my door behind you." I gently closed her door as I exited, and began the hour-long journey back to my unit.

It felt like I had just gotten sucker-punched for the second time, my ego bled profusely from my nose, and a legion of those little blue-and-white humiliation spots flashed like a strobe light behind my eyelids.

As I walked into the unit at Northern State, I was still in a confused daze about our meeting. There was still an explanation that was locked away from me, and Debbe had the key. I wanted to know if there was any justification for forcing me to go to through those evaluations. An explanation or an apology was long overdue, but if my verbal question elicited that kind of a reaction, what would be the fallout if that question was memorialized in the form of a written complaint.

I tapped into my well of advice. Jack.

"Hey, Jack, got a minute?"

FOURTEEN

The Shot Heard Around the World

"Take a night to think about it, kid." Jack knew what I was about to discover. "Once you send that letter, there's no going back." Jack was clear in his warnings to me and I understood everything he was saying. "Debbe takes everything personally. And if she comes after you, you'll be on her and every other ass-kissers' piss-list for the rest of your life."

As payback, Melendez became a pawn for the chief and helped to set up fellow piss-lister William Blake, making him look incompetent, lost, and unable to run a unit. IA's trademark of retribution was extremely effective. Blake was demoted, and slandered throughout the department. Everyone considered him a moron who was "too" nice, and easily intimidated. Blake finished his career an old, scared, shell of a man,

"What would you do?" I asked Jack.

"My money is my money." Jack said, and I was in full agreement. I was about to have my check garnished, and to me that was totally unacceptable. Jack saw in my eyes that I had no intention on backing away from the fight, and so he gave me a rough blueprint outlining how to make a formal complaint.

"Kid, keep the letter short and sweet. Stick to the issues,

and don't forget to say thank you. Always." I had planned to do that anyway, but it was good that Jack emphasized those and other points.

That night, I sat home and typed my first letter dated for the next day, which was June 17, 1999. I stayed up late and, although I called it an "interoffice memorandum", it was later dubbed by me as the "big-bang" and by others as the "shot heard around the world". Simple and direct, it read:

> *As per our conversation on 6/16/99, I am forward-*
> *ing this memo to you. I am trying to understand al[l]*
> *the circumstances, departmental policies, etc., sur-*
> *rounding the department's decision concerning me*
> *during the summer of 1998. These include, but are not*
> *limited to, those decisions concerning mandatory psy-*
> *chological evaluation sessions.*
>
> *I would like to thank you in advance for your*
> *prompt response.*

On the morning of June 17, I brought that letter with me to work and faxed it to the Chief. Jack also suggested that I notify my union representative about what had transpired so they couldn't deny knowledge of the situation, which I did.

I arranged to meet with our union president, a character named Barney Dyrnes, the following Monday in Brigantine, New Jersey, which was about an hour and a half drive from Northern State.

Barney was typical of those in the department whose only goal was retirement and its accompanying benefits. Corrections was definitely one of New Jersey's best-kept secrets. Barney would make noise during the union meetings to give the im-pression that he was an advocate for the members, but everyone was aware of his Sunday-brunches with Debbe and those in her inner circle.

"Hey Brother! What's up?" Barney greeted everybody that way, even those sporting dagger wounds in their backs. "Let me take you on a tour and show you what Trenton is smiling about."

The prison in Brigantine was a new facility with all of the bells and whistles that any career criminal and Jersey-fresh politician would enjoy, but for opposing reasons. We toured the jail and I saw first hand just how much of a business the correctional system was.

Our talk began in earnest after we returned to Barney's office deep inside of their IA Unit. I was weary of Barney because he and my supervisor, Terry Diller, were bosom-buddies, but what I didn't know was that Barney was even closer to Debbe.

"Last summer, I was forced to see this psych, okay. Now, I got a warning in the mail that they might garnish my paycheck in order to pay for it..."

Barney interrupted me with his own insight. "Yeah, man! That was when you were having problems with your wife, right brother?" Somebody obviously had been talking and I quickly switched gears from transmitter to receiver.

"Something like that. So what's your take?"

"About what?" Barney's facial expressions were easy to read, especially when he was trying to play dumb. At that point, there was no reason for me not to be direct.

"You know, about forcing me to see a psych." Barney slowly and deliberately rocked backwards in his chair, coming to a choreographed halt.

"Yeah, well, you were looking real bad, brother." A partially covered smirk peeped across his mug. "I mean, you were crying about your wife fucking around on you. Then you shit your pants, right? After you fell on the floor and Chuck had to clean you up, right, brother?"

The mentioning of my wife's infidelity struck a strained chord that bound tightly around my soul, a shrewd reminder of the tears I shed during my eternal-summer of turmoil. I quickly surmised that Barney attached an addendum to his painful song.

"Shit your pants" was something unexpected, one of a series of the department's vulgar clichés, not meant to be taken literally, but often expressed precisely that way. A built in "Catch 22".

Nothing of that sort ever happened, but any attempt to accurately explain what really occurred would have shifted the focus from what I was actually seeking, and it would have given Barney more ammunition for gossip. In disbelief, I grudgingly restrained any hint of my heart's disdain, and urgently concentrated on what was more important to me.

"Who told you that?" I asked.

"It happened, right?" Barney was avoiding my question, stalling for some reason, and obviously searching for any sign of weakness.

"No, it didn't go down like that. But you still didn't say who told you that lie."

Barney gambled on my friendship with Thaddeus by throwing his name out just to observe my reaction, but I was better than prepared for such a sloppy effort.

"T.C. told us you were in bad shape, brother. They were just trying to help you out, you know."

Amateur! He'd violated two more basic rules of interviewing an individual: you must (1) remain focused on your topic; and (2) ensure that each specific question was completely answered without any ambiguity. When confronted with union situations, he was exceptionally witty and intelligent, but Barney was definitely off his game that day. Moreover, since Barney had so tactlessly tried to alter the topic of our conversation by evading my question, I figured that, as a courtesy to him, I would guide him back to the right path.

"So, you're telling me that Thaddeus said that I crawled around on the floor and took a shit in my pants, correct?"

"I didn't say that!"

"But you brought up Thaddeus, correct?" Barney was looking for the nearest cave to hide inside, but there were none.

"I never said anything about T.C."

"Wait a second." I shook my head, outwardly displaying my disbelief. "You didn't just say that he told you something about me?" No response was offered. I nodded, but not in agreement. Pointing at his telephone I said, "Let's call him and see if he remembers."

Now Barney was in a fix. He knew that I regularly talked to Thaddeus, for whom he and all of Central Office held an affinity. Thaddeus was not a threat to them, and Barney wanted to keep things that way.

"You're fucking trying to change my words around! I never said that T.C. said you shit yourself."

"Then who did?"

"Chuck told us." I should have known! My angst peaked without revealing any evidence of itself on my brow. Everybody knew that Charles "Chuck" Walters was not to be trusted, so nothing he said surprised me, even if the thought of him managed to piss me off. Now it was time for me to get out of that conversation as quickly, even if not as subtly, as possible.

"Chuck lied." I stoically gravitated from my seat, adjusting my firearm that had shifted its position on my belt.

"I may have been upset, but Chuck is a liar." Well, subtlety was never my specialty. Feeling that I had gotten one up on him, Barney wasn't simply going to watch me walk out unfettered, especially since I had just pushed him to give up Chuck's name.

"You mean you didn't do any of that shit, Kenny? Your own boy, T.C., said you were in bad shape." His hands and voice leaped towards the ceiling in utter confusion. He was grasping for bubbles of satisfaction, randomly tossing names at me. "And so did Randy. Now you're saying that *nothing* happened last summer?"

Barney already had his mind made up on that script, with me starring as the unrepentant and ungrateful villain. Even still, I couldn't figure out how Barney could have had such a fresh recollection of an incident that didn't involve him, and occurred almost a year ago. I had to tread lightly, and watch for traps.

"All I'm saying is that what really happened is different from what you're saying Chuck told you." It was clear that Barney was now interviewing me. So, I immediately changed the topic.

"Hey, when are we having that union picnic?" Perfect execution. His anger slowly melted as dollar bills danced in Barney's eyes, and his union-persona took over. Like all union presidents, Barney fussed about how nobody supported the union and how good the union was for the unit. That slight shift in topic effectively side-stepped any further questioning from him.

I headed back to Northern, an exhausting drive in modest traffic, with animosity building inside me the entire time as I recalled the specifics of my chat with Barney. As soon as I stepped in the unit, I confronted Terry about what Barney told me.

"Barney's a goddam liar, that's what he is." I hadn't given Terry any specifics about what Barney told me, and Terry was already denying it all.

"You didn't say anything to Barney about me and my wife?"

"Me and Chuck never said that you should divorce that bi...I never said anything about you and her." Terry's face was flush red, a normal state for him, but he looked lost, which was abnormal to say the least. I hadn't mentioned Chuck's name, nor had I mentioned Barney's statements about me getting a divorce. Nevertheless, since he brought up Chuck's name, I thought I'd toss it back at him.

"And what about Chuck? I heard that he..."

"Don't worry about Chuck, and I'm going to straighten Barney out for lying, okay?"

Walters needed his behind kicked in the worst kind of way, and with so many people anxiously waiting for that honor, my turn would be a ways off. However, I had a much bigger problem. My union president should have contacted me last year if he thought that there was something that might affect me, but he didn't. I was on my own without a detailed strategy to follow.

So, once again, I headed back to my unit where I could tap into Jack's savvy—a shrewdness that always included a blueprint.

FIFTEEN

People Ought to Know When They're Conquered

June 23, 1999 should have been no different from any other Wednesday, coming exactly one week after my meeting with Chief Faunce and only two days after my ad hoc interview with my union president.

"Kenny…" Terry was calling for me from his office. As I stood from my desk, I saw Terry coming from the short corridor that extended from his office into the general area of the unit.

"Debbe wants you to go to Central Office to get your money." With that announcement, Terry casually returned to his office as every astonished eye fixed upon me.

"Way to go, kid!" Despite Debbe's curious generosity, Jack was as elated as was I.

"He didn't say anything about those policies, though." I replied quickly, almost dismissing the fact that I had won the first battle. This was destined to be my day of vindication.

Jack was more focused than I was.

"Slow down, kid." He grinned at me. "First get your money, then you can talk about everything else." Jack's advice had merit and I trusted him.

I put my things away and started towards the door. "Congratulations kid. But watch your back." Jack's final warning was well received.

Upon my arrival at Central Office, I noticed the secretary's area was empty. This wasn't strange in and of itself, but I had grown accustomed to greeting either Colleen or Sharon whenever I arrived. A voice suddenly came from the doorway of Chief Faunce's office. It was Assistant Chief Willie.

"Hello, Chief. I'm looking for Debbe…"

"She's gone for the day." His large head tilted upwards. "Come on in." Assistant Chief O'Brien was standing inside the office waiting for me and it didn't take long for me to figure out that something bad was about to happen. Jimbo took his royal seat, let out a gross sigh, and began tapping his fingers on a flat, greenish-brown folder that lay on the desk, open end facing the window. We stared at each other, neither ever blinking. Finally, I cast my eyes upon O'Brien who quickly responded.

"Kenny, I'm really disappointed in you." Chief O'Brien shook his head in dismay. "We really thought that you were going to have a long career with us."

Instinctively, I started firing questions back. "You're talking past tense, O.B. Am I being fired?"

Jimbo hurriedly took the lead from the more passive O'Brien. "Why are you always starting problems? You should've already been fired!" Jimbo tightly pinched the edge of the folder between his thumb and his forefinger.

"Nobody's firing anybody." Chief O'Brien was trying to sound like the voice of reason, performing a good chief to Jimbo's bad chief. Jimbo was a hothead, and O'Brien was charged with keeping him in line. "We're just concerned about the way you've been acting, Kenny."

O'Brien didn't stop there. "Debbe thinks you're just going through the same kind of problems that you had last year and she just wants you to talk to a friend of ours."

This had the writings of a set-up all over it, but I was determined to gather as much information as possible without hurting myself.

"What friend?"

"Dr. Cevasco is a good psychiatrist and a personal friend of ours. He agreed to speak with you." Chief O'Brien nodded, looking for him to agree, but Jimbo was too busy turning red.

Dr. Richard Cevasco was the department's head of psychiatry for the entire state, and he was waiting to evaluate me in an office that was next to Chief Faunce's office. Jack's warning to "watch my back" quickly became relevant.

"You go in there and talk to him for a few minutes, and you can have your job back."

"Just like that."

"Just like that!"

That day, I must have had the word "fool" written all over my forehead because both chiefs actually looked like they thought I would agree to their request.

"So, I am being fired." I said.

"We just want you to talk to him."

"Let me get this straight. You want me to go for *another* psychological evaluation?" My left eyebrow crept towards my hairline.

"Yeah, brother, he's cool." O'Brien nodded agreement with his own assertion as he grinned incessantly. "Piece of cake."

"Is it mandatory?" My questions caused Jimbo to boil until he had to interrupt. "Well, let's see. Give me your gun and badge." A lump formed in my throat. Was I being fired? For what? I refused to let Jimbo intimidate me or to see me quiver. I removed my badge from my wallet and placed it atop of the greenish-brown folder that sat on the desk. Then, I pulled out my firearm by the handle, removed the magazine filled with eight hollow-tip rounds, unceremoniously ejected the ninth round that was still lodged inside of the gun's chamber, and set my Smith & Wesson 4053 next to my confiscated badge.

Jimbo never expected me to comply so easily. I had called his bluff and my refusal to panic was making him look desperate. He paused for a moment to gaze down at my gun before speaking to me.

"So, you're going to talk to the psych now, Kenny?"

"Is it mandatory?" I kept my question simple, without any attitude. That folder was too interesting to him, and his fingers never stopped fumbling over it. I knew that whatever was requested of me had already been decided.

"No, it's not mandatory." Chief O'Brien answered.

"Well, do I have the right *not* to talk to your friend?"

"You really should talk to the doctor, brother." O'Brien irritated me enough on any normal day, but as much as I hated him calling me brother, I had to stay focused on the matter at hand.

"But do I have the right to decline?"

"Sure you do."

"Well then, thanks, but no thanks."

"You're suspended! Right now!" Chief Willie exploded, the blood-induced crimson from his flushed cheeks now dominated that huge, oval-shaped forehead and could be seen through the stringy comb-over that decorated the top of his mammoth-sized cranium. He pulled a memo from that greenish-brown folder, pre-signed and dated, stating that I was suspended immediately pending a pre-scheduled psychological evaluation. As I looked at the memo, I realized that my intuition was correct. That interview with their "friend" was predetermined, and I had failed the evaluation hours prior to my arrival.

"No, wait." O'Brien tried to calm Willie before turning his attention to me. "Debbe said to…"

"Fuck him! I told y'all!"

"Kenny, c'mon." O'Brien tried to stay with Debbe's plan. "Why don't you talk to your friends about this?" Waiting outside the door were two investigators, Ellis Allen and Houston Miggins. Both, coincidentally, were African American.

They were surprisingly well versed on what was happening, which gave me even more reason to be careful.

"What are you doing, brother?" Allen asked. "O.B. is cool. Don't fuck this shit up."

"Yeah, man. O.B.'s just trying to look out for us." Miggins' said. I didn't know that this was an "us" situation. It seemed that "I" was the only one being suspended for refusing to be evaluated voluntarily.

"I don't trust any of you as far as I can spit at you." I had just been suspended for refusing to voluntarily see a psychiatrist and was not worried about hurting any feelings. That statement would have stopped anybody with integrity. However, Allen and Miggins were under Chuck Mueller in the Fugitive Squad.

"Don't say that, brother. I saw Dr. Cevasco when I had that domestic shit with my fuckin' ex. O.B. gave Cevasco a call, and they made it go away. I'm telling you, O.B.'s gonna look out for you."

Miggins was emphatic, "O.B. is on our side, brother!" The pair did everything but put on black face and tap shoes and start singing "Mammy!"

"See, Kenny." O'Brien never ceased to nod at his own accolades. "You talk to Richard, and you go back to work. Alright?" Chief O'Brien was clearly getting desperate, but I had already read Chief Willie's suspension notice. That memo was signed before I had arrived at Central Office. The deck was stacked against me in that office and I knew that I needed an out.

"Is it alright if I call a union rep?"

"Go ahead. Barney's waiting for your call." Judging by the reaction on O'Brien's face, I didn't think that Willie was supposed to tell me that. I had planned to call PBA vice-president Officer Enso, who wasn't my union representative, but was well versed in department matters. But I figured that since Barney was patiently awaiting my telephone call, I'd call him and see how much more information I could get from him.

"Barney, they just handed me a suspension notice. What's

up?"

"Brother, they're going to suspend you. Did you talk to the psych?" Barney didn't wait for my small talk, rather going directly to the matter at hand. I never mentioned the psych to my union president, but I knew what time it was.

"Why didn't you warn me about what I was walking into?" I asked.

"What are you talking about?"

"You are my union president, right?" I asked.

"Kenny, if you don't want my help…"

"You're my union president, aren't you, Barney?"

"Yeah, brother, but…" Barney stuttered, and I lit in.

"And you should warn your members if there's a trap waiting for a fellow member, correct?"

"This ain't no trap!" There was a brief pause, allowing just enough time for Barney to regain his weathered composure. "Hey, they said they're worried about you, and so am I." After that kind of reply from my union representative, nothing else needed to be said. My fate was already sealed.

"Take care of yourself, Mr. President." With a press of the receiver, I ended the call, and remembered to stay calm.

Allen quickly chimed in, "So you ready to see Cevasco?"

"Ellis, you're pushing awfully hard. What's in it for you!?" Allen looked as if I found Waldo on the back of some comic book. "Sell out. The answer's still 'No'." I looked O'Brien in the eyes. "I'll be evaluated only if you or Willie order me. But I'm not volunteering for anything."

Jimbo ordered me to hand over the rest of my credentials, which I did. I was then ordered to drive back to my unit and turn in the state vehicle, which I also did.

On the way back, I had plenty of time to think about what had happened and what I would do about it. Somehow, instead of forming a plan, I wasted my time wondering how I could have been suspended for refusing to volunteer.

By the time I reached my unit, I wasn't in much better shape than I was when I first left Central Office. Terry met me as soon as I stepped inside of the unit.

"Kenny, come into my office. I need you to sign something."

I followed Terry into his office, and saw Jack sitting on one of the chairs facing Terry's desk.

"What's up, Jack?"

Jack shook his head, indicating that there was something unclean about what was going to happen.

"I told Jack to come in here so that he could be a witness."

"A witness for what?" As I spoke, Jack's expression reprimanded me.

"Chief told me to give you this." Terry said. It was a memo ordering me to be evaluated by a different psychiatrist, Dr. Walden Holl, in two days. The evaluation was prescheduled and to take place regardless of what happened with Dr. Cevasco. Terry wanted me to sign his copy as proof that I had received it, but I was skeptical about anything that had to do with Central Office.

"I'm suspended, and I'm not signing anything."

I turned and walked out of the office. Jack followed behind me and caught up with me in the small corridor.

"Keep your head, kid." Jack had a rude smirk on his face.

"Did you know about this?" I didn't think that he had, but with all of the foolishness that I had witnessed it seemed like a good question.

"No, but right after you left, Chuck, Randy, and T.C. had their statements in Terry's office." Jack looked at the secretary as she sat by her computer, unable to restrain his thoughts. "Mother-fuckers! This shit never changes!" Disgusted, Jack walked back to the work area of the unit. The secretary looked up at me in disbelief.

"They are so dirty." She looked ashamed for them. "You

know they wrote those reports against you, right?"

"What did I do?"

She maintained her whisper, as though our office was bugged by the NSA. "Thaddeus didn't say anything to you?"

"About what?"

"He's your friend?"

"About what?!"

"Last summer..." She leaned forward across her desk to see if anybody was standing within hearing distance. "Call me later." She was nervous about talking too much inside of the unit. "And, hey, don't do anything stupid."

I exited the office completely dejected. I had never been suspended before, and their reason for suspending me made my comprehension that much worse.

The trials from the summer of 1998 had dauntlessly woven patience into my life, and now that patience gave me a crude type of experience with matters that should have clearly devastated coworkers and remembering how I had withstood their attack once before encouraged me to defend myself again. I refused to be ashamed of standing up for my rights, and I was ready to let the world know it.

SIXTEEN

Hit 'em Up Style

I have never been the type to go looking for fights. But if I ever found myself confronted by that type of a situation, I believed that I had the right, no obligation, to not only defend myself, but to make sure that my aggressor never forgot the cost of attacking me. I remembered from my youth that the only thing a bully understood was his own pain, not reasoning. Simply hitting him back wasn't enough. You had to hit him back harder than he hit you, and then you had to keep hitting him until you couldn't fight any more.

So I analyzed my fists, and started jabbing. My most effective punch was rationally seeing this as nothing more than a game of chess, although I was forced to play without my three most powerful pieces—my Queen and both Rooks/Castles. I complained about being forced to have mandatory psychological evaluations and they countered by suspending me. Now, it was time to defend against their attack by acting in a way that was consistent with the "reasonable person" test.

The three chiefs were interested in more than my mental status. The department's ultimate goal was not to only discipline an employee they considered troublesome, but to inconvenience and to punish me in order to discourage others from not playing ball. Encroaching on Jimbo's dominion regarding Aburami required true penance in the form of outstanding performance, but questioning Debbe Faunce's sovereignty was blasphemy and unpardonable. Yes, they could have just ordered me to talk to Dr. Cevasco, but Debbe didn't account for my defiance and never gave O'Brien or Jimbo a "Plan B".

Dr. Holl was located an additional hour and fifteen minutes away. I anticipated nothing positive from Dr. Holl, so I prepared a counter-balance from anything that he could or would say or do. The first step was to have an evaluation performed by somebody that had no relationship with the state. I went to the J.P. DaSilva Psychiatric Center.

At the center, I scheduled an evaluation with Dr. Jorge Quintana, MD, in his Rahway, New Jersey office for June 24, 1999. I had never met Dr. Quintana prior to that Thursday, which would insulate me from being accused of collusion by the department.

Dr. Quintana was very pleasant and professional. He gave me a thorough "fit-for-duty" evaluation, determined that nothing was wrong with me, and recommended that I be returned to full duty without any restrictions, specifically noting that my firearm should be returned. With Dr. Quintana's evaluation in hand, I quietly prepared myself for Friday's slaughter.

That morning, I drove to Dr. Holl's office for my mandatory 11:00 am appointment. Before I left the office on Wednesday, Celeste had mentioned that they wrote reports against me. I didn't talk to her about what was in those reports before my meeting with Dr. Holl as I should have, but I didn't want to risk anybody overhearing me speaking with Celeste after I had been suspended. They would have undoubtedly started to bother her about everything under the sun.

Although I didn't know what those reports contained, I decided to bring other statements about my behavior prior to my suspension, such as peer assessments and evaluations. They were less than a couple of weeks old. Among those peer evaluations were two official evaluations I received from my instructors at the state's Division of Criminal Justice.

I arrived on time and entered a makeshift office that looked like it was converted out of a nursery or something. The lights were dim, and the stained wood raced throughout. After a few minutes, Dr. Holl greeted me only by telling me to have a seat in his office.

He started with mundane questions about my age, my family members, and how and where I grew up. But later on during the evaluation, a red flag rose. Dr. Holl began asking me questions about my daughter and my thoughts immediately switched to the questions of Dr. Quack Kahn from the summer of 1998.

I was almost grateful that Dr. Holl didn't go to the extremes the Quack went to, but my thankfulness was curbed after I spied the legions of documents he consulted prior to each of his questions. While he was asking one of those questions, I interrupted him.

"May I ask a question?" His pen froze in his hand as he stopped writing, his eyes fixed on mine.

"Sure."

"What are those?" I asked, pointing at the documents with a tilt of my head.

"These are reports from your co-workers and supervisors." He straightened the reports with both hands, tapping the bottoms on his crossed knee as he held gently to the sides.

"About me?"

"Yes." Dr. Holl barely nodded as his attention returned to the documents.

"May I see them?"

"No." Dr. Holl didn't look to answer me.

"Well, can I at least know what's on them or what they're about?"

"I said no." It didn't take much to know that there was

something in those documents that was not very glowing and the psych wasn't telling me anything. Therefore, I tried to take charge of the session, attempting to direct it towards my peer evaluations.

"I went to a state training class, and I was evaluated by my classmates and my instructors." Dr. Holl never lifted his head nor responded to my statement. "Would you like to read some of these?"

"No." Clearly, Dr. Holl was not just working for the state; he was focused on protecting the interests of his employer, and appeared determined to give an opinion that presented me in the worst light. So, right then, during the latter part of the hour-long evaluation, I began mentally planning my next move. One report wouldn't be enough to offset his evaluation, which meant that I had to have a third doctor evaluate me. That way, I would have two unbiased evaluations to discredit Dr. Holl's report. But that third evaluation had to be done with all haste.

I needed somebody that the state could not refute as incompetent or biased. So, the next morning, I called Dr. Daniel Williams, the same psychologist that the department had forced me to see a year ago and scheduled an emergency session. Dr. Williams was not pleased with my outstanding bill, but I trusted him, and the fact that the department handpicked Dr. Williams was the frosting on the cake.

"Kenneth, how are you?" Dr. Williams asked.

"Not good, doc. I've been suspended." I said.

"For what?"

"I asked if I had a right to refuse counseling, and they told me that I did. However, when I said thanks, but no thanks, they suspended me. And yesterday, they forced me to have another evaluation."

"They can't do that!"

I smiled as I exhaled. "Yeah, that's what I thought. But here I am."

I had no intention of hiding anything from Dr. Williams.

He was straightforward in the past, and I believed that he would continue to be so.

"I met with another one of their guys yesterday. Dr. Holl in Haddonfield, NJ."

"Why would they send you all of the way down there?" His question was merely rhetorical.

"Ever heard of this guy?"

Dr. Williams shook his head. "Um-um."

I sighed and refocused myself. "I need a complete evaluation, today, if possible."

"Sorry, I can't help you."

His words were like splintered wooden-nails going through my stomach, ripping apart my disbelief. "Why not?"

"Your bill, Kenneth. It's almost a year old. Way overdue. I can't do anything until this bill is paid. I'm sorry." Business was business and I clearly understood his reasoning, but he didn't understand my resolve.

"That's not my bill, but I'm going to the bank right now to withdraw my mortgage money, and I'm coming here to pay that bill. Okay?" I couldn't take no for an answer, not at that point.

"I'll be here when you get back, Kenneth." Dr. Williams didn't expect me to return as quickly as I did. I paid for the past bill and for the cost of that evaluation.

"I know that these peer evaluations may not be relevant, but would you like to see them?"

"How recent are they?" Dr. Williams reached for the documents.

"A couple of weeks old, if that."

"Of course they're relevant." He laughed at my expression, then drew suddenly serious, concerned about my question. "Why wouldn't you think that these would be relevant?"

"Probably because Dr. Holl refused to even look at them." Dr. Williams stopped moving, his jaw hung open.

"What do you mean he refused to read them?"

"I asked if he wanted to see them, and he said no. He only

read the department's statements."

"From co-workers, huh?" Dr. Williams was starting to piece together the puzzle.

"Yeah. Something like that."

"And what did they say about you?"

"Don't know." I shrugged my shoulders and shook my head.

"Don't know?" Dr. Williams was growing more and more disgusted with my answers. "What do you mean you don't know?"

"He wouldn't let me read them and he wouldn't say what was on them."

He took a deep breath. "We can't do anything about that now, so let's focus on this session. You're the youngest of seven children, correct?" And with that, my evaluation commenced.

At the conclusion of the evaluation, he informed me that it would take a little time to write up the evaluation.

"Once again, Kenneth, there's nothing wrong with you." Dr. Williams shook his head as if to say I was wasting my money and my time with repeated visits. While at the same time, he seemed to understand why what would have been wasteful under normal circumstances proved to be a necessity. "You seem to believe that you've been treated unfairly, but based on recent events, your concerns are more than justified."

I left his office reassured of what I considered to be the obvious. And, all along, I couldn't help but wonder if I had any recourse.

After leaving the doctor's office, I stopped at a grocery store in Newark to pick up a few items that my wife had missed when she went shopping days earlier. It wasn't by chance that those items were forgotten because I was predestined to be there on that particular day at that specific time.

Upon leaving the store, I bumped into a man who was a very unlikely source for legal advice. Officer Norm Trent was

my adversary in a case that dated back nearly a year, which I
initially wanted reassigned to another investigator. Teamed
with PBA Vice-president Luther "Gunny" Gregg, they formed
the most formidable duo of representation in the state.

Trent represented two cops at the center of a racial controversy, Officers Nutall and Bongo. These cops, who were white,
were alleged to have assaulted and injured a black inmate
named Covin. Although the administration really didn't care
about racial equality, the brass had a tangible disdain for that
pair of officers because the officers had chosen not to "play
ball". That, coupled with their reputations for being more than
a little aggressive against darker-skinned inmates, didn't help
their cases.

However, I loathed the idea of concluding a case based
solely on reputation, without verifying the facts. The case was
closely watched by quite a few low-level department brass because Corrections was being monitored closely due to Covin's
"Special Needs" designation. The state was forced to provide
separate and secluded housing for inmates with diminished
mental capacity, and the rules regarding the handling of those
inmates differed from that of the rest of the general population.

I might not have been that curious about the circumstances
of the case if it were not for Edwin Melendez instructing me
to hang them out to dry before I even conducted my first interview.

"Here's a case you're gonna love." Edwin was grinning as
usual, passing Scott Russo's desk and coming directly to me.
I sighed as he laid the folder on my desk. I opened the folder
and began reading the complaint.

"Both of those racist assholes finally screwed up. They had
no business inside of that gate without a supervisor. They beat
that brother's ass, and Barbo gave us the green light to fire their
asses!"

Barbo was the administrator of Northern State at the time.
He didn't seem stupid enough to come out and tell Edwin that,

but you sometimes had to wonder whether Edwin was making things up as he went along.

"I got a lot of cases here, Ed."

"Fuck dat shit! If you didn't spend so much time on the phone chasing pussy, you'd be finished your work!"

Yep! He was still pissed off because his woman thought I looked better than he did. Nevertheless, I hung up the telephone and started working. After skimming over Covin's complaint, I was troubled by a couple of inconsistencies in his version of events. I interviewed Covin immediately and noticed that he was missing the "ring of truth" that was usually obvious in most interviews. I later returned to the unit and did some research. His answers were almost identical to an account that another inmate had given about the same two officers not even a month prior. A greater coincidence was that the inmate from the earlier complaint was housed in a cell adjacent to Covin on the date of the incident.

There was an inmate housed in the unit who remembered me from my days as an officer at Rahway State Prison and really wanted to be my snitch. I didn't want any pets, but if he was willing to deliver without costing me anything, I figured why not. I had the cops pull him out of the unit and take him into an area away from the other inmates.

"Don't listen to Covin's crazy ass!" His shoulder twitched subconsciously, a reaction from not being allowed to have free access to the medications that the state used to throw at inmates for the asking.

"Well, what happened?"

"D'ey beat his ass, d'at's what happened." I never said he was eloquent, only that he wanted to be my snitch.

"You don't seem too broken up about it."

"Fuck Covin. His ass smells like shit! He won't take a shower for shit. He keeps piss in d'ose milk cartons to throw on the CO's n'shit. I'm glad d'ey kicked his ass." I had to change direction in order to see if he was playing me.

"What, you blowing Nuttall and Bongo now?"

"Fuck d'em racist crackers! He called me a nigga!"

"Who? Both of them called you a nigger?"

"Not Bongo. He too stupid. Dat fuckin' cracker Nuttall did." It never ceased to amaze me why, if the racial slur "nigger" was unacceptable, the slur "cracker" or "honky" was merely par for the course. Maybe George Jefferson could explain that better.

"Then tell me what happened." I sat back and watched the first clear record of events unfold right before my eyes.

"D'is whole unit smell like shit! N'we was telling d'em crackers d'at d'ey need to clean Covin's ass with a fire hose. N'dat's when d'em crackers got d'at nigger out of his cell. But when d'ey took d'em cuffs off 'em, d'at nigger kicked Nuttall's ass."

"I thought you said that the officers beat him."

"Hell, yeah, d'ey beat Covin."

"When?"

"After d'at nigger beat d'ey asses. D'en d'ey gonna call a code n'shit."

Three other inmates on the unit, after lamenting how racist the officers were, all emphasized the "good" punches that Covin got in before he was "beaten".

Later, I interviewed Covin a second time, and after asking him the same questions in different ways, his story eventually mirrored my would-be snitch's account. I had Covin moved to an interview room that was out of direct sight of any officers.

"Covin, what's goin' on, black man? I thought you had skills."

"What the fuck you talking about?" He looked confused, and very interested in where I was taking our conversation.

"The 4-1-1 going around your house is that two white boys broke their foot off in your anal cavity. What's up? That's why you got that limp or what?"

"White bastards." Covin was definitely aggravated. "Ain't

nobody kickin' my ass."

"From what I heard, it's too late. They already did."

"Last man that beat my ass was the bitch who delivered me, and I'm still looking for him." Truly not original. But Covin wanted to make sure that I thought he was tough, even though I had heard the biggest punks yelp that line a million times before. I felt I could use his aggression to my advantage.

"Relax, Nubian King. Ain't no shame in letting two Klan-rejects punk you. Where's home? I'm going to get you out of here. Which jail you want to hide in?" Covin asked the obvious questions, but his demeanor was a guarantee that he already knew the answer.

"What the fuck you want to know where I'm from for?" he asked.

"C'mon, man. You can't stay here. I'm gonna hook up a transfer." I made my last comment with a wink. "Now, everybody knows you can't fight. It's just a matter of time before they test your chin."

Covin looked at me, trying to think of something clever to say, but he was a few sandwiches short of a picnic. He kept gazing as I continued with my diatribe.

"What? You *want* to stay here and be everybody's ho? You want to blame me for losing your virginity to the Kings or Five's?" referring to two of the stronger gangs at Northern. "Not happening. Just tell me where you want to go?"

Covin exploded! He stood up from the table, slammed his hand down, and started rambling.

"Nutall always fuckin' with me. I don't be sayin' shit to his ass. I'm tired of that shit." Covin then laid out the entire incident.

"When those punk bitches let me out, they talking about we gonna clean your cell. Right? I was like, 'Ight, cool.' But as soon as I got out, I was like, '*Bam*, bitch! Talk shit now, mother-fucker!' His ass was done!"

Covin was very demonstrative, swinging his fists to mimic

his descriptive words.

"*Bam!* I cracked that bitch in his face. Bongo tried to grab a nigga', but I fucked him up, too. *Bam!* I was knocking them red-bitches out. Then they grabbed me, and I still kicked *they* asses."

His yelling was so loud that Officer Tyson, no pun intended, opened the interview room door quickly.

"Mr. Freeman, you straight?" Some of his concern was knowing that I normally interviewed inmates without any hand-cuff or leg-iron restraints, a practice that was frowned upon but never directly addressed.

"I'm good. I'll be done in a few."

After my interviews concluded, I still needed to speak to the officers for their versions of the incident. At that point, the only problem they had was not following procedures for having a supervisor present during the movement. However, if they lied about anything, then the possibility of termination returned.

Union representative Trent represented the two cops. During their interviews, both officers proved forthcoming and honest in their accounts, and I was fair with them in reporting what I found. When asked, I recalled that the officers were guilty of violating standard procedures regarding having contact with Special Needs inmates, but not of a racially motivated assault. Of course, I was later labeled a social worker, but this case was used as supporting evidence for not seeking to have the cops fired. My conscience was clear because I was told to investigate that particular incident, and that meant that I was not to seek retribution on those cops for the two prior cases that the administration had bungled.

Jimbo made it clear that I was doing African Americans a "disservice" for allowing a couple of racists to remain officers. But, I knew that I would have been doing all of society, not just African Americans, a disservice by allowing politics and grudges to dictate my conclusions, especially without consideration of the relevant facts. If those cops screwed up in the past, they should have been disciplined in the past. I won the quiet admiration of my peers, the very vocal respect of officers I would have to investigate, and an indescribable loyalty from Norm.

"Damn, man. Where the hell have you been?" We shook with our right hands and embraced with our free arms. "Luther and I thought that they got rid of you or something." Norm was kidding, but he was too close to being accurate for my taste.

"Well, almost." I smiled, but my look didn't fool him.

"What did they do?"

"I've been suspended pending a psychological evaluation."

"Domestic violence?" Norm knew the procedures for officers that were accused of battering their wives or girlfriends, so that would have seemed reasonable.

"N'all. I'm not that stupid. They got me for refusing to voluntarily see their psych."

"What?" There was nothing wrong with Trent's hearing, but he needed more information.

"They wanted me to volunteer. They said I could refuse. Then they suspended me when I did."

We talked about the specifics of my situation and I expected him to be shocked and appalled, but he wasn't.

"None of that shit surprises me." We walked towards Springfield Avenue in Irvington, discussing many aspects of the department's politics.

"To be honest with you, I don't understand why they hadn't come after you sooner. You're a liability for them."

I thought he was alluding to the fact that I was African American, but he wasn't.

"Honest men can't be controlled, and they need to control their people."

Norm called PBA president Luther Gregg, and they put me in contact with an up-and-coming young, local politician. His name was Wayne Smith, President of the Irvington City Council. Mr. Smith had already amassed a reputation for fighting bureaucracy, and he didn't mind falling out of grace with New

Jersey's top political dogs when they were wrong.

I sat down with Mr. Smith in his office, and spoke frankly with him. He asked me questions regarding how was it possible to be suspended without ever being charged with any offense, and his response was, well, predictable.

"They can't do that!" He released an involuntary chuckle, which ended almost as quickly as it began.

"Would you believe that I've heard that before?"

"If what you say is true, then they've got a huge problem."

"Oh, it's true." I handed him copies of the letters for him to keep. "Can you help me?"

Without hesitation, he began writing two letters on my behalf. One was addressed to Governor Christine Whitman and the other to Commissioner of Corrections Jack Terhune. Mr. Smith also spoke to me, in confidence, about my plight and gave me some extremely insightful advice for dealing with the state as well as for my personal life. His final comment encouraged me to continue to fight, "Understand, integrity has no equal." I left his office believing there actually was such a thing as a decent, trustworthy politician.

The following Tuesday, I received a telephone call from Chief O'Brien, ordering me to appear at Chief Faunce's office on June 29, 1999. I arrived as scheduled and requested that a union representative be present. Upon arriving, I was greeted by Chief Willie.

"Good morning, Chief. Did you want me to contact a union rep to be a witness?"

"I'm your fuckin' witness", replied Jimbo. This was clearly not going to be a cordial gathering. I sat down in front of Chief Faunce's desk, and listened to her and Jimbo's explanation of what my evaluation meant to them.

"I spoke to Dr. Holl yesterday, and he told me about your condition." Debbe took the lead and tried to look sympathetic.

"And I'm not upset at you, because he explained to me that you are suffering from a type of short-term memory block."

"Memory block." Although I had planned not to say a word, I couldn't help repeat her folly. A sharp ache rushed passed my temple, forcing me to blink one eye.

"Yeah…" Faunce actually looked convinced that I was convinced that she had a clue. "…you had a tough time last year with your wife and all. And what you have done to cope with that kind of trauma was to, involuntarily, mentally block out the circumstances and specifics regarding your breakdown."

Breakdown. Mental blocks. Postponed trauma. All of that had the markings of a great defensive strategy in case of litigation. They both nodded, waiting to see if I would nod, but a completely different thought swirled around in my mind. *If either of you believe any of that crock, maybe I'm not the one who needs a psychiatrist.*

"Dr. Holl wants to see you in thirty days, you know, to make sure that you don't have a relapse. Until then, you'll be on restriction status and you won't be allowed to use or carry a firearm, Okay?" The mentioning of a possible relapse was their way of informing me that if I brought this matter up again, they'd plaster me to the unemployment wall. With that knowledge, I knew that this wasn't the time for asking questions, but stupid and ridiculous people were my weakness.

"Is it mandatory?" I know what you're thinking. *When will this guy learn?* But that question jumped out of my mouth before I could stop it, and Jimbo was pissed.

"What is it with you Kenny? We're trying to cut you a break. Do you want stay with IA or not?" Willie stared at me as I stared at Faunce. "Just tell me 'cause I don't like your attitude."

I paused briefly,

"Yes. I want my job." After that, there were no more words. Just looks. Jimbo at me. Me at Jimbo. Faunce at the ceiling.

"Are we finished?" I asked. As you could have guessed, that question didn't go over well either. Jimbo's hothead got the better of him, and he couldn't help it either. Thinking was his weakness.

"We're finished when I say we're finished, you got me?" No response was necessary, but since my new agenda was simply to get out of the meeting calmly, I nodded my head.

Faunce left the office, then returned with some papers.

"I'm sending you to East Jersey [prison] for a while. It seems that you've never been able to get along with any of your co-workers, and none of your co-workers want to work with you."

"And rightfully so." said Jimbo. This was the first that I had ever heard of a problem between my co-workers and myself, but I thought that before I doubted anything that Faunce said, I had better see what was in those three letters.

"You'll work under Chris for a while." The truth of it all was that Debbe Faunce was transferring me because I wasn't playing ball the way she, and the entire department, was accustomed to playing ball. Chris Hamner was more intelligent than Diller was and also being positioned to become the next assistant chief, so Chris had a vested interest in adhering to Faunce's every whim. My destruction was at hand.

SEVENTEEN

Who was Sun Tzu?

As ordered, I reported to Chris Hamner for work at Rahway State Prison. Since I'd worked at Rahway as an officer, I was already familiar with the layout of the jail as well as the way it operated. Nothing much had changed in the short time I had been away, and since I had never dealt much with Hamner as an officer, my only knowledge about him had come from other officers. Now, all of my information came from those inside Internal Affairs.

Rahway's Internal Affairs Office was an old, two-floor, wooden house with cracking white paint. Hidden behind large tree-like hedges, it was situated across the street from the main jail. I entered Hamner's office on the second floor of the house and stood facing the man who would have a dramatic impact how I would come to understand life's dramas.

Hamner was a good fit for Rahway and relished an unusual rapport with the prison, as well as with Central Office. He had a well-guarded secret that Faunce tried to cover regarding racist statements Hamner made about another investigator named Essie Williams. It almost proved to be his undoing. Faunce coerced Essie into accepting a modest payoff and the promise that Hamner would never again supervise Essie in exchange for Essie's silence. Faunce's coercion included a veiled threat to disclose an embarrassing aspect of Essie's personal life. Faunce had saved Hamner's career, and so Chris owed Debbe big time.

Hamner was viewed as the "brains" of Internal Affairs because, at age of 40, he earned a law degree from Rutgers University. I admired Chris because he worked full time and had a young child. Less admirable was his much flaunted past intimate relationship with the sister of an old high school buddy of his, the Mayor of Woodbridge, James McGreevey. Additionally, since many believed McGreevey would eventually re-place Christine Whitman as governor, Hamner deemed himself untouchable.

"Investigator Freeman. Hi, I'm Chris." He never stood up from behind his desk. He barely even looked up from a single sheet of paper under his hand, nor did he shake my hand, but I didn't see any of it as being rude. "Have a seat please. I want to go over some rules." Talk about straight to the point.

"I only have two rules. Be on time, and never lie to me. I also expect you to do whatever I tell you to do without questions, okay?" That was actually three rules, but who was counting?

"No problem." Hamner was warning me that I would not be given a second chance to make a mistake, something I had anticipated from the moment I learned of my transfer. Since we were clearing the air, I decided to make it known that the same would be demanded of him.

"If I disagree with something you tell me to do, I'm gonna to let you know." I paused to see his reaction, then I tied up my loose end. "After I do it, of course."

"I've got no problem with that." Half of a smile grew on Hamner's face as he responded.

"Anything else?"

"Nope. Not right now, anyway." Hamner shuffled the paper on his desk that kept his attention. "Skippy will show you your office." I left the office with investigator Wayne "Skippy" Everret, Hamner's second in command and all-around help.

Everret had the most seniority of the investigators at Rahway, and he was routinely left in charge in Hamner's absence. He gave me a tour of the office, the evidence locker, and showed me the type of equipment they had available for surveillance exercises. Hamner's connections gave the unit the ability to get equipment that other units on the inside only dreamed about. Part of my standard issue was a miniature tape-recorder, extremely reliable and virtually undetectable. I was told that I needed it for my conversations with the cops, inmates, and staff, and I was warned to never disclose that I was recording every word.

Everret later walked me through the prison, reintroducing me to the front office personnel as well as the ranking officers. However, since I had worked there as an officer, it was less like a tour and more like a reunion.

Later, I was granted access to their N.J. State Police NCIC database located inside a rear office that belonged to an old friend from Northern State, Bob Karkoska. The database gave state and federal criminal and personal information on practically anybody at the push of a button. Bob was transferred to Rahway because of some foolish comments he made regarding an officer who was caught in a drug-sting operation with whom Bob assisted the State Troopers. I spent a good deal of that afternoon talking with Bob about our plights, and somehow, the name Aburami surfaced.

"That punk mother fucker came through here on a medical or something."

"When?"

"I don't remember. Look him up." Bob was more interested in reminding me how "fly" His Royal Fly-ness still was, but I was wondering why Aburami was not in protective custody.

"How can you tell if he's in PC?"

Bob rolled his royal chair to the computer and looked at the screen. "You see these charges he got? They're for refusing to pack up his shit and get his ass back into General Population so he can get his ass kicked!"

Bob laughed harshly, no sympathy for Aburami in any way. I looked at him in disbelief, not about his disregard for Aburami, but because Aburami shouldn't have had to catch any charges in order to remain locked away from the rest of the prison population. However, I never let Bob know my thinking.

"That's what I do to my bitches! They get fucked!"

I knew that Jimbo had guaranteed that Aburami wouldn't have to return to General Population, but now I saw that things weren't always what they appeared, especially in this state.

I went home and contemplated everything that happened to me in the past year and a half. I vaguely recalled passages in a book I had read some time ago. There was an eerie echo in the pit of my gut reminding me that I had been warned about this type of situation, but I failed to study that warning. I knew that I really needed to study the warnings explained in *The Art of War* by Sun Tsu, instead of simply reading it, in order to discover the treasures hidden within its pages.

I was formally introduced to *The Art of War* as a Marine while on Embassy Duty. I had a lot of free-time to read during the rotating night shifts in Cairo, Egypt, but that was twelve years ago. Until that point, I hadn't applied the lessons of Sun-Tzu to anything professionally or personally. The military strategies he discussed transcended that specific use and could be applied to any combative situation. So, later that evening, my daughter and I went to the public library where I began researching what I should have studied twelve years earlier.

The first lesson that caught my attention was that of "Tao". It described warfare as "the greatest affair of state, the basis of life and death, the Way (Tao) to survival or extinction. It must be thoroughly pondered and analyzed."

There was no doubt that I had considered what the department's response to my complaint would be, but the question was had I "thoroughly" considered their response and pondered and analyzed my own survival. The department had declared war on me, and I hadn't made proper preparations to defend myself against a stronger foe with greater resources. I had to assume a defensive posture and I knew that I had to prepare myself to preempt every accusation they could fabricate.

That didn't prove as difficult as one might have expected. I decided to concentrate my efforts, adjust my thinking and focus my time on getting to know my supervisors, understanding their habits and noting the minutest of details.

I then pondered what I considered the most important aspect of my struggle. Sun-Tzu noted that being victorious was the goal of every general. However, not every general puts the time and effort into defining victory and, therefore, ends up ineffective and insecure. Over the past weekend, I had considered what being victorious entailed and, amidst the multitude of thoughts, confusion, and desires that I had, one prominent goal remained—I wanted my $800.00 back!

It seemed ridiculous to wage a war, destroy my reputation, and possibly end my career in law enforcement over $800.00, but somehow it mattered to me more than anything else did. The principal of accepting a thief's explanation was Greek to me. They stole my money, plain and simple. Faunce promised me that I would be paid when I was told to drive to her office not a week earlier, and I was determined to get my $800.00 from her or the state in her name. Nothing else would suffice.

Faunce and Jimbo were nocturnal creatures of habit, not wanting anybody to see their actions, but I decided to shed as much light on them as possible. Taking a cue from Mr. Smith, I stayed awake that night and wrote letters to New Jersey Governor Christine Whitman, U.S. Senator Frank Lautenburg, Commissioner Jack Terhune, and others about what happened to me.

In my letters, I let them know that I was suspended for

questioning the validity of a previous psychological evaluation that occurred over a year ago and for refusing to voluntarily submit to another evaluation. I also included how Jimbo ordered me to falsify my report on Aburami, only to later deceive me by leaving Aburami in harms way in the general population. Moreover, I told them all that I wanted my $800.00 returned to me.

I also filed a formal complaint with the department's Equal Employment Division claiming that I was treated differently than other employees, against promulgated rules and regulations, and against the public good.

After I began forwarding my disclosures to public figures, my years of note taking were about to be used against me in a way I could have never predicted, my unrevealed weakness would be exposed, and my own carelessness would be at fault.

EIGHTEEN

Keep Your Enemies Closer

Some time after I arrived at Rahway, I overheard a new investigator named Danny Klotz make a joking comment to Everett about two incidents that involved the department's Fugitive Squad as Everett laughed, but added nothing. Sure, the incident was well-known inside of IA, but there was something weird about the words that Klotz had used. His description and diction reminded me of the way I would have described the incident. In fact, it was exactly the way that I had described that particular incident about a year ago. Klotz was young and foolish, and the only person in the unit that trusted him enough to tell him anything was his best friend Chuck Walters. And that's when I realized I had left my journal in my desk at Northern State Prison.

I made a b-line to Northern in order to retrieve it, but I was too late. My desk lock had been forcibly opened, and my security blanket was gone. I filed a theft report with the State Police because the theft took place on state property, making a permanent record of the theft, but none of that mattered. The department's position held that my former supervisor, Terry Diller, along with Walters, searched my desk for some undisclosed case that they couldn't find. Coincidentally, the search was conducted on the same day I was suspended.

I was furious with myself for not keeping my journal at home or at least having made a copy of it. My desk was always locked whenever I left the office, even if only to use the toilet, on the advice of Pam Trent. I kept my open cases, which were kept in file folders, on top of my desk, and my completed cases were returned to the main files as standard procedure. The only things in my desk besides my journal were pens, pencils, and blank forms. All of my writing utensils faced the same direction, and the departmental forms I kept were color-coded. I hated for anybody to mess up the inside of my desk, which was why I left anything that might interest my supervisor on top of my desk.

After Faunce found out that I reported the journal missing, she ordered everybody within a hundred feet of me to write reports, documenting my every action. Kevin Bolden, who was in charge of the unit on that particular day, was put to the test by Faunce.

"Kenny," Kevin stuck his head inside of my office a couple days later. "...stop by my office when you get a chance, alright?"

"Give me a minute." I put away the books that were on my desk. "I'll come now."

We walked to his office, which was located next to mine, and looked much nicer.

"Watch your back, man, because they're gunning for you."

"That's no news flash." I smiled to lighten the mood.

"No. You don't understand. They just got finished raking my ass over the coals about you. They're trying to say, you left on state-time to do personal shit without permission. I told them, "Fuck that shit, I gave him permission." But they're still going to try to hang you. Watch your ass."

I saw how aggravated Kevin was by all the foolishness, but it was becoming second nature to me. I regretted them involving Kevin in their battle against me, and I realized that I, too, had involved him.

"I should have thought about asking you for ..."

"Handle your business. God ain't pleased with their shit!" Kevin cut off my apology with the same forcefulness that he always exhibited. "You didn't do anything wrong and I didn't do anything wrong. Those bastards got it in for you and they're trying to recruit help, especially from other brothers. But they won't get me to do their dirty work."

I came to work everyday and was given very little responsibility and even less work. Morning meetings were informally held in Hamner's office. We also ate lunch there on a daily basis, except for Kevin, who chose to eat in his own office. I found hanging around Hamner's office very interesting. For the most part, I sat and watched Bob and Klotz have their daily battle of wits, similar to Bob and Antinoro's intellectual jousts. As amusing as those fencing matches were, the real story came after Hamner explained the intricacies of the children's cartoon "Cat-Dog". The more Hamner spoke, the more I realized that he wasn't nearly as intelligent as everybody thought.

But, he had an unmistakably absent tolerance for stupidity and excuses. He drove over an hour and a half to work every day, yet still arrived thirty minutes before work. That meant that he had no tolerance for anyone being late. He endlessly researched information he was questioned about in order to gather proof. That meant he had no tolerance for foolish lies that could be proven false.

One day while the group was discussing an incident in which Klotz was caught lying, which happened frequently, Hamner remarked to us that we can never submit any reports without independent written evidence supporting our opinion.

A guilt-faced Klotz called out in pain, "But I admitted that I lied to you, boss."

"Yeah, right." Bob wasn't going to miss an opportunity like that. "You admitted *after* your dumb-ass got caught, you lying ass-wipe."

Bob's crude humor may have drawn laughter, but my attention remained with Hamner's revelation. In law enforcement, official opinions require evidence. Although Hamner was definitely my adversary and had a history of racist comments and bigotry, I still found qualities about him that I admired.

In like fashion, hanging around his office I discovered that although Hamner owed his allegiance to Faunce, his loyalty was as hollow as was his opinion of her.

"Nobody questions Debbe. All of her orders are over the phone." Chris shook his head as he informed us of some changes that Faunce had implemented for the state, changes that he silently opposed. It was clear from his expression that Faunce was not used to answering questions. If my letters were persuasive enough or in a high enough volume, she would be required to answer questions that she didn't want to answer. Hopefully, my complaint and letters would foster her arrogance and expose her weaknesses.

Nobody forced Faunce to put her words in writing, which meant she could deny everything and admit nothing. Both Hamner and Diller learned Faunce's credo, "If it ain't in writing, it didn't happen." That prompted the joke "Debbe only gives orders over the phone", meaning that if you got caught, you're on your own.

Near the middle of July 1999, my letters had gotten the attention of a few of the brass, but not enough for them to play fair. My complaint received the attention a distracted preschooler would give Alan Greenspan, while my letters were pretty much ignored. The department Equal Employment Office acknowledged that, based on the statements of witnesses, Lieutenant Tessenholtz used the racial slur Sambo in regards to me, but noted that being called "Sambo" wasn't as bad as being called "nigger". Faunce was determined to ensure that

Tessenholtz never spent one day out of work for my ridiculous sensitivity.

Infuriated with the investigation, Faunce immediately wrote to the investigator handling the case and offered her own reasons about why my complaint shouldn't be trusted. She elected to assert that I was suffering from delusions, ignoring the three psychological reports she and the Teflon Don had received. The problem with her assessment was that none of the department's doctors agreed with her. But that never stopped Faunce from getting what she needed. "Don, this is Debbe." When in trouble, Faunce always reached out to Teflon Don.

"What's up?"

"These damn doctors don't know what the hell they're talking about. Kenny's delusional, right?"

"I hope so. Why?"

"Yeah, well, I need a favor?" From that point, the conspiracy began in earnest. Teflon always created a buffer between himself and the rest of the department. As Hamner was seen as the brains of IA, Teflon was the brains of the entire department.

The problem Faunce faced was that she had evaluations from Dr. Holl, Dr. Kahn, Dr. Williams, and Dr. Quintana in possession at the time she made her own diagnosis. In order to have her way, she needed one of the doctors to change their official report, corroborate her statement, and agree that I was delusional. Therefore, Faunce and Teflon sought an expendable scapegoat to do their dirty work, Dr. Richard Cevasco.

Dr. Cevasco knew he couldn't alter his own report because not only hadn't he evaluated me, he wasn't a real psychologist or psychiatrist. His degree was in education and he was only assigned to be the department's head of psychiatry because there weren't any psychiatrists or psychologists that wanted the job. Whomever they chose had to be someone that I wouldn't object to, somebody that I had paid to see. Dr. Quintana was out of the question because he had no financial affiliation with the state. However, there was another person, who had benefited financially from the department—Dr. Daniel Williams.

"Good morning, Dr. Williams?" Dr. Cevasco said.

"Good morning and how may I help you?"

"I want to thank you for all of the fine work that you have done in the past." Dr. Cevasco's reminder of their past relationship was merely camouflage for his treachery. "But I have some questions about an evaluation you did on one of our employees, if you can remember." Dr. Cevasco was clumsy. "Kenneth Freeman. You remember him, right?"

"Sure."

From that point, Dr. Cevasco began asking general questions, being friendly and persuasive. However, a venomous adder was lurking in the the tall grass.

"His chief and I believe, well, it just seems that Kenneth doesn't remember things quite the way that he should. We don't think that *you* did anything wrong, because Kenneth is very manipulative, you know?" said Dr. Cevasco.

"What is this about?" Dr. Williams relaxed in his seat as he held the telephone securely to his ear, thinking that Dr. Cevasco's statements were overtly unprofessional.

"Chief Faunce was wondering if you could help us to help Kenneth."

"And how's that?" Dr. Williams was more interested in just how far somebody would go to harm another than he was in anything that Dr. Cevasco had in mind.

"Well, if you wouldn't mind adjusting a portion of your evaluation to kind of mirror the chief's concerns about Kenneth, you know, so we can get him the help that he needs." There was a brief silence on the telephone line. "We just don't want to take a risk on somebody that *you* cleared, who may be suffering from delusions to walk around with a gun, right?" Dr. Cevasco said.

Dr. Williams understood what was being asked of him, as well as the ramifications of not agreeing to falsify his own official report. "Sorry. I can't do it." Dr. Williams said.

"What? You do realize that three other psychiatrists said that he was clinically delusional, you understand that, right?" Dr. Cevasco asked.

"I thought you said that he *may* be delusional. Now, you've got three psychiatrists agreeing with you?"

"No. That's not what. . . Well, yeah, we all said he's delusional, and we wanted to give you the opportunity to reconsider your…"

"My report stands." Dr. Williams ended the conversation, slamming the receiver onto the base, fully knowing he would not receive any more business from the department.

Dr. Cevasco immediately contacted Faunce with the bad news.

"Debbe, he didn't go for it."

"Dick?"

"Yeah."

"What do you mean he didn't go for it?"

"Dr. Williams won't change his report. But we're okay, as long as you don't put your statement in writing."

"Idiot! I already did, and they're not going to just give it back!"

"Who did you give it to?"

"Why don't you let me worry about that." Faunce was done with answering questions, and she needed to advise Teflon of Dr. Cevasco's failure. Without Dr. Williams, Teflon and Faunce decided to get their wishes through Dr. Holl. The follow-up evaluation was quickly scheduled for me on August 25th and I was given a written order to appear in his office on that date.

I immediately contacted the same two psychiatrists that I had used in June. Dr. Quintana agreed to evaluate me without any reservations or comments. However, scheduling an evaluation with Dr. Williams brought another surprise, as if my life wasn't eventful enough.

Dr. Williams sounded aggravated at me for reasons of which I knew nothing.

"Dr. Williams, it's Kenny." There was a brief pause. "Kenneth Freeman from Corrections."

"I know who this is."

"I wanted to know if it were possible to schedule another evaluation. They've me scheduled to see their guy again." I laughed into the quiet telephone. "I've scheduled one with Dr. Quintana again and I was hoping that you would see me, also." I was somewhat numb to the chaos by that time, able to shake off much of my frustration through laughter and sarcasm.

"Sure." I waited to see if he would add anything to our short conversation, as he normally used small talk to relax me, but I got nothing.

"Did I do something wrong?" His voice told me that something was up. I just hoped that I was able to duck the punch.

"Get yourself an attorney." Dr. Williams was adamant, and I wasn't expecting that kind of advice.

"I plan to, but why are…" I started to ask him for more information, but he interrupted me, with a sense of urgent compassion.

"Your employer just called me and asked me to change my report," Dr. Williams said. A glob of air left my lungs as if I was in an Abbott and Costello movie.

"You've got to be kidding me!" I said that fully knowing that he was as serious as he had ever been. My stomach tightened, and I felt the same sharp headache I experienced in Debbe's office a couple months earlier. This headache had more force, but later subsided.

"No, I wouldn't kid about something like that." There was no compromise within Dr. William's voice. "They're probably going to get somebody to say that you're delusional if they haven't already. Who are you supposed to see?"

"Dr. Holl." I said. "I don't believe this."

"Just relax." he said. "First, come on in and let me complete an evaluation on you now. Do you have any paperwork from them?"

"I got a couple of things."

"Bring them with you." I got my money ready and drove to Dr. William's office. We discussed everything from soup to nuts. Many of the questions regarded exhaustive matters that were already evaluated and he was extremely specific, almost adversarial, but I understood that he was just being thorough, covering all bases.

After my evaluation with Dr. Williams, I decided to speak to somebody who had plenty of experience in dealing with corrupt leadership, somebody who wouldn't hold back any good advice from me, somebody trusted. That's when I called Delacy.

Sgt. Delacy Davis was not only a great officer with the East Orange Police Department, he was also the founder of B-CAP (Black Cops Against Police Brutality). We were formally introduced to each other after he received a copy of my letter to Senator Lautenberg, and we spoke frankly with each other regarding a few different matters about Corrections. We were only a few years apart in age, but on that day, he talked to me in a way that he'd never done before—almost as a nervous father would caution his eldest son.

"They'll be looking for you to deny that certain events occurred. Don't get tricked into lying. Your greatest advantage is your honesty when it comes to telling the facts of your situation coupled with your resolve. Even if it seems to paint you in an unfavorable light, tell the truth!

"If the details are inaccurate, say so. Then explain your perspective. If you remember the setting of the events, let him know that first. Remember to paint a complete picture. Watch your eye-movements, control your breathing, limit your facial expressions, and for God sakes, don't tap your finger."

"I do that a lot, don't I?"

"Yeah. You do."

"What does tapping mean?"

"In itself, probably nothing." he said. "But if he's trying to hang you, he'll use that to determine that you're suffering from nervousness and that you have inhibitions regarding whatever he happened to be talking about at that particular moment. Remember, you're nothing more than a lab rat under their trick microscope, inside of their lab. Trust me, based on the documentation I've read, they're not going to play fair. Be yourself, and you'll be fine."

I was ready to defend myself against Dr. Holl, but I wanted to be able to go on the offensive if the opportunity presented itself.

"What are psychiatrists afraid of?" I asked.

"What?"

"No. Not specifically. In general. If you were a psych, what would scare you?" I asked Delacy to consider his own plight if he were a psychiatrist as he shook his head.

"I don't know." He paused for an extended amount of time, reflecting introspectively. "I guess I'd be afraid of what any other profession might be afraid of. I don't know."

Sgt. Davis was an honest man, a professional with integrity, which probably made him the wrong person to ask.

Sun Tzu said that you could use the enemy's weapons and fears to increase your own strength. Dr. Williams was a captive of his own morals and ethics, and Dr. Quintana was a student of professionalism, making them both of little use in discovering a psychiatrist's worst fear.

The state was more powerful than I was, had a bigger budget, greater legal advice, better access to the courts, and controlled the rules as well as their application. I understood their advantage well, but my advantage was that they underestimated my resolve. The playing field for the evaluation put me at a great disadvantage, rendering me nearly defenseless to Dr. Holl's critique. And that's when a plan emerged that had the potential to counteract some of Faunce's shrewdness.

"Delacy, what if I could have you evaluate Dr. Holl's evaluation. Would that stop him from hanging me?"

"There's no way he's going to allow you to bring anybody with you, especially not me." Sgt. Davis laughed. "He wouldn't even look at your peer evaluations last time, right?"

"Yeah, but I'm not talking about you coming with me. I'm talking about bringing his evaluation right here to you?"

Before Delacy could ask me another question, I changed the subject, never disclosing to him how I planned to bring my evaluation to his office.

NINETEEN

Bring the Mountain to You

There was no conceivable way to legally bring Dr. Holl to East Orange to conduct my evaluation. However, I had a way of leveling the terrain, so that even if I lost the battle, I might later redeem myself to some extent. I arrived at Dr. Holl's office on time and ready to go. I sat erect in the chair with my hands placed solidly on my lap. My eyes focused on the doctor, and I prepared for his onslaught. While he prepared himself, I decided to allow him to really get into his evaluation before I began interviewing him. It all would backfire if I appeared too aggressive, so I watched for my opening.

Sgt. Davis' answer that a psychiatrist would fear what any other profession would fear was correct. However, I should have asked, *What scares a liar?* Delacy had given me the answer and the state had issued me the solution. I kept it in the inside pocket of my suit jacket. The strength of the department forced me to assume a perpetual defensive posture, but my pocket companion gave me the confidence to defend myself in a more constructive manner, preserving myself for the next battle.

"Good morning, Dr. Holl." I remembered not to tap my

fingers showing my impatience, but I couldn't wait to see if he agreed with me about what scares liars. He looked up from the documents on his lap until his eyes met mine, but he said nothing, totally ignoring my greeting. His eyes then returned to his documents and note pad.

"Your name is Investigator Kenneth Freeman, correct?" he asked.

"Yes, sir." I said.

"And you are…"

I interrupted him, "Excuse me, Dr. Holl?"

"…a 33 year old male, correct?" He tried to continue, not missing a cue.

"Dr. Holl, sir?" I was determined not to go any further without telling him about the "solution" I brought with me.

Dr. Holl again looked up at me. "What!"

I reached inside of my jacket and removed my miniature tape-recorder. I pushed record and began to speak, loudly and clearly, right into the built-in microphone.

"My name is Kenneth Freeman. And today is August 25, 1999 and I'm in the Haddonfield, New Jersey office of Dr. Walden Holl."

Now, I had his full attention. The documents on his lap were worthless, his questions didn't matter, and neither did my answers. You see, the answer to the question of what a liar fears is, simply, truth. Yes, liars hated the truth, and no matter what the profession, the truth was the Achilles for all liars. My solution was my tape-recorder, an unbiased witness for such truth and verifiable proof of everything that either the doctor or I said during evaluation. My recorder allowed other people to evaluate Dr. Holl without having to enter Dr. Holl's office. Moreover, the best part about my solution was that it took the focus off me and placed it squarely on what my solution might reveal. Hence, the tape-recorder was effectively interviewing the psychiatrist.

"Dr. Holl. Would you mind if I tape this evaluation?" What

was he going to say, no? The good doctor nodded his head, gesturing to me that he gave me permission to record him. That was an old trick that savvy defendants used in order to protect their appeal if convicted. If you motioned with your head or hands, nothing was recorded in the official transcripts. Nevertheless, I was aware that the recorder was conducting that interview, and every action had to be recorded, even if I was the one who explained them.

"Dr. Holl, I acknowledge that you just nodded your head essentially giving me permission, but the tape-recorder can only understand your verbal responses. Is that okay with you?"

"Yes." Dr. Holl in a very different voice than the one that he used when he was in charge. He had lost control and was clearly not a happy camper.

"So, is it alright for me to tape-record this evaluation, doctor?" I had to make sure he agreed aloud and I wouldn't accept anything less.

"I said, yes." Dr. Holl barely separated his teeth in his response. Temper, temper. He stopped writing, and just stared at the recorder.

"Dr. Holl? Is everything alright?" I wanted to make sure to record the atmosphere, closing the long pauses with descriptive explanations.

He gazed at me and grudgingly continued my evaluation. The session was nothing like our first meeting. None of his questions was probing, and Dr. Holl rushed through them at a dizzying pace, intent on just getting the evaluation over.

Dr. Holl asked me about my family, just like before, and my answers matched exactly what was recorded in the documented history resting on his lap. What's your daughter's name? What's your mother's name? How many siblings do you have? How old is your wife? Do you have a stepson? How old is he?

All of these questions were asked and answered two months ago, and as I reflected on the absurdity of it all, I made a monumental error, a flaw that would define my entire mental status. I smiled.

Dr. Holl's countenance illuminated the way children behave on Christmas morning. His voice shrieked and a few of the documents flew off his lap, as the tape-recorder noted his words.

"You smiled!" He tried to gather the fallen documents without taking his eyes off me. "Tell *me*, why did you *smile!*?"

"Sixteen."

"Sixteen? What do you mean sixteen?"

"He's sixteen years old." The smile wasn't big, my lips never parted and the corners of my mouth barely wrinkled, but that didn't matter to him.

"No!" Dr. Holl responded. "You smiled! What were you thinking about? Tell me!"

"I was answering your question."

"But you smiled!"

"If my smile offended you, please forgive me, Sir." Dr. Holl refused to acknowledge his true intent regarding my smile, so I continued with my answer. "He's sixteen years old." My face returned to its original, stoic state, and no more expressions followed. Nevertheless, that wouldn't be the last time that I heard about my smile.

Soon, Dr. Holl completed my evaluation, and as was customary, he asked if I had any questions.

"As a matter of fact, I do, if you don't mind." I said.

He nodded. Then, he quickly responded, "Go ahead."

"Did you ask Dr. Williams to change his report and say that I was delusional, for Chief Faunce, that is?" I asked. I didn't take any time to warm-up before I dropped that bombshell.

Dr. Holl was clearly on the defensive, and he took some time to answer me. "Dr. Holl? Did you understand my question?" I asked.

"Are you accusing me of asking another psychiatrist to change his report?" His laid-back persona was eroding, and I watched his anger build.

"I'm only asking a question. You said that I could ask a question, didn't you?" I said.

"No, I did not ask him to change his report. Did he tell you that?" Dr. Holl asked.

There was no way that I would answer that question. The evaluation was done, and I was free to leave.

"It was just a question." I said. "Thank you for your candor, doctor. Have a good day." And, with that, I stood from my seat, spoke into the recorder to note that evaluation had concluded, and pushed stop. Then, without saying another word, or making another smile, I left his office never to return.

After my exit, Dr. Holl telephoned Central Office to question them about my statements.

"Who is this?"

"It's Bill. What's up?" Chief O'Brien was the only one left in the office at that time.

"I need Debbe. Now!" Dr. Holl was in no mood to deal with O'Brien.

"What happened? Did he fail to show?"

"Oh, he showed up. With a tape-recorder." Dr. Holl was furious.

"What!"

"That's the least of your troubles. Who called Dr. Williams?"

"We did. Why?" asked O'Brien.

"Tell me you didn't ask him to change his evaluation." Dr. Holl may have been willing to play ball in times past, but now the stakes were rising, and his professional reputation was at risk.

"No, no. We simply wanted a degree of clarity on a couple of things." O'Brien was never very convincing, but Dr. Holl needed anything to cover himself.

"Clarification? On what?"

"Well, you know…"

"Never mind." Dr. Holl couldn't believe that he could

ever have agreed to help such a foolish group of individuals. "You'll get your evaluation."

"Can you make the bi-polar disorder stick?" O'Brien asked.

"Not without any evidence. And he didn't do anything while he was here." Dr. Holl thought for a moment about any inconsistencies in my behavior, and then had an idea.

"Well, he did smile."

"Good enough! Send it up A-SAP."

And Dr. Holl did just that, composing his evaluation in a way that maximized every wish that Chief Faunce and Teflon Don could have conjured in their corrupt wayward minds. However, the measures that Dr. Holl would go to in order to justify Faunce's desires while placing his own practice in jeopardy was greater than I ever imagined.

TWENTY

Don't Worry, Be Happy

Labor Day weekend had arrived. With some time away from the psychiatrists and the pressures of Faunce & Crew, I did quite a bit of soul-searching regarding my personal life. My marriage was in severe trouble, but it wasn't stressing me the way it had only a year earlier. My desire to stay married wasn't a third as strong as it had been in the past. And, by all indications, Priscilla wasn't that interested in our marriage, either. We kept up appearances, maybe a little for the children's sake, but more likely for our own interests.

My personal goal was to live a drama-free personal life and I was well on my way. With neither partner desiring anything of or from the other, there was nothing left to fuel arguments. Actually, there wasn't anything at all for my wife and I to even discuss. Living that way would have made me miserable a year earlier.

Once again, South Street Seaport in lower Manhattan was reclaimed as my favorite hangout. In the past, I spent endless nights reading my favorite novels beneath the stars, and laying on the reclining chairs of the third level outside of the mall area just a few steps away from virgin pina coladas. My daughters and I enjoyed the Bourbon Chicken with spicy rice and a Snapple—a truly priceless existence that I cherished.

My wife repeatedly called my pager, obviously wondering where I was and why I wasn't waiting for her to return from wherever she had been. I'd call her back to let her know that we were fine and to ask if she wanted to see the girls, but that's as far as my concern stretched. It didn't matter to me whether or not she was at work or some other place, or if she was alone or had a companion. I had made it back from being less than zero and did not intend on visiting that dark corner of my life ever again.

All I cared about was hanging out with and protecting my little girls. My wife, on the other hand, was a grown woman with the freedom and the ability to make her own choices. That was the key—everybody was responsible for his or her own choices. She never *made* me do anything I didn't already want to do and I never *made* her do anything she didn't already want to do. That understanding was a long process, but it finally opened the portal to my peace.

After we returned home, I carried both sleeping girls upstairs as they had fallen asleep on the ride home. I wiped their faces and arms with a warm face cloth, and then I laid one in her bed and the other in her crib. I took a hot shower, and started to dry off before I heard the alarm being disabled downstairs from the kitchen. I put on my pajama bottoms and left the bathroom. On my way out, my wife and I passed each other without a comment or glance.

I went downstairs and entered the kitchen. After surveying the refrigerator, I remembered that I had left the doggie bag holding the rest of the spicy rice in the back seat of the car. I got the bag from the car and stepped back into the house only to find Priscilla waiting for me in the kitchen.

"Where are you going?" She asked as I stood there wearing pajama pants, no socks, no shoes, no t-shirt, and no underwear. So, I ignored her and headed towards the microwave.

"You didn't get my last page?" Things had been peaceful and now she was asking me the same kind of questions that she ignored last year.

"Yeah, I got it."

"Well…" She didn't finish her sentence, and I was not about to help her grill me about why I wasn't chasing her any longer.

"Well what?"

"Well, why didn't you call me back?" she asked.

"I did call you."

"Earlier, yes. But what about my last page?"

I wanted to eat, and I knew this conversation could possibly last for hours. So, I cut to the chase for her.

"Like I told you earlier, we were at South Street. We bought some food, cooled out for awhile, now we're home." I turned on the microwave and started heating the rice.

"Who's we?"

"I'm not fighting with you anymore. I'm going downstairs in the basement to watch TV so that you can argue with yourself." The microwave bell rang as I took out my food, and then I closed the door behind me as I went into the finished basement.

Priscilla was not used to the new me, and I was slowly adjusting to myself. She hated the thousand question assaults I used to fire at her, but now I embraced a method of not asking any questions to which I did not already know the answer. If there was anything that she wanted me to know, she would tell me without my having to ask her. Soon, Priscilla followed me into the basement, and stood between my big-screen television and me.

"You don't want to know what happened?" She asked the question in order to provoke my curiosity, but it sounded like somebody who wanted to justify, or maybe explain, her where-abouts and actions. But I was having none of that. And even if there was a half dozen fragmented remnants of concern swimming inside of my heart, I didn't *want* to care about her any-more, and I refused to show any pain. I had enjoyed a peace-fully, tiring day with my kids and was determined to unwind while they slept soundly, with only my thoughts and that spicy rice as company. So, I set my face like a flint and spoke up.

"Would you like to have some of this rice? It's not too spicy?" I was determined not to allow myself to be drawn into trusting her, which I knew was more than possible. My heart loved her and minimized my pain, desiring, longing, wanting her for a lifetime. However, I no longer trusted my heart—es-pecially when it came to making rational decisions about my life—and I wasn't going to give her the opportunity to show her softer side, and shame my common sense.

She stared at me and grinned as she gritted her teeth. Her head nodded stiffly as a warning to me as she silently glided up the staircase, softly securing the hollow door behind her.

I stayed awake almost two hours after our encounter, watch-ing the late-night television shows, then allowing some of those shows to watch me as I sat still on the recliner and fought back love's tears. My true desires had betrayed my drama-free existence, reminding me of everything good and decent that we used to enjoy together. I lived in an emotional cesspool that friends called a good marriage, and it was just as much my fault as it was hers. And, sometimes, I believed that it was more my doings than hers. Unfortunately, none of that mattered any longer. What had occurred over the past few years couldn't be undone, and our choices, my choices, were long lasting and life changing.

TWENTY-ONE

There's More Than One Way

The failures of Faunce and Teflon Don were beginning to mount, from the first mandatory psychological evaluation, which could have been explained away as an innocent error made in good faith, all the way to their attempt to have another psychologist change an official report to justify Faunce's unsupported clinical determination of "delusional". All of that could have been avoided if Faunce had done something excessively out of character for any governmental agency. Apologize.

An apology was a stranger to Jimbo, who figured that he'd take matters into his own hands. While I was at home in my den, I received a telephone call. I checked the caller ID to get an idea of who called before I answered, but it read "unknown", as was common at that time, and I answered the telephone anyway.

"Hello."

"Kenny!" The familiar voice asked for me, but I couldn't quite make out to whom the voice belonged.

"Speaking."

"Why don't you cut the shit?" The caller's voice was unusually quick, rambling, very agitated.

"Who is this?" I asked.

"Just cut the shit, alright? That Sambo remark was way off, but your little letter campaign is really fuckin' pissing us off. So knock it off!" he said.

I sensed his bravado from his choice of words, but wanted to be certain nonetheless.

"You know who I am, but I don't know who you are. That makes you a coward." I said.

"Who the fuck you calling a coward?"

"Just identify yourself. Stop hiding under Debbe's skirt." I said.

"Yeah, I'd be a coward if they burned down your fuckin' house and your fuckin' daughter got killed, right?"

I snapped! "You're going to do what, Willie?!" *Slam!* He hung up. I ran to the front window and looked outside to check for any state vehicles. I immediately called my brother and told him what happened. He wanted me to take my daughter to his house while I went to the police department to file a complaint.

I called Hamner to officially notify him of the telephone call. Then I drove to the police station to file a report. They told me what to do if I ever received another call, but that was about all they could do at that time.

In the meantime, Hamner called back.

"Kenny, I'm sorry about what happened. But did you say that Willie called you?" Hamner asked.

"Yeah, it was him!"

"Did he identify himself?"

"No. But I know it was him."

"How? Do you have caller I.D. or something?"

"The number was unavailable, but I know it was him."

"Let me get this straight, you are alleging that Assistant Chief Willie from Internal Affairs threatened you, correct?"

"Come again?" I shook my head, trying to shake off my anger while recapturing my senses.

"You are alleging that it was Assistant Chief Willie who threatened to kill you and your daughter, correct?" Hamner wasn't simply asking for clarity, he was planning. I was plenty pissed off, but there was something else lurking in the midst of our conversation. There was anywhere between a twenty and thirty minute interval from the time that I first notified Hamner of the telephone call until this particular conversation. In our first conversation, I had told him that Jimbo had threatened me, but I didn't tell him that he threatened to kill both my daughter and myself. Nevertheless, somehow, Hamner now had the specifics of the incident smoldering in his arsenal.

"Listen carefully," I admonished him, as an intense headache pounded relentlessly, the stress of holding back frustration. "It's my earnest belief that it was Willie who called me."

"No! That's not what you said in your official complaint!" Hamner had revealed his hand. "I heard you say that Willie threatened your lives. Now didn't you!"

By that time, I was completely in control of my emotions, my logic, my position.

"It's my belief that Willie called. Can I prove it, or did he identify himself, no."

"Now, you're saying that you're not sure. How can you..."

"Am I being charged with anything?" I interrupted him abruptly, not allowing him any room to wiggle.

"What?"

"Am I the possible subject of any type of disciplinary action?" There was no comment from Hamner, only silence. "No response? Then, I'm hanging up. Good bye."

"I want to see you first thing in the morning."

"I'm hanging up the telephone." Hamner hung up his telephone before I could finish telling him that I was going to hang up. I knew where all of this was headed. When my journal went missing, what I did could've been compared to reporting the theft of some gourmet cheese to the nastiest sewer rat in the Meadowlands. I laid across the leather sofa for an hour, eyes closed, constantly massaging my temples, relieving the stress behind the headache. I screamed until tears danced around my cheeks, and conjured a thousand ways of vengeance.

As promised, the next morning Hamner called me into his office to inform me that I had to submit a written statement about the telephone call. He said that he was assigned to investigate the questionable circumstances surrounding the threat, and that Faunce wanted to assure me that she would personally follow the investigation's progress closely. Hamner interrogated me inside of his office, without a representative, intermittently for three days, each time followed by an order to write another statement. The interrogations continued until on the third day, Hamner informed me Chief Faunce decided that unless I directly accuse the assistant chief, I would be considered an evasive and uncooperative complainant and the case would be closed.

"Kenny, we want to help you. If Willie did it, Debbe wants you to know that nothing will happen to you. We just need you to say that it was him."

"Can you put that in writing?"

"You know how Debbe is. Telephone orders only." Hamner laughed, momentarily forgetting whose side he was on.

"Didn't you say that if it's not in writing…"

"I'm not going to play games with you, Kenny."

"And I'm not playing games with you. Why don't we let the local cops take a look at it first?" That approach was more than logical; it was a wise thing to do considering I had no reason to trust my department.

"You can wait for Irvington PD to look into it, but those morons couldn't find their assholes using both hands." Hamner had a trifling disdain for Irvington, Newark, and East Orange police officers, believing that they were inferior because of where they patrolled. I had a profound respect for those officers *because* of where they patrolled, which made his comments all the more deplorable to me.

But I didn't comment about his remarks as I was getting a more detailed picture of Hamner and his loyalty. I left his office and returned to my own, located a short walk down the stairs, when Hamner called me again on the telephone for the second time that morning. I returned to his office for more abuse.

"Kenny, I just spoke to Debbe and she told me to relay this message to you." Hamner looked at Everett who had entered his office after I had left. "You are ordered to go to Central Office, immediately. No detours and no telephone calls."

"No problem, Chris. Did she say what it's about?"

Hamner smiled shyly.

"Don't shoot the messenger. I'm just passing the word." Everybody knew that he was more than the messenger, but it was still too premature for me to confront him, especially since I could still get information from him. By my remaining calm, Hamner strangely thought I still had a measure of trust in him. In fact, I knew that he was lower then a snake, and more lethal, too.

"No problem, Chris. Let me get my things." I knew that there was more than a high probability that I wouldn't be coming back to the office to work, and the memory of the events that transpired the last time I was ordered to go to Central Office hovered tirelessly over my attaché case.

I discretely called my friend, Debbie Davies, who was now the union vice-president, as quickly as I could dial. Speaking low, I covered my mouth and the speaking end of the phone receiver.

"Debbie. It's about to go down."

"Where?"

"Central Office. Debbe ordered me to go there immediately." I had updated Davies on everything from the evaluations to the telephone threats. Neither of us trusted them, and she was sure that if they decided to hang me, they would go through Teflon Don. I had put my money on Hamner, but I guessed that I was about to lose twice that day.

"Move slowly, Kenny. I'll meet you there. But I don't know what I can do." She was confused about what anybody could do to stop a charging behemoth.

"All you have to do is be a witness." Liars hate the truth.

"Move slowly, okay?"

"Routes 1-and-9 are always congested. I think I'll go that way."

I hung up the telephone without saying or waiting for a good-bye as I heard a knock on my closed door.

"What's going on, man?" Kevin peeked inside my office, almost dazed. "They told me that I have to escort you to Central Office?" Kevin laughed in disbelief. "What the fuck is that all about?"

I shook my head.

"Doesn't surprise me at all." I grabbed the box holding my personal effects and picked up my case. "Let's bounce."

Kevin stood in the doorway, not moving, wondering why I was walking towards him and the doorway.

"What the fuck?"

"Kev. It's cool. Let's bounce." There was boldness in my attitude and it had "sick-and-tired" written all over it—enough to make Kevin nod his head.

As we were walking out of the front door of the building, Hamner called to Kevin, telling him to come closer to the secretary's desk, where he whispered into Kevin's ear. Hamner's thick eyebrows danced in confidence, but Kevin just laughed.

"What the hell are you talking about?"

"Just…" Hamner pointed to me with his eyes, ending his sentence while Kevin put his hands high to signify that he had heard enough nonsense for a lifetime.

"Alright, alright, alright!" Kevin shook his head and let out a hearty laugh, then his whole demeanor transformed to a seriousness rarely displayed by Kevin, especially in front of

Hamner.

"This shit is fucked up." Kevin took two steps towards the door, then he stopped. "And, I don't appreciate y'all sticking my ass in all this bullshit." Kevin turned to me as I stood in the doorway, cradling my belongings as if I was homeless; he tapped me on my shoulder, breaking my stare at Hamner. "Fuck him, Kenny. Fuck all of them." My sentiments exactly.

We got into the government cruiser as ordered, and I had to leave my car parked there. I packed my things inside my trunk and locked it back.

"You good, Kev?"

"What?" Kevin let go of a frustrated breath, painted with laughter, which he had held since Hamner first gave him the order to be my personal escort. "I hope you're taking notes on all this bullshit." Kevin shook his head in disbelief, muttering to himself the word "bullshit" every few moments.

"Relax, man. I'm good." Kevin was definitely taking this as if it was him going to the cross to be crucified, but that's just the type of man Kevin was.

"You must be a praying mother fucker, cause I'd..." His head never stopped shaking. "They're coming after you, man." Kevin took his eyes off the road to emphasize his statement.

"Don't you think that I know that? I had a job before corrections, and if this is my last day, I'll find a job after corrections, okay?"

"You know what Chris' punk ass told me?" Kevin completely ignored my calm spirit. "He told me that Debbe said that I'm to call her, immediately, if I have any trouble with you!"

We sat quiet for a moment in that cruiser, nodding, glaring out the windows at the truckers passing by, letting Faunce's ridiculous caution seep in.

"I'm in no rush to get there. Want to take the scenic route?" We looked at each other, and then, as if we had choreographed this scene for months on end, laughter burst from the deepest wells of our stomachs, tears raced along our cheeks to the point that Kevin was ready to pull the cruiser over for loss of vision.

"Dumb-asses!" Kevin wiped his eyes frantically in order to see the roadway. "Yo, man. Just handle your business."

We gave each other dap with our fists.

"Thanks for the concern, but I'm good."

"Alright. If you say so."

"I say so."

And that was the last Kevin and I spoke of the nonsense surrounding me for the remainder of the voyage to Central Office. We stopped at a convenience store, which was fine with me, especially since it allowed Davies additional time to get to Central Office. However, as I bought a Gatorade, I wondered if all the delays would work?

TWENTY-TWO

This Is for Your Own Good (Teth)

When Kevin and I arrived at Central Office, nobody (except for me, of course) could have guessed who just *happened* to stroll inside the office area.

"Hey, Kenny." Davies wore a smile that illuminated some extremely wearisome investigators, who stood afar and watched our arrival. Her illuminating smile was rivaled only by the one I displayed. "What are the odds of seeing you down here, *union* member Kenneth Freeman?!"

I figured I would play along with the full name bit.

"Debbie Davies! What in the you-know-what could you be doing down here, *union* vice-president *representative* Debbie Davies?!" Our smiles were contagious, affecting Kevin, who must have figured by now that something was up.

"Well, Kenneth Freeman, I am *officially* dropping off this old report that I just felt needed to be *hand-delivered*. Today. By me. Here. At Central Office." What a comfort her smile proved to be as our nods reinforced her every syllable.

She and Kevin greeted each other happily.

"Oh, by the way, have you met my personal escort? His name is Kevin." Davies looked astonished and her playfulness ended.

"No way!" Both Kevin and I traded nods as Davies' jaw finished dropping. "What in the world is going on!"

Before we could speak another word to each other, Sharon Jarrel, the secretary whose desk we had serendipitously gathered near, spoke to me.

"Hey, Kenny." Sharon's voice was gentle.

I shared a decent rapport with her ever since I came into Internal Affairs, or at least that was what I thought. "Hi, Sharon. How are you?"

"They're waiting for you in the upstairs conference room." Very politely with her smile cemented on her face, Sharon's attention immediately returned to her desk area, refusing to acknowledge me any further.

Ignoring Sharon's slight, I spoke to her anyway. "Thank you." I turned to Davies and shrugged my shoulders. "Are you ready for this?"

"Does it matter?" Davies chuckled at my question as we entered the hallway. Jimbo entered the hallway and confronted Davies, who had known him for a considerable amount of time.

"What are you doing here?"

"I'm doing great, Jimbo. So nice of you to ask."

"Fuck that, Debbie. What are you doing here?" The assistant Chief's eyes were glued on me, as was his question, but Davies stayed cool.

"I had some business to take care of. But since I'm here, I don't want Kenny to meet with you guys without representation." Debbie knew Jimbo well, and more importantly, Jimbo knew Debbie. "You weren't about to talk to an investigator without a union rep, were you?"

"Well, he wanted Kevin to be his witness."

"Says who?" I couldn't let that one slip through. Jimbo looked flushed. Davies squeezed my wrist.

"Well, since I'm here, and I *am* the Vice-president, I might as well come along and sit in. You don't mind, do you?" Davies was so smooth in her dealings, providing exactly what I needed.

To my surprise, Teflon Don was anxiously waiting inside the conference room, fumbling through a small stack of papers that sat before him. He looked up worried and spoke to Jimbo.

"Chief Willie. What is she doing here?"

"Hello, Mr. Doherty. I'm his union rep. What's going on?" Davies didn't need any introductions, she knew who she was, and she knew what Teflon was there to do.

Jimbo closed the glass paned doors behind us, and that's when "The Don" started his verbal attack on fair play. However, all motion inside of that room ceased as soon as I pulled out my tape-recorder. I sat my solution on the large wooden desk in front of me and pushed record.

"Mr. Donald Doherty, director of Employee Relations, do you mind if I record this meeting?"

Teflon looked only slightly confused as he folded his ashy, yet well manicured, hands on top of his papers.

"No recording devices are allowed for the purposes of this meeting." The setting resembled the shady dealings that proceeded in the dark corners of the governor's office. I complied with Teflon Don's instructions, turned the recorder off, and waited for the next anvil to drop onto my head. And it didn't take Teflon long to let go.

"Mr. Freeman. We've just received the results from our psychiatrist regarding your mental fitness, and I'm just a bit concerned that you've relapsed." I glanced at Debbie Davies from the corner of my eyes, then I returned my focus to Teflon as he continued. "It appears that you are suffering from a bi-polar disorder. Chief Faunce and I agree with Dr. Holl that you may present a significant risk to both yourself, as well as your co-workers. You know, handling a firearm and all," he said.

Davies looked over at me as I shrugged my shoulders and shook my head in exhaustive disbelief. She then twisted inside of her seat and questioned Teflon Don about his last statement.

"You're saying that he's bipolar?" Davies asked.

"That is correct."

"And your psych says that he can prove that, right?"

"Sure."

"What could he have possibly found this time that he didn't find the last time?"

"During Kenneth's evaluation, Dr. Holl noted that Kenneth's bipolar disorder manifested itself through an inappropriate smile near the completion of the session." That one smile during Dr. Holl's hour-long session had returned to haunt me and was documented to be 100% proof of a bipolar disorder.

"What in the hell is an inappropriate smile?" Davies smiled at Teflon Don, who, in turn, smiled back. "You and I are both smiling right now. Are we bipolar, too? Or does that only apply to Kenny?" Teflon didn't respond to Davies' question, but he managed to nod his head in pain, appearing sympathetic to my regrettable predicament.

"But now, unfortunately, we have an even greater problem. Since you can't carry a firearm, departmental policy mandates that you can't work as an investigator."

Davies leaned forward in her chair completely disgusted by what she was hearing.

"And what policy is that?!" Davies' question had little effect on the direction that my position in the department was headed. Teflon and Jimbo looked at each other.

"It's a new policy."

"How new?"

"New."

"I've been in the business for twenty years and I've never heard of any policy like *that* before!" Debbie said.

"It hasn't been written yet, but the commissioner has assured me that it will soon be policy." Teflon said.

I never blinked. I was getting used to retaining my composure as I heard inconceivable explanations. But not Debbie.

"What the hell is this?!" She turned to Jimbo. "You're

enforcing a policy that doesn't even *exist?*" Jimbo tapped his fingers on the desk wanting to respond, but Teflon was the diplomat of the pair running the show. He completely dismissed Davies' inquiry as less than small talk and continued with his own disgraceful agenda to punish, humiliate, and, ultimately, terminate me.

"Let's try not to confuse Kenneth with these minor administrative matters. Instead, we want to help Kenneth with his medical leave." I touched Davies' hand, trying to get her to calm down just a bit, but she was already very angry. Whatever Teflon had planned was predetermined, and there was no possible way that anything either Davies or I said could have changed it. Nevertheless, Davies still believed that Teflon had a shred of decency left in his soul.

"How did we get from imagined policies to medical leave?" Davies was beginning to sound the way that I had felt for the past year. By this time, I had a death-grip on Davies' wrist. I was mentally spent by all of their foolishness and I wanted Davies to allow Teflon to give us the rest of whatever he had for me so I could get out of there.

"Kenneth, the chief and I agreed that you should take a medical leave for maybe three to six months so that you can deal with your *problem*. Then, when the time is right, we'll have a doctor clear you to return to work."

"And just how long will that take?"

"No more than three to six months, or so." Teflon's pacifying attention returned to me. "We're committed to you getting better. These doctors want to help you."

Davies interjected again. "With what?"

"You know, with your problem."

"The bipolar disorder, right Don?" Davies was growing increasingly sarcastic.

"Yes. The bipolar disorder." Teflon announced. "There's nothing to be ashamed of, Kenneth. We spoke to the Commissioner and we all want what's best for you."

"As long as he doesn't smile, right?" Debbe had reached her end with Teflon's explanations, but something else bothered her. "Now, this medical leave, is it voluntary? I mean, does Kenny have a choice?"

"No. Departmental policy mandates it." Teflon said. Davies looked at me and exhaled, knowing full well that there wasn't then, nor had there ever been, any such policy.

"So what you're telling me is that Kenny can come back to work if another psychiatrist clears him, right?" Debbie asked.

"That's correct."

"And, we've got your word on this?"

"Of course. We're just trying to help him." Teflon Don was so concerned with my health.

Debbie started grinning. She looked at me and started in with her questions to me.

"Kenny, didn't you get an evaluation from another psych the day before you saw their doctor?"

"Yes." I kept my responses short and sweet.

"And he cleared to you to work and to carry a gun, right?"

"Yes." Davies smiled at Teflon after I gave my answers.

"Well, I guess everything else is moot, right? A second psychiatrist saw him and cleared him to work. So, he can go back to work right now, correct?" Davies and Teflon Don laughed, but Teflon's laughter was more nervous than hers. Jimbo was almost forgotten until then. He started to turn beet red again, breathing heavily with all the girth and pre-explosiveness of an agitated Mount Saint Helen.

"Well, if you get me the proof of what you've just told me, as per departmental policy, we'll have to schedule a third opinion, since one doctor said one thing and the other said something different. Then, if he's cleared by a *third* doctor, I'll have no problem bringing Kenneth back to work." Teflon's eyes began to quickly shift towards Jimbo, who sat quietly.

I looked at Debbie, as if to remind her of my other evaluation, but Debbie was on point. She laughed, "Funny you should mention it, you know, about having that *third* evaluation? Well, Kenny just happened to have been evaluated by a *third* psychiatrist the day *after* he saw your doctor." Davies exhaled, "So, I guess all of this really is moot, according to what you just told us. Okay Kenny, you can go back to work. Right Mr. Doherty?"

"The same psychiatrist?" Teflon asked.

"No, of course not. A different one, with no connections to the first, or to Kenneth, or the department." Davies paused. "An unbiased psych."

Teflon Don chuckled.

"Wow. I didn't expect that." He looked at Jimbo, but by now, Jimbo was giving his impression of an overweight turtle trying to hide in his shell.

"What's wrong? You don't want an unbiased doctor not affiliated with any of us?" Davies' sarcasm was sharper than a two edged sword, and oh-so precise.

"No, that's fine. But you can understand that the department wants a third opinion from one of our doctors, right?"

"Departmental policy again?" Davies asked. Teflon Don didn't respond verbally, but his breathing echoed off the ceiling. "Well, you would agree with me, Don, that there's no way that Kenny should ever go back to see Dr. Holl, right? Because he's already got his mind made up about Kenny and this peculiar, bipolar disorder smile, right?" Davies asked.

Teflon fiddled his earlobe with his thumb and index finger. "We'll get another doctor for him." Teflon finally conceded to reason, but not enough to change what was planned for me. "But we need him to get me those other evaluations as quickly as possible."

"No problem." Davies said. "But six months is crazy, especially since he's already got a third psych saying he's fine. How long will he be out of work? The man's got a family to take care of."

"No problem." Teflon said. "I'll schedule his evaluation

immediately."

"But what about his pay?" Davies asked.

"All he needs to do is request Family Medical Leave, and I'll make sure that he gets approved. Just get that paperwork in." Teflon paused, and we all just visually surveyed the room, each waiting for the other to speak. "Any questions, Kenneth?" Teflon Don asked me.

"Is that all?"

"Yeah, that's all from me." Teflon was done.

I turned my attention to Jimbo.

"Hey Chief. Am I still in Investigator Kevin's custody? Or am I allowed to leave under my own power?"

Mount Saint Helen finally erupted, spewing fire and brimstone, shaking the very foundation of the large conference room.

"There you go again, Kenny. I never said that you were in custody. Kevin was your witness to make you feel better and you…"

"Mr. Freeman, we asked Kevin to drive you down here to this meeting because we thought that since it was raining outside, you might not feel like driving, or you may have been a bit tired." Such compassion made me nauseous. Teflon was obviously trying to curb Jimbo from saying something else stupid, as was Jimbo's reputation. "You don't have to ride back with him if you don't want to, okay?"

Davies stuttered at Teflon's admission. "So, *you* chose Kevin to bring Kenny here?"

"Sure. They said they were friends." Teflon shrugged his shoulders.

"And, *Kenny* didn't *want* him as a witness, right?"

"What idiot told you…" Teflon's glance methodically joined ours, as we unsympathetically planted our sights on Jimbo. Boy, he sure looked like he could use a friend. Teflon sighed heavily as he closed his eyes in frustration, and once again, covered for the moron. "He doesn't have to ride back with Kevin."

I felt like smiling, just to rub it in Jimbo's red face, but I had accomplished what I set out to do without gloating and thought that a little humility might bring me a bit of peace in my own mind. The vengeance I had desired when Jimbo threatened my daughter and me dissipated. He may have made the threat, but Jimbo was only a bigheaded puppet with the Teflon Don and Faunce pulling his strings.

"Gentlemen, have a good day." I walked close to Davies as we exited the room, and whispered into her ear. "Walk me to my car please." She nodded in agreement.

After I left, Davies went back in Central Office and was approached by Teflon Don.

"I'll make sure that his Family Leave is approved, okay? But we need him to request it quickly."

"I'll fill it out for him myself." Davies offered without realizing that Teflon had another agenda other than my health.

"No!" Teflon Don caught himself and changed his tone. "No. It's important that Kenneth requests Family Leave, personally. Okay? Policy stuff."

"Okay. I'll tell him." Despite what happened on that second floor, Davies continued to believe Teflon Don wouldn't go along with Faunce and would call for fairness in the matter.

"You know, he's nothing like what I expected." Teflon said. "I was told that he would flip out, start hollering and screaming, maybe even throw a few things."

"Not Kenny."

"I see." Teflon wiped his brow. "First, they're calling him our Rising Star, now he's the Anti-Christ."

"Give him a chance, Don. You'll like him."

"Sarcastic as hell, but seems like a decent kid."

"He really is decent, but you know this department. Piss off the wrong person, and all hell breaks loose." Davies said.

"Well, let's try to help him out a little bit." Teflon said. "I just need that request, and those other evaluations, alright?"

Debbie Davies reassured him that I would get those documents signed as soon as possible, and why not? She trusted him even though his reputation as the department's hatchet man was almost legend, and his exploits well documented in the many disciplinary actions against other employees.

As her conversation with Teflon ended, Davies noticed Jimbo standing near the secretaries' area, laughing with other investigators assigned to Central Office.

"Chief, can I ask you something?" Davies asked.

"If it's about Kenny, fuck no." Jimbo said. "I can't believe that you're helping that bastard."

"I'm his union rep, and he's my friend."

"Kenny don't have white friends. He hates his own kind. He wouldn't even listen to his closest friends."

"Ellis and Houston? Are you kidding me?"

"He's a fuckin' racist!"

"You're calling *him* a racist? Oh, don't even bother going there!"

"He's protecting a fuckin' terrorist!"

"What in the hell are you talking about?" Debbie couldn't comprehend the hatred Jimbo had for her friend.

Jimbo glanced at Ellis Allen, who was still confused about why Sam-I-am didn't like green eggs and ham. "Don't ask me shit about him!" Jimbo shook his head in disbelief.

Allen chimed in, "Fuck him! Kenny deserves everything his ass gets!"

However, Debbie wasn't going to let a minor thing like "no" derail her.

"Whatever, Ellis." She dismissed Allen and turned her attention back to Jimbo. "But since you don't like him, Chief, you're going to allow one of *your* investigators to be put out of work based on a policy that doesn't even *exist*?" Jimbo kept laughing, never responding to Davies as the other investigators slowly dispersed.

"Chief!"

"If he can't carry, he can't work."

"Ed Melendez worked without a firearm for a long time, and so did I. And so did a whole lot of other investigators. But you're going to put Kenny out." Debbie kept speaking as Jimbo started to walk away. "Chief…"

"We got to start somewhere, don't we?" Jimbo was through talking about a deal that was already decided. He returned to his office and closed his door. Davies eventually left Central Office and returned to her own office at the A.C. Wagner Correctional Facility in Bordentown.

Later that day during our daily telephone chat, she and I discussed the events that had occurred, including what transpired after I left. I offered her some advice about Teflon Don, and then informed her that if I were to "voluntarily" submit the Family Leave request he was so adamant about, the department could later argue that I had requested medical leave because I agreed that I suffered from a bipolar disorder. In addition, they would use my request as proof that I was never forced out of work.

Debbie was reacting the way most cornered people would. She was hoping against hope for somebody in authority to stand up and say "no" to the madness. But Teflon's help reminded me of a cat in the story about a bird who began his journey south about a month too late. The cold weather arrived and, during his flight, his wings froze and the bird fell from the sky, landing on a farm. A cow came along and crapped on the bird, and the bird became depressed.

However, the bird soon noticed that the heat from the manure melted the frost from his wings. Along came a cat that licked the bird clean of the manure, and then proceeded to eat the bird. The moral of the story, "everyone that craps on you ain't your enemy, and everyone that gets you out of crap ain't your friend."

Unfortunately, Davies would only discover how treacherous "The Don" really was when she faced her own public demise.

TWENTY-THREE

Is There a Doctor in the House?

I hand delivered copies of the evaluations from both Dr. Williams and Dr. Quintana to Teflon Don's office a few days after the Central Office meeting, a gathering that commenced my mandatory medical leave of absence. Teflon was on the telephone when I arrived, but I was still able to hand the evaluations directly to him. He thanked me for the evaluations and asked if I had signed the Family and Medical Leave Act (FMLA) documents, which I had not, and then he continued with his telephone conversation.

A week later, I received a letter from Teflon Don telling me that another psychological evaluation was scheduled for September 27, 1999, with Dr. Leslie J. Williams, PhD, of the Institute for Forensic Psychology in Oakland, NJ. Unsure of what to expect from the fourth psychiatrist, I contacted Dr. Daniel Williams to ask his advice on how to approach the evaluation.

"It sounds good. He's not in private practice." he said.

"So, why is that good?" I asked.

"If he's working for a center, then he has to answer to somebody."

"But what if he owns the center?" Dr. Williams laughed at

my questioning, which I felt was more than reasonable, considering the hoops that I had to jump through.

"Then you've got your hands full." he said. "Try not to worry about it too much, Kenneth. Get yourself a good night's sleep and just...just be you." That night, I did just what the doctor ordered.

Early the next morning, I arrived at the center ready for my evaluation. Unknown to me, I had been scheduled for an extensive battery of tests designed to search every crevice of my imagination, exposing me for the bipolar, manic depressant, delusional, serial deviant that Teflon Don and Faunce knew I was. First, there was a series of multiple choice and written exams. The first exam consisted of over 800 questions and the second was another 500 questions long. Two written tests measured my ability to draw pictures about myself, about women, men, children, houses, flowers—you name it, I drew it.

After all the written work was completed, Dr. Leslie Williams, who was a bit reserved, but pleasant nonetheless, examined me. I was subjected to a hearing examination and a retina examination. Dizzying beams of light were rapidly shot into my corneas as I was questioned about the multitude of colors I observed. For reasons I've never understood, it seemed important to the doctor that each color illicit a deep emotion or put me in touch with a particular "feeling".

"Kenneth, is there a particular thought or feeling that you're having at this moment?" You cannot possibly imagine how bad I wanted to bellow out a line from the great philosopher and orator Austin Powers. *"Psychedelic, baby! Yeah!"* But any response that included groovy words would have made my single, inappropriately bipolar smile look like, well, like a smile. So, I decided not to take any chances, and instead, I focused on a more important issue like what would I cook for dinner.

In total, Dr. Williams questioned me for about an hour during our discussion session. A clear third of his questions surrounded why would I spend a significant portion of my mortgage to pay the department's $800.00 bill. My credit rating was also deemed significant criteria for being bipolar and of paramount concern regarding my ability to carry a firearm. None of it made any sense.

After reviewing the close relationship between bipolar disorders and a person's FICO score, I was summarily instructed that Dr. Williams had only begun to evaluate me.

"Was there something about your childhood that could have affected your decision to give your mortgage payment to a stranger?" Dr. L. Williams was definitely made from the same mold as Dr. Holl, but with one obvious exception. He was secure in his profession, not begging for anybody's approval, making him a much more personable individual than Dr. Holl and Dr. "Quack" Kahn.

"My apologies, doctor. But, I'm not intelligent enough to understand the connection between preserving my livelihood and my childhood desire to have a Johnnie Lightning set of my very own."

He laughed at the absurdity of my response, but never lightened up with his questioning. Hence, a second evaluation was scheduled the following Monday. As mental homework, I was told I must use that time to consider the effects of my upbringing on using my mortgage for the psych bill, and to prepare for any questions that might arise as a result of my undocumented illnesses.

By this time, I was taking three to four doses of headache medication a week. I tried several different brands, but the headaches dominated each pain reliever. So, I put my quiet time to good use.

With nobody home but me, and plenty of time on my hands because of my mandatory medical leave of absence, I spent my time writing poetry and cleaning different parts of the house. When I needed an occasional laugh, I took a break by watching Damon Wayans and David Allen Grier in *Blank Man* while stretching out on my recliner. But that was rare during the week because the attic's clutter had earned the majority of my attention.

The attic was the one place in the house that had accumulated so many boxes and bags of clothing that it was almost impossible to find anything without getting frustrated. While I was straightening up the attic, I ran across some old photos and memorabilia from the year and a half of my Marine Corps deployment in Cairo, Egypt. I sat on a rectangular box in the warm attic for hours reliving those memories. For a while, it felt as if I had actually returned to Cairo, and was sitting on a funky camel, staring at the great Pyramids of Giza and wondering how the Sphinx was originally constructed. I remembered the construction of the New Office Building on the main compound at the embassy and recalled the nighttime security sweeps on the CIA's floor, ensuring that no sensitive documents were left unsecured.

I smiled endlessly about my experience because I had no regrets. Whatever life had waiting for me after my trials, I chose to accept it gracefully, with many pleasant memories embedded into my consciousness to direct me to peace. Those memories carried me for the entire week and reminded me that God had blessed me. *How many kids from Newark can say that they viewed Moses' birthplace, or went to the magnificent museum in Alexandria, or saw a Pharaoh's tomb, or rode on the Nile River? How many have watched the set-up for the musical "AIDA", having the base of the Sphinx as a background?*

Monday arrived too quickly and I returned to Dr. Leslie Williams' office for some more of the same. I didn't flinch when he told me that we had another hour-long interview and more paperwork to trod through. I just prepared myself for whatever new tricks he had planned.

Right away, I knew that my brother, Keith, would burst out in laughter when I later described the thought that came to mind as soon as I saw the doctor's newest trap. Ink blots! He emphasized, and then reemphasized, how unimportant my responses to the inkblots were and how I had nothing at all to worry about, while all the time he watched me for another one of those inappropriate bipolar-smiles.

The doctor held the bunch of hand cards above his desk. I sat frozen as I recalled how the nerd in *Blank Man* related every inkblot to insects or bugs, anything except what the doctor considered normal. The possibilities of what could result from those thoughts were hilariously infinite. For the past week, I inundated myself with the sights, thoughts, and memories of Egypt. Again, sitting before that doctor, I escaped to that ancient land and marveled at the red, sand storm skies.

"Tell me, Investigator Freeman…" Dr. Williams asked as he reached for the first inkblot, "what do you think of when you look at this?" The doctor gave me a way out by the way he formulated his question. The inkblot actually resembled two dancing bears, but he didn't ask me what it resembled or what I saw. He asked me what I thought of when I saw it, which was entirely different. Subconsciously, I wasn't even in North America. I was climbing the largest of the three Great Pyramids of Giza, staring at an opening that one of the Egyptian locals told me was the sacred entrance to the tomb of the Pharaoh Ramses. Moreover, with all honesty according to his *question*, I answered him accordingly.

"I see an inscription, over the doorway entering Pharaoh's tomb, on a pyramid in Egypt." Dr. Williams stared at me with a smile, then he lifted up and swiveled the card towards himself, as if he were trying to decipher the inscription. After he looked at the card, his eyes glanced back at me, then quickly returned to the card. He smiled a second time, then placed that card behind the others, revealing the next.

"And what do you think of when you look at this one?" Another perfect question. At that point, I had left the pyramid and was riding a camel towards the mighty Sphinx. "There's a disfiguration right here, in the area that was the nose of the Sphinx." I pointed at the card, my forehead wrinkled and showed my uneasiness at the disfiguration. Dr. Williams was no longer smiling to cover his bewilderment. And my answers only got better with the other cards.

"Hey, doc! I think about the mouth of the Nile River"..."A camel, doc"..."A severe sand storm." All of my answers were consistent with my memories of Cairo, and all were honest. After we finished with the inkblots and another question-and-answer session, he reviewed a few of the inkblots.

"Doesn't this look like two dancing bears?" he asked.

"If you say that they're two dancing bears, then I guess I agree."

"That's not my question." He began to explain himself, but I cut him off.

"I'm just trying to keep my job. Forget what I said earlier. It's dancing bears."

"No, no. I mean, can you see two..." I interrupted him again.

"Definitely, sir. I agree with you. It is definitely two dancing bears." Dr. Williams sighed heavily and pulled out a second card.

"What about this one? Can you see a woman?" See a woman? I saw a beautiful, curvaceous diva in that card, a figure that any man would dream about—men would kill to caress her and women would die to be shaped *like* her—and that's what I told him.

"Definitely, doctor. I agree with you. It's *definitely* a woman!"

"I know what I see, but do you see a..."

"Definitely, sir. A beautiful woman, right there. Yup! I don't want any trouble for not agreeing with you, sir."

"Never mind." Dr. Williams shook his head and stretched as he laid the other cards down. His shoulders relaxed and he let out another heavy sigh.

"They really don't like you, do they?" I was careful to answer his question, focusing on the inkblots instead.

"If you want dancing bears or beautiful women, fine."

"I'm not talking about that. I'm talking about your employer."

"You'd have to ask them, sir." I said. "All I see is beautiful, bear-shaped, dancing women, doc. Whatever you say."

He sat the cards on his lap and sighed. "Kenneth, would you mind just talking to *me* for a little while?"

"You ask me as if I have a choice, that is, without being fired. Sir." The doctor nodded his head in defeat, surrendering any attempts at winning my trust.

"I'll give Mr. Doherty a call to tell him my findings." He said.

"Will I be able to get a copy of the evaluation?" I asked.

"Not from me." Dr. Williams said. "You'll have to get it from your employer, unless…"

"Unless what…"

"…unless your lawyer subpoenas my records. Then you can have all of them."

"But I don't have an attorney."

"Shame." His eyebrows flashed up quickly, then returned to their common place. Not having an attorney was proving to be a problem, a problem that didn't have to remain. "Do you have any more questions for me?"

"Are you done with me, doctor?"

"Sure. We're done." And with that, I left his office, and my thoughts remained in Egypt for the long drive home.

The next day, I received a telephone message from Jimbo ordering me to return to work. After returning, I was told that once Faunce received the official, written evaluation from Dr. Leslie Williams, I would be notified of her decision regarding my firearm. I was placed on restricted duty without any explanations about what kinds of activities were actually restricted.

Union Vice-president Davies was irate. She wrote letters

that questioned why I was put out of work in the first place, seeing that I was in the exact same predicament that I had been in prior to the implementation of the policy that never existed, with one exception. They took nearly every hour of the sick time that I had accrued, claiming that I voluntarily agreed to use it.

In October 1999, I was ordered to return to Central Office to get my firearm. Any officer or investigator that had to retrieve a weapon for nearly any reason would have just been told to go get the weapon, sign for it, and return to their duty station. But for some reason, Hamner made it clear that I was being "ordered" to retrieve my weapon from Internal Affairs. I was even warned that my failure to comply with the order would most likely result in disciplinary actions. I knew that with their mounting failures, the stakes would eventually increase, but I didn't know how rapidly that would happen or the assistance the Teflon Don and Faunce would receive.

TWENTY-FOUR

Good Advice, Counselor

When I arrived, I was told to report to another investigator, Michael Mancuso, who would sign the weapon over to me. I walked into Mike's office and he told me that Chief O'Brien wanted me to report to Chuck Mueller (MBM) before he could release my weapon.

"Why?"

"Hey, Ken…" Mancuso said, "I guess it's got something to do with one of your letters." At that point, their order for me to report to Central Office was beginning to make sense. The charade had all the markings of an ad hoc investigation, a witch-hunt, hoping to snatch an unsuspecting employee. Internal Affairs had changed its name during that time to the Special Investigations Division (SID), but their tactics proved consistent. Same package, different wrapping.

"Hey, brother. How you doin'?" the Muscle Bound Moron asked. Mueller was the same guy who called investigator James "J.R." Reynolds his "brother", but told everybody J.R. was incompetent and stupid. Mueller would have similar stories about two of J.R.'s three closest friends: "Fatman" Randolph and Houston Miggins, but not about Allen. Allen may have been an idiot, but he was foolishly loyal to Mueller and O'Brien.

I wasn't sure why Muller despised J.R. that way, but Mueller kept the four Musketeers extremely close to him. Unlike Allen, they had mastered the art of "shuck-n-jive", and were so incompetent that they posed no true threat while filling a quota. They were rewarded regularly for assisting management with trumped up reports on dissidents of all nationalities.

In one instance, Miggins called a meeting of the African American investigators when Faunce discovered that Miggins lied after shredding reports he couldn't understand instead of asking for help. Facing termination, Miggins struck a deal to save his job and told Faunce that some "disgruntled" African Americans had gathered over the weekend to start their own racist union designed to disrupt Internal Affairs' daily operations. It forever caused a chasm between the unit and the unit's few African American investigators. Transfers, tougher assignments, and lowered proficiency ratings followed those investigators for years—all of whom our union president Barney Dyrnes and Mueller commonly referred to as "brother". However, in an ironic twist, it was later discovered that Fatman Randolph and J.R. were the ones who informed Faunce about Miggins' misconduct.

"Good morning, Mr. Mueller. But my name's not brother." This was not a cordial meeting, and I was not in the company of friends. That phony smile melted from his face and I continued with my question. "Why am I here?"

Just as quickly as the smile disappeared from his face, it reappeared.

"Ah, c'mon, brother. Have a seat. I just want to talk to you a minute." Mueller said.

"My name's not brother. Please stop calling me that."

"Kenny, c'mon." The Moron balled his fists to playfully punch at me. "We're all on the same team, right?"

"That depends."

"Depends on what?"

"If you're here to investigate me. If so, then we're obviously not on the same team."

His smile permanently left his face, and I witnessed disgust.

"Okay then, have a seat, investigator." Now, that was more like it. "I was told to ask you a few questions about a letter that you wrote to the governor [Christie Whitman] as well as to [U.S.] Senator [Frank] Lautenberg." Mueller had questions already written for him on a notepad on the desk. Right then, I knew I needed a lawyer, but with departmental inquiries, the department wasn't required to allow you to have a lawyer present. However, they were required to allow you to have a union representative.

"You said that we're on the same team, right?" I asked. It should've been obvious to Mueller that I didn't consider him my teammate. However, a horse could only see what his master's blinders allowed.

"Yeah, man." Mueller said.

"Then you won't mind if I called our other teammate, Debbie."

"The Chief just stepped out for…"

Can this Moron *really* be that stupid? "I'm talking about Davies! I think my union representative should be present, if we're on the same team." He looked confused, which was normal, as he let me telephone Davies from the office. It would take her less than an hour to arrive. We both sat in the office waiting for Davies to arrive, looking at the walls, the floor, each other, and never saying a word.

When she arrived, Mueller restarted the interview. He placed a tape-recorder on the top of his desk. I asked if he would mind if I also tape-recorded the interview, just in case his recorder had one of those "edit" buttons. He refused, but said that he would send us a copy.

Mueller continuously reminded Davies that I was the complainant, and not the target of any kind of investigation.

He attempted to reassure us that I was not being disciplined for writing to the governor or to the senator. The interview was supposedly about the confidential informant Muhammad Aburami. But, it wasn't. It was the most blatant witch-hunt ever conceived, and I was undoubtedly its sole target.

Davies was great, as usual. She interrupted Mueller with speeches, comments, and anecdotes as regularly as possible. Mueller was none the wiser because he lacked her experience with investigations and union representatives. She was a seasoned player at their game, and I had a lot of confidence in her. Davies also knew the history of SID, and she reminded him every chance she got.

In one instance during the interview, Mueller pretended to be shocked that Chief Willie would ever order somebody to alter or change an official report.

"Kenny, you're talking about Jimbo? He might yell some times, but, hey man, he really likes you." Mueller's face shown dismay that I could tell on somebody as wholesome and good as ol' Jimbo. Mueller had to be stunned because he was promised the Chief's position when ol' Jimbo retired. But Davies wasn't shocked at all, and she told Mueller why.

"Well Chuck, I've been knowing ol' Jimbo a lot longer than you have, and *Jimbo* ain't no saint." Davies leaned over as she, once again, took over Mueller's investigation. "You remember that time that he told me to go back and change certain evidence entries in our logbook before we sent it to the Mercer County Court? The trial? When ol' Jimbo didn't want us to look as incompetent as we were?" Davies adjusted herself as Mueller crossed his arms. "I told him no, remember? But y'all never told that prosecutor what *you* did."

As Mueller sat quietly, Davies continued with her history lesson.

"Remember when Timmy Dill testified about how Chief Faunce shredded those documents *after* they were subpoenaed? Timmy just didn't mention ol' Jimbo's name in all of that. But he was there, too, remember?" She sat back in her seat and glanced at me while checking her watch. "So let's not act like this isn't something right up ol' Jimbo's alley."

At the conclusion of the interview, Davies and I walked down the hallway to Mancuso's office to retrieve my weapon, but there was a problem. Mike was told to give me my gun, but nobody wanted to give me a receipt for the weapon, nor was there any written record of when it was taken away from me. Also, nobody gave me the authority to either have or carry my weapon. Ray Charles could have seen the problem with this, but not Chief O'Brien.

"Kenny, why are you making trouble for yourself?" Since I had a union rep with me, I foolishly figured that logic would work.

"I received a letter telling me that after Debbe got the written evaluation from Dr. Williams that she would let me know of her decision. But, standing here now, Chief, I haven't heard a thing from her."

"If she said that you'll hear from her, then you'll hear from her." O'Brien said.

"What does that mean, Chief?" I had a tough time accepting double-talk, especially when it came from little men.

"It means she'll let you know when you can carry."

"In writing?"

"Sure." O'Brien said. "Go ahead and sign it out now, and Debbe will notify you about carrying it later." I then turned my attention to Mancuso.

"Now, who's gonna note that I haven't had my weapon since June 23rd?" Mancuso handed me the weapon's receipt. Like Kevin, Mancuso had no idea why they had involved him in the chaos.

"Kenny, I don't know why they're doing all of this. Just note on the receipt the day they confiscated your weapon, and then write today as the day you got it back. That way, they can't say that you didn't inform them."

Davies agreed with what Mancuso offered and so did I. After I signed the receipt, with all of the information, Davies quickly snatched the receipt and hurried down the hallway to make a copy of the receipt for safekeeping. Next, I hid the copy inside my jacket and showed O'Brien the original receipt with the dates that I noted on the receipt.

"Can you sign this chief?" O'Brien wasn't too pleased with my notes, but he initialed the receipt and wrote the word "noted" above his initials. That original was then handed to Mancuso, and I took custody of my weapon. O'Brien permitted me to take my weapon to McGuire's Air Force Base to re-qualify for firing my weapon, but I still required authorization from Faunce before I could carry my weapon.

TWENTY-FIVE

Their House, Their Rules

I worked nearly a month without a problem after the return of my firearm, but mean people lay in wait for prey. Authorization from Faunce hadn't come by that time and Hamner had placed me on the "on-call" rotation. Hamner trumped Faunce and gave me permission to carry my firearm at specific times. When Chief Faunce found out, she was livid.

And, just like that, I became the target of an internal investigation. I was charged with lying about needing any authorization in order to carry my weapon. Investigator Richard McHort, a former trooper of Hamner's, conducted the investigation and interviewed me in Hamner's office. Jack Dale wasn't a union representative, but Faunce chose him to sit in on the interview as my witness. Throughout the interview, Jack kept asking one simple question:

"What the hell are you investigating?" My sentiments were the same. I told him about the weapon's receipt, but that didn't seem too important to McHort. The only thing that interested McHort was if I personally spoke with Faunce and if she personally stated in words, not in a letter, that I needed authorization. The documents aside, it was clear where they were headed.

After the interview ended, Jack had a few questions for McHort.

"Rich, you still haven't answered one question. Can he carry a gun or not?"

"If Kenny feels that he should carry, then he should use his best judgment." McHort may have used that line on a child in a candy store, but this was Jack asking questions.

"What the fuck are you talking about? Can he carry a gun or not?" Jack was getting very upset, and his voice echoed with frustration.

"Hey Jack, why are you asking me? It's up to Kenny?" McHort looked in my eyes, and with a straight face, he asked me, "Can you carry or not?"

"You've gotta be shittin' me!" Jack said. "Who the fuck's in charge here?" No answer was offered as Jack surveyed the incompetence, focusing on McHort. "Why don't you call Debbe and ask her?"

"Debbe told me to investigate him."

"Why are you asking Kenny when you're trying to discipline him? Whatever he decides, you're just going to say that it was wrong. What kind of fucking sense does that make? Geez!" McHort stood, and headed out of the office. "And while you're at it, ask her why the fuck am I here? Barney's supposed to be his union rep. Make his ass do some work for a change!"

McHort went into another office and supposedly telephoned Chief O'Brien. He returned moments later and gave us a news flash.

"Debbe wasn't there, but O.B. said that if Kenny feels capable of carrying a gun, he should use his better judgment."

In one of the few displays of commonality, Hamner and I both broke out in a burst of ridiculous laughter.

Jack spoke through his laughter. "We've got to be on fucking Candid Camera! You can't make this kind of shit up." Jack looked frantically around the room at Hamner, then at McHort, pointing at me with his thumb. "Will somebody tell this poor kid if he can carry a fucking gun?!" All eyes zoomed in on Hamner, the senior investigator of the four present, the one who had previously given me permission to carry at certain times.

"Fuck that. Don't look at me." Hamner may have been a jerk, but he knew when to bow out. Immediately, all eyes switched to McHort, the eyes and ears of Central Office.

"Well, I'll tell you what. If you feel…"

Jack quickly interrupted.

"Fuck that. Yes or no."

McHort wanted to slither back into his hole at Central Office, but Jack refused to release his scaly head.

"Ah, yes."

"Can I get that in writing, or do I have to trust you?" I asked.

"He ain't going to give you nothing in writing. But I heard him say it, kid." Jack stood from his seat, shaking his head while he looked at Hamner. "You know that none of this makes any sense." McHort asked me to leave the office while the three of them spoke in confidence. A short while later, Jack came out with the same perplexed look on his face.

"I heard him say it. Go on and carry you gun. But watch yourself, kid. They think you've got a short fuse. I told you they'd be coming after you." Jack had a wicked laugh that everybody recognized. *Hern, hern, hern!* That sound bounced off the walls as he left the building. And, so did his warning.

The investigation was only a formality. The department used investigations to legitimize actions that were decided. The joke regarding investigations was, "What do you want to tell me before I find you guilty?" That joke was hilarious when hearing officers used it on inmates making frivolous allegations. Truth was, the joke's not funny unless it's on somebody else. True to form, within two weeks, I received notice that I would be suspended for five days for making a false statement against Faunce.

My union president, Barney, told me that officially the union wouldn't help because no union rep was present for my interview. Thank God for the officers' PBA representatives, who put me in touch with someone that I called Jack Dale with a law degree. His name was Andrew Dwyer, counselor at law.

Andrew was tall, clean-cut, and extremely sarcastic. His first reaction to what had happened during my career with Internal Affairs was disbelief. That was, until I handed him the large box of reports that documented Faunce's exploits. After reading the documents, he gave voice to my feelings.

"Not only are they arrogant enough to feel they can get away with this kind of behavior, they even put most of it in writing. And there's no telling what documents you haven't seen yet."

He agreed to represent me and researched the Contentious Employee Protection Act (CEPA), better known as the "Whistle-Blowers' Act" as well as the Law Against Discrimination. His advice and guidance was a great comfort to me because, as much as I thought that I was able to defend myself, my health suffered from all of the stress. The headaches had increased in their severity and were becoming more and more regular. The over-the-counter headache medication I depended on was less and less effective, and I began feeling nauseous from the taste. And, I began losing my appetite.

Jack's warning didn't take long to be proven true. Right after the New Year, Hamner started trying to push my buttons. He and Faunce resurrected the telephone call that I got from Willie that past August. Nothing was ever mentioned about the investigation for over five months, but it was now a very hot item.

"Freeman, Debbe told me to order you to state, specifically, who threatened you on the telephone." Hamner had summoned me to his office, telling me that he had an urgent message from Faunce.

I answered him the way that I answered him half a year ago. "It is my belief that Chief Willie called me, but I can't be sure."

"Wrong answer. Debbe wants you to be specific." I was clear about what Hamner wanted me to say, but there was no way that I would walk into a lion's den voluntarily.

"I can't. Unless you're ordering me to lie." Hamner nodded his head slightly, thinking of what to say next.

"You said your caller ID read unavailable, right?" Hamner asked.

"Something like that. Unknown or unavailable."

"Good. Then you are ordered to bring in your caller ID and all of your telephones." Hamner said.

"For what?" I asked.

"We're going to see if they are capable of registering "unavailable" or not. I need to see if your phones have caller ID." Hamner had long passed ridiculous, and was well on his way to absurd. "And I need another statement from you saying that you specifically claimed that it said 'unavailable'."

I sat back in the creaky, wooden chair in front of Hamner's desk. "Let me see if I understand you. You want me to just give you my personal telephone and caller ID? The same one that I bought with *my* money, and for me to go without a telephone until *you're* ready to return them?"

"Are you refusing to comply with an order?" Hamner smiled, hoping that I would refuse to agree to deliver my telephones to him. "Refusing an order" was the basis of most disciplinary charges. However, I had no intention of giving Hamner my home telephone, nor did I intend to defy his ridiculous order.

"You know what, Chris? I would bring them in . . ." I paused to watch Hamner's grin gradually dissipate. "But there's a slight problem."

Chris sat there motionless, barely breathing.

265

"What problem?"

"I'm glad you asked, Chris. Sir, are you ordering me to break the law?"

Hamner sighed heavily.

"Break what law?"

"You know, steal?" I said. "You see, if I just *take* those things from my home, without permission, that would be stealing. And I don't want to steal from my wife. Are you ordering me to steal?"

"You just told me that *you* bought it, with *your* money, remember?" Hamner said.

"Oh, but I do remember." I began rubbing my chin and looking up at the lights. "But, strangely enough, I recently gave all of that stuff to my wife. So, you'd have to ask her if I could bring it in and give it to you. She might agree to sell it to you for, I don't know, maybe $800.00?"

"$800.00?" From the look on Hamner's face, I could tell that he remembered that dollar amount and was roasting in anger.

"Now, Mr. Hamner, if you like, I can give you her answer right now."

Hamner grinned.

"When did you give them to her?"

"Just now." I said. "Can I help you with anything else?" Hamner was stumped, but he didn't give up.

"You've got until tomorrow to bring them in."

"No problem. Permission to contact the Irvington Police to tell them that I plan to steal equipment for you? I will notify Debbie Davies, you know union stuff, about your order, and I will need that order in writing just in case Irvington PD asks. But maybe first I'll give my wife a call to see what she says. Okay?"

I returned to my office and called home. "Hello?" My wife answered the telephone.

"Priscilla. Congratulations on being the proud owner of

whatever the department orders me to bring in!"

"Oh my God. What are they trying to do, now?" Priscilla witnessed Faunce's treachery from the front row. Although we weren't on the best of terms, hard times had a way of uniting us.

"I'll explain later, but Chris and Debbe want you to give them all of *your* telephone equipment for how ever long it takes them to do whatever they want to do."

"Tell Debbe and Chris that if they want it, come and get. They know where I live."

"Good enough."

I relayed her message to Hamner who was already very angry that he couldn't trap me, an anger that got the best of him shortly after I returned to my office.

Hamner walked past my downstairs office and peeked inside, seeing me adjust my tie in a mirror behind the door, which was slightly ajar. We made eye contact as he passed, but I thought nothing much of it. A few moments later, there was a crash against my elbow and forearm. Hamner stood back from the door, waiting to see my reaction. Jack's warning overcame my desire to retaliate. *They figure you've got a short fuse.* Would I have been justified in striking him back? The answer was a definitive "no". I would be deemed a delusional, bipolar troublemaker who makes false statements against superiors. In situations such as that one, the truth rarely mattered.

My poker face was in full swing as I extended my arm and grinded my teeth to sooth the pain. I strained to pull my stare away from Hamner's jaw. Then, I backed up slowly until I reached my desk, I picked up the telephone with the uninjured arm, and dialed my attorney. Hamner snickered at me, disappointed that I didn't lose my cool, and then walked away.

While talking to my attorney's answering service, I realized that my lip was bleeding. The door hadn't come anywhere near my face, but I bit down so hard on my lip that my incisors cut through. As mad as I was that I didn't go at Hamner, I was proud that I had restrained myself and scored one for the good guys.

I wrote a memorandum to the Chief detailing what happened, as was required, and I went to have my arm treated by a physician. The injury was severe enough to keep me out of work for a few days, so I took that information to the local police department and filed a formal complaint about the assault. I was leery about dealing with the Woodbridge Township because Hamner's much-flaunted friend, James McGreevey, was mayor, and everybody understood that McGreevey watched out for his friends.

The information regarding my criminal complaint against Hamner hit one of many nerves in Central Office. Faunce transferred me to the Adult Diagnostic and Treatment Center (ADTC) in Avenel, a sex offender facility located near the rear of Rahway State Prison and a two-minute drive from Hamner.

I worked with Pablo Alicea, who was near retirement, and Gloria Cunningham, who was out of work due to a severe injury. The IA unit's offices were apart from the main prison facility, and housed inside of a long, white trailer. There were three modest-sized offices and a general area for our secretary, the incomparable Irene.

I wasn't there a full day before I received a transferred telephone message from my insurance company requesting I verify some information my *advocate* had sent them. I called back my insurance company, pronto, to see what was going on and to find out the identity of my advocate. The person on the telephone warned me that due to the nature of our conversation, our telephone call could be recorded or monitored or both.

"Yes, Mr. Freeman. We just need to verify the dates of your crisis intervention."

"What are you talking about?" I asked.

"I received your request", she said, "for assistance regarding your doctor's bill. We declined it the first time your employer submitted it. But then you resubmitted some changes to your request, and now we just want to verify the accuracy of those changes."

I never sent a letter to my insurance company, but I had a good idea who did.

"We might have a problem. Could you fax me a copy of that letter, please?" I asked. She agreed without any hesitation, and faxed it to the office. There was no big surprise when I saw the name of the person that sent the letter. Kathleen VanSteen, one of Teflon Don Doherty's people. The letter stated that I was having "emotional difficulties" in 1998 and again in 1999, and that I, without any coercion, felt a need to seek psychological treatment for my mental illness. VanSteen went on to note that I authorized her, to act as my advocate, or confidant, in such matters. Then, she included a copy of Dr. Daniel Williams' invoice, dated October 1998.

What puzzled the insurance company was that VanSteen wrote that I paid the $800.00 invoice and just wanted to be reimbursed for my out-of-pocket expenses. However, there was no proof that I had paid the invoice until the insurance company received another copy of that same invoice with an April 26, 1999 payment entry. The invoice was printed six months before that entry could have occurred, plus I paid the bill on June 26, 1999.

"Did you submit this document with these changes?" she asked.

"No way. This is the first time that I'm seeing this."

"Well, it seems that you're trying to get us to reimburse you for your expenses after we informed you that your claim was denied, Mr. Freeman." The representative wasn't being nasty, but she had questions about the request that she had assumed was mine.

The set-up had the consistency of Teflon, and I didn't like it. My words were being recorded and I had to be sure that I put on record what actually occurred.

"I never authorized anybody from my employer to act on

my behalf, with my insurance company, for any medical matter. I didn't pay the $800 in April, I paid it in June. Also, I never altered this invoice nor did I have any idea that anybody else was doing that or intended to do that." I wanted to be exceptionally clear about my position, and she understood.

"Are you saying that you didn't try to collect this money from us?" She asked.

"I mailed you copies of my bill in the fall and winter of 1998. But I never sent *this* letter that you faxed to me. This is my first time ever seeing it." I said.

"Who would do this, Mr. Freeman? And in your name?" she asked.

"Please write these two names down. Donald Doherty and Debbe Faunce." I told her. "The author of this letter works for Doherty, and Faunce is my supervisor."

We talked for a while longer about the letter. I requested that she report the matter to her fraud department, and she agreed after giving me her full name. I also wrote a letter reporting the incident to the department.

I thought I had witnessed it all—the mandatory leave of absence, confiscation of sick time, ghost-policies enforced for my benefit, and refusal to clearly authorize me to carry a gun. But, what awaited me in the year 2000 made all of the events of the 90's seem like small potatoes.

TWENTY-SIX

Now, It's Time for the Hard Stuff

The celebration of my second daughter's first birthday should have been exciting, but several comments from some of the Faunce loyal guard were a perpetual reminder that my peace of mind would be constantly challenged. Those comments, often made during meetings or other gatherings, were more than vicious and laced with malice.

I tried to smile as we sang *Happy Birthday* to my daughter and blew out the candle, but I couldn't shake off those thoughts. I watched my wife, who was almost two months pregnant with our third daughter, laugh as she cut slices of cake and made jokes. At the same time, I recalled the conversation between two of those A-K's during the Christmas party. They discussed which "time slot" each had with "her", referring to a schedule they would put in place to sleep with my wife.

All of their comments were blatant enough for the rest of the world to recognize, but were determined too vague for the department leadership. I refused to let any of them see my anguish, but as the stress manifested itself exponentially, my headaches and health worsened.

This wasn't the first personal event that I couldn't enjoy,

and it wouldn't be the last. My marriage was doomed. All trust had vanished, and respect had diminished to a level so low that glimpses of admiration could only be noticed during large social gatherings. My career was destroyed because I dared to question Faunce's sovereignty. My anger about it all simmered on a daily basis and my most sincere poetry horribly reflected inner frustrations that no man should have to face. My private sanctuary rested in the positive tests results proving my paternity—a fact I declined to make known to either my enemies or my wife. Soon, the party ended, and my thoughts instinctively returned to the battle.

On February 9, 2000, exactly one week after my daughter's birthday, I wrote to the Commissioner to officially notify him about the insurance incident. The letter read, in part:

> *I must inform you now that Ms. Kathleen V. Vansteen, Employee Relations, attempted to fraudulently collect compensation from an insurance company and, without my authorization, misrepresented herself and accessed my private medical information from my insurance carrier.*
>
> *A spokesperson from the company informed me that Ms. VanSteen presented herself as my authorized [representative] prior to the insurance agency releasing such confidential information.*

The letter went on:

> *Sir, this act has eclipsed that of being intolerable. Assistant Chief William O'Brien acknowledged that the department contacted one physician and that physician informed me that he was asked to change his conclusion in favor of the NJDOC's Internal Affairs Unit. Must I accept that also?*

No sooner had I finished signing that particular letter, that I received an unannounced visit from the Attorney General's office. A new hire, Alex Atkins, had recently graduated from the same state Criminal Justice Academy, and was trying to learn on the job. Atkins met with both Faunce and Hamner about his plan of attack, and then he appeared at my office door.

"Good morning. Is there an investigator Freeman here?" Atkins asked my secretary Irene. Irene was nervous most of the time, and this day was no different. I came out of my office when I heard his question.

"I'm Freeman. Who are you?" I asked.

"Hey, my brother. Can I speak to you in private?" Atkins had all the trimmings of trouble, and when he referred to me as his "brother", I knew he had no plausible discernment or professionalism. Incompetence was, and always should be, intolerable.

"How do you know that I consider you to be *my* brother?" He smiled at my bluntness.

"I'm investigator Atkins from DCJ." His grin didn't falter as he handed me his business card. The card confirmed that he was from the state division, but I didn't know exactly why he was visiting me.

"I'm investigator Freeman, Mr. Atkins. Now. How can I help you?" I handed back his card.

"Can we talk somewhere in private?"

"Sure. Come this way." He followed me into my office where he took a seat. I removed the jacket to my suit that was draped across a visitor's chair so that he could sit comfortably, walked behind my desk, and sat down. I folded my hands and placed them on top of my desk, and said nothing, waiting for him to make the first move. Atkins looked around my office at the pictures on the walls, as well as some of the newspaper articles I had cut out.

"You have a very interesting office." Oh, Yes. He was definitely minor league material, but I had other things I needed to do, so I helped him along.

"Would you like to question my interior designer?"

"That's funny." He laughed as though I was on *Late Night with Jay Leno*. "But I just wanted to talk to you about what's going on."

"That's fine. So, talk." I said

"No. I want you to tell me." Atkins said. I was bored with his stupidity, and I didn't like entertaining morons so close to quitting time.

"Why don't you tell me whatever you want me to say so that we can get whatever this is over. I've got other things to do before I go home."

A stumped Atkins sat there a few moments, then sprung to life after realizing that Affirmative Action wasn't going to help him any longer.

"I just heard that you were having some serious problems, and I thought that you'd like to talk about them."

"With whom, you?"

"Yeah. We can just talk for a while. Maybe I can help you." What a doo-fus! There was no way that he could have graduated from the academy and made that kind of a state-ment, especially since he took a few moments to plan what his response would be. I sat back and sighed, as I stroked my hair firmly with both hands until my palms covered my aching eyes. In distress, I surmised that Atkins had stolen the idiot-crown from Mueller, and would reign supreme for many years to come.

"What serious problems do you want to discuss, Mr. At-kins?"

"Any problems that you want to."

"Such as…"

"Well, you're having problems, correct?" Atkins said.

"Sure, I have a problem."

"Okay then! Tell me about it!" Atkins perked up, scooting to the edge of his seat, gripping the arm rests as if he was about to win a birthday with Blues Clues.

"My problem is being questioned without my attorney being present."

Atkins sat deeper in his seat and grinned wickedly.

"I just wanted to ask you a few questions, okay."

"Of course. But since you had no problem introducing yourself as my brother, then you shouldn't mind having my legal brother sit in on our little jam session. You feel me on this, my strong, black, Asiatic, two-fisted, collard greens and ham hock-eating brother?"

Atkins didn't know if I was insulting him or complimenting him, and I wasn't telling.

"I guess it would be okay, but…"

"Perfect!" I quickly cut him off, effectively ending our meeting. "Take this," I wrote down Dwyer's name and telephone number. "Set up a mutually agreeable date, time, and place, and I'm all yours." I swiftly stood and started out from behind my desk, extending my hand to shake his hand. "Thank you for your time and patience. I'll follow-up with my attorney to make sure that everything runs smoothly from our side. Okay, sophisticated black man?"

Atkins wasn't thrilled at being verbally hurled out of the trailer, but I was losing eleven brain cells for every minute that I speakededed to him. I mean, that I actively engaged in conversation with him. Oh, my God! I'd better hurry!

"Good-bye, Mr. Atkins, and have a good day."

TWENTY-SEVEN

Please, Don't Testify

On February 25, 2000, my appeal hearing regarding an official determination about carrying my gun was held. There was nothing out of the ordinary presented at the hearing. Angry that the department refused to allow us to use any type of recording instrument at the hearing, my attorney paid for an official court reporter to be present, whose costs were passed on to me.

The hearing officer shared the name of the famous playwright. Eugene O'Neil. His note taking was slow, causing the hearing to stop on several occasions while he asked us to repeat what had just been said. Mr. O'Neil didn't hide his support for management, evidenced by an argument that he had with Mr. Dwyer about the department's copy of the weapon's receipt signed by Ellis Allen. The original receipt had my handwritten notes on it and was initialed by Chief O'Brien, but Jimbo, who presented management's case, was allowed to enter a copy of a different weapon's receipt. The copy of the receipt that O'Neil allowed management to enter not only didn't have O'Brien's initials, it didn't even have Mancuso's or my signature on it. Andrew leaned closer to me to whisper.

"Kenneth, who the hell is Ellis Allen?"

"Andrew, I told you, we're not in Kansas anymore."

He was livid, and could barely refrain from presenting our copy of the actual receipt; a receipt that management's witnesses had already acknowledged was signed by Mike Mancuso and me.

"You're accepting fraudulent documents from management?" Dwyer hoped to get O'Neil's response to that question, but came up empty.

"It's accepted." And with that, management's unsigned document was admitted. To add insult to injury, O'Neil ruled that since he accepted Jimbo's receipt, he wouldn't accept our real copy, a copy that had both Mancuso's and my signatures on it. Dwyer wasn't finished with the incident, which was why on direct examination, he placed knowledge of our receipt into the record.

"Now, investigator Freeman, when did you receive your firearm?" Dwyer asked.

"On or about October 22, 1999, after I was ordered to be interviewed by Charles Mueller regarding a snitch named Aburami." I said.

"Did you accept your weapon?"

"Not at first."

"Why not?" Dwyer asked.

"Because they weren't going to give me a written receipt documenting when my gun was taken from me and when it was returned."

"And why was that important to you?"

"Because just in case somebody was shot or murdered with my weapon during the time that I didn't have it, I didn't want to be held responsible."

"And so, you noted on the receipt the date that the weapon was confiscated as well as the date in which the weapon was returned to you, correct?"

"That's correct."

Andrew had succeeded in exposing the absurdity of the

state's disciplinary system. A feat that wasn't as difficult as one might have believed. He was intelligent, but my attorney was naïve about the way Faunce and Teflon Don conducted business. Although neither was present at the hearing, Teflon was the hearing officer's supervisor, and Faunce dictated whatever she wanted Jimbo to remember. Right after the hearing ended, Faunce's recollection of my testimony that she didn't hear, manifested itself into more disciplinary charges.

Almost immediately following the hearing, I received two notices in the mail. The first was the hearing officer's decision that I was guilty and would be suspended for three days instead of five. The fact that the department had presented a false receipt was somehow deemed moot.

The second notice was much more interesting in that it notified me that I would be suspended for an additional 15 days because of my testimony at the hearing. Faunce decided that I lied during my testimony, claiming that,

> *On February 25, 2000, you stated during your Disciplinary Appeal Hearing that you had been ordered by Assistant Chief Investigator James Willie to have an inmate murdered. This comment was witnessed by two Department of Correction's employees, Assistant Chief Investigator James Willie and Hearing Officer, Eugene O'Neill.*

Mueller's investigation was used declaring that I never told Mueller during our interview that I had been ordered to have Aburami killed, and that my letters to Governor Whitman and Senator Lautenberg were malicious lies.

Dwyer told me not to worry about the charges, but he wasn't the one being disciplined. I could tell that he was more inspired to take my case before a Superior Court now that he had a taste of their treachery. He believed that Faunce and Teflon Doherty wouldn't have any input into the outcomes at that level.

"I remember what you testified at the hearing. Now, they'll have to wait." he said.

"Wait for what?" I asked.

"Wait to review the transcript." Dwyer said. He was a good guy, but he just didn't get it.

"They don't want to see the transcript. I've already been found guilty." I thought Dwyer understood that those notices were only for show.

"I think you might be acting just a little bit paranoid, Kenneth."

"You might be right. But Delacy Davis told me that just because a man is paranoid doesn't mean that somebody's not chasing him." We both laughed.

"I guess you have a point." Dwyer said. "I guess you have a point."

My February 9, 2000 letter had reached the Commissioner by that time and a meeting was held giving Teflon Don and Faunce specific instructions to put an end to my employment —a charge they gladly accepted. On March 23, 2000, they met with their old accomplice, Dr. Richard Cevasco, to discuss how to approach my letter. During that meeting, it was decided that their debacle with Dr. Daniel Williams had to be sanitized, making my letter to the Commissioner a lie and grounds for my termination. Teflon decided to give Dr. Cevasco another shot.

"Good afternoon, Dr. Williams. This is Dr. Cevasco from the New Jersey Department of Corrections."

"Good afternoon, Dr. Cevasco." Dr. Williams said. "How can I help you?"

"Well I just wanted to follow-up on a few matters regarding investigator Kenneth Freeman. Do you remember him?" Dr. Cevasco asked.

"That was last summer, right?"

"Yes."

"Not specifically, but let me get my file on him."

"That won't be necessary." Dr. Cevasco said. "I just wanted to follow up about when I asked you before if you were making a differentiation between a corrections officer and an investigator. It was sort of unclear in your report."

"I'm sorry if I implied that. But, I wasn't making any differentiation between the two." Dr. Williams was at a great disadvantage at that point, and had no clue where all of this questioning would eventually lead. "I believe that I cleared him to return to work. Correct?"

"Yes, you did. But, we're sad to report that Mr. Freeman has had a relapse."

"Oh, I'm sorry to hear that. He seemed like a very nice young man. What happened?"

"You're a psychologist, not a psychiatrist, right Dr. Williams?" Dr. Cevasco asked.

"That's correct. Why?"

"Because Mr. Freeman claimed that he got some information from somebody that I asked a medical doctor to change some entries for me. And that couldn't have been you because I only called you about the differentiation, remember?"

"Well, I vaguely ..." Dr. Williams said.

"I don't mean to bother you. I mean, he couldn't possibly have been talking about you because he said a doctor told him, and you're not a doctor, right? You're a psychologist, right Dr. Williams."

"Yes. That is correct. I am a psychologist, not a psychiatrist."

"And, if he was talking about an MD," Dr. Cevasco cut in.

"Then he didn't mean me!" Dr. Williams finished Cevasco's sentence.

"We didn't think so, but we just had to check. Sorry for your time." Dr. Cevasco said. "But could you do me a favor?"

"Sure."

"I'm going to fax you some information. Could you write

just what you told me, and fax it back to me now? It would really help him. Kenneth agreed to see one of our psychiatrists on a regular basis, and finally get the help he needs." Dr. Cevasco said. Dr. Williams complied with Dr. Cevasco's request, not fully understanding exactly what punishment Teflon and Faunce had in store for me, and what part they had manipulated Dr. Williams into playing. The trap was laid and the bait was set.

The next day, I received a fax from Faunce stating that the Commissioner was profoundly disturbed by the serious nature of my letter to him. The mere idea that anybody would subject me to such atrocities was deplorable. Subsequently, the Commissioner ordered the Chief, herself, to personally complete a thorough investigation of my complaint, and to report her findings directly to his office. Faunce claimed that the department had no clue who I had referred to in my letter to the commissioner, and in order for her to be thorough and fair, I needed to put that doctor's name in writing and forward it to her.

I responded by asking, in writing, what rights I had regarding any possible disciplinary actions I knew would undoubtedly result. My request was a reasonable one, especially since departmental policy dictated that I had to be at least informed if I was the target of the investigation, and, if so, be allowed representation.

But Faunce was not having any of that, her fangs fully extended, she salivated in anticipation of her next victim. I received her final ultimatum in the early part of April 2000 to name Dr. Daniel Williams, which I did under protest. Miraculously, one day after I faxed Dr. William's name to Faunce, I was again charged for making a false statement with the penalty being my termination from the department.

As the hearing neared, what I thought was good news surfaced. Internal Affairs became a lodge within the Fraternal Order of Police, a nationally recognized entity whose members extended from coast to coast. However, our union maintained control over the vital areas such as negotiations and other crucial services that could have protected me.

Through the legal plan, I was assigned an attorney named Mike Gogal from the law office of Fusco & Macaluso in Passaic on April 20. I chose to go with the plan in order to save money. He immediately noticed that the department had violated their own policy for scheduling the hearing, and requested that the charge be dismissed, as was mandated by the state. Not a chance.

Prior to the hearing, I received two copies of the official transcript, a sealed defense, or at least I thought it was. The hearing progressed the same as the first did, except the new hearing officer was Dennis Wertz, another subordinate of Teflon Don. Wertz had come over from the Parole Unit, and was trying to retire without ruffling anybody's feathers.

Eugene O'Neil didn't testify quite the way management would have liked, but I needed my attorney, Mike Gogal, to dig a little deeper and see why his testimony was different from what my charge alluded.

"Mike. Ask him exactly what did he hear." I said. However, Gogal never pressed O'Neil on any specifics.

"He didn't say anything that could hurt us."

"But we've got a smoking gun over here." I referred to the transcript. "Force him to commit to something."

Gogal didn't respond to me, nor did he ever ask O'Neil for any specifics about his testimony, and that worried me. But, in a strange twist of fate, Mueller testified about what Jimbo and O'Neil had heard.

"Yes, that's what Kenny stated. He stated that he was ordered by Chief Willie to have an inmate murdered." Mueller said. My attorney handed Mueller and Jimbo, who was again presenting the department's case for Faunce, a copy of the transcript and asked him to show the hearing officer my comment.

"Mr. Hearing Officer, would you mind if we take a break to allow management to go over the transcript?"

I couldn't believe what I had heard. Jimbo didn't request a break, Gogal did. Mueller was on the ropes, we had him in an impossible situation, and my counsel requests a break?

"No! No break! Ask Chuck to prove that I said it!"

I was ignored. Gogal tried to pacify me by telling me that it was protocol, but I knew that there was something else going on. I left the room and walked downstairs furiously, with Gogal close behind me. After I went downstairs, the hearing officer joined Jimbo and Mueller as they sat in the break room to review and discuss the transcript. I thought of staying on the front porch area to cool off until I realized that I had just handed a smoking gun to my enemy, and my attorney was no where to be found.

I raced back to the meeting room, occupied only by the transcriber that I had scheduled to record the proceeding.

"Excuse me. Did you see the hearing officer?"

"He went that way," pointing towards the break room, and I used a speed walk to look inside.

And there they were, the hearing officer, Mueller, and Jimbo.

"Is this a private party?" The hearing officer looked down at the floor as he shuffled past me without comment. Jimbo then stood and looked back at Mueller.

"I have to take care of something. Take the transcript back to the hearing." Jimbo and I stared at one another as he walked past me and headed to the main staircase, leaving Mueller behind. I shook my head and went into the restroom next to the break room, splashed water on my sullen face, and gazed aimlessly into the full mirror above the sink. The faucet dripped slowly, unable to be completely shut off. As I stood silently, another thought raced through my mind. *I'd better tell Gogal what I saw.* Clearly, that meeting had to be improper if not prohibited.

I grabbed a couple of paper towels to dry my face and hands and skipped down the back staircase. I didn't have to search far for Gogal. He and Jimbo were in a remote area of the hallway whispering and nodding. After a short time, Jimbo noticed me and nudged Gogal, who quickly moved away from Jimbo and threw on an instant smile.

"Mr. Freeman. I didn't see you there." *No shit, Sherlock!* "You about ready to go inside?"

"What the hell is going on?" I asked.

"No, no, no."

"No, what?"

Gogal laughed, but it was obvious I wasn't trying to be a comedian.

"No, he was just asking me about another case that I'm handling. I wanted to take care of some logistics."

"What case is that?"

"Nah. It's not here. I mean, I could be handling it." I could smell a foul stench coming from Gogal. I questioned if saving a little money was worth having a union lawyer that was suspiciously fraternizing with management, and the answer was clear. I watched Jimbo head back upstairs using the main staircase and spoke to Gogal out of the corner of my mouth.

"Maybe we should just go back inside, huh?"

When we returned, Mueller offered a different reason for that statement not being in the transcript. He stated that the court reporter must have missed it, and that he was certain I made the comment because that was similar to the things that I thought.

Jimbo testified, but for some reason never even commented about the statement. Gogal's job was not rocket-science, and I pressed him to ask Jimbo about what he witnessed. All of my comments to Gogal were written on a note pad.

"Ask him if I said that I was ordered to have an inmate murdered. Now!"

"I think we've made our point." Gogal whispered.

"Ask him if he is lying or did the court reporter lie. Ask him, now!" I placed three and four lines underneath my comments, highlighting the urgency, but understanding that the fix was in. "Pin him to the wall!" I clutched my pen in my fist and pounded the pad, making an echoing bang against the wooden table. Gogal shifted himself to me in an irritated fashion, showing his disgust with my interference with such a spirited defense, and released the words that every client yearns to hear about their accusers.

"Calm down! Jim's really not a bad guy, you know?" I was floored. Devastated. Unsure where to turn. Just when I thought that I had seen everything, I discovered another billion corrupt galaxies left to be explored. Everything inside of me shut down, except for the throbbing pain between my temples.

"Mr. Freeman. I think that you should testify. What do you think?" Initially, I wasn't going to respond to Gogal's ludicrous suggestion, but I decided to scrawl my comment under my earlier request for Gogal to pin down Jimbo. I wrote,

"Do you need my testimony for the fix to be complete?" I calmly laid the pen on top of the pad, and swiveled it so that my counsel could see it. His eyes knew what it read before he had a chance to comprehend it.

"Mr. Freeman would like to exercise his right not to testify." Jimbo and Wertz looked confused at Gogal's revelation, and closing arguments began. At the conclusion of the hearing, Dennis Wertz, Mueller, and Jimbo all met with Faunce in her office and decided how to address my refusal to testify in my own defense, the time-limit violation, and what to do with the transcript. With Faunce, where there's her will, there will be a way.

Dennis Wertz issued his findings, which concluded three peculiar decisions. First, there was no time-limit violation because Faunce claimed that Gogal, himself, set the hearing date, even though I received Faunce's notice of the hearing date two weeks prior to my first contact with Fusco & Macaluso. Secondly, Wertz decided not to charge me for not testifying, but did make clear that I was not doing my best at helping the department to become better. Finally, in regards of the transcript, it was determined that I "probably" didn't make that specific comment, a determination that should have warranted that the charges against me be dismissed, right? Wrong! Teflon and Faunce determined that even if I didn't make the statement, I was thinking about them, and that my inner *thoughts* would have come out if I had agreed to testify.

A fifteen-day suspension was my penalty for thinking too loudly and for refusing to admit my thoughts under cross-examination. I remembered wondering if this nightmare would ever end, but was sobered by the reality that I had another charge on the horizon, and the goal for that punishment was my final termination.

I reported Gogal's actions to two attorneys at his law firm, who were incensed at Gogal's behavior, but the damage had already been done.

TWENTY-EIGHT

The Third Time Is No Charm

The first two disciplinary hearings were weak appetizers for Faunce and Doherty, while their main course was my ultimate termination. I became the subject of multiple investigations, allegations, and discipline. I was repeatedly accused of minor infractions with major consequences. Once, I was accused of not reporting for over a week that an inmate had escaped from a halfway house. An investigation was completed and found that it was somebody in Central Office that had dropped the ball, but they weren't even verbally reprimanded. Instead, I was warned to review the department's policies and was cautioned about committing any further violations.

But Faunce's bread and butter rested the Cevasco trap. This termination hearing accused me of making another false claim—that a doctor told me that he was asked to change his medical conclusion. For somebody who had never been in trouble, I was about to stand my third trial in four months, surely it had to be some kind of a record. Dennis Wertz was again assigned to serve as the hearing officer, against our objections. I understood that you got what you paid for, and this time I had no desire to take the cheap way out, and neither did Dwyer.

"I'm taking this case! And it's not up for discussion." Andrew Dwyer couldn't fathom what Gogal had done, more, what Gogal failed to ask. He requested disclosure of management's evidence, and discovered that missing in all of the documents Faunce had forwarded to him was two particular letters that were the absolute foundation of our case.

We were a bit puzzled because the department listed no witnesses to testify at the hearing and, of course, no evidence can be entered without a witness testifying that the evidence was an authentic and true copy of whatever it purported to be. However, inside of a department where corruption was a mainstay, there was no reason for me to have believed that this hearing would be any different. My attorney felt the same way, and was prepared for battle.

The hearing barely got started before the fireworks began. Dwyer questioned Wertz's overrule of every one of his objections regarding the admissibility of evidence that nobody authenticated, as well as the way Wertz accepted testimony from a witness that wasn't present, and therefore couldn't be questioned by the defense. Obvious, but this is New Jersey.

"How can you accept as reliable what somebody says who you haven't heard and we can't even cross-examine?" Dwyer asked.

"I'm going to allow it anyway." Wertz sounded like a broken record. Prior to the start of the hearing, Dwyer gave the court transcriber specific directions, in the presence of both the hearing officer and Jimbo, to record every word that was said inside of the room, even if the hearing officer wanted to go off-the-record.

"I want a *real* judge to hear the mayhem that goes on inside of these hearings." Dwyer said.

Jimbo submitted more documents, Dwyer made more objections, and Wertz ruled more in the department's favor. And when it was our turn to put on a defense, Dwyer requested that the hearing officer order Jimbo to turn over all of the department's documents. The basis of the charge was that Faunce had completed an investigation into the matter, but according to Jimbo, there was no written investigation indicating what was done or what conclusion was reached. Jimbo emphatically stated that they had sent us a copy of everything. Dwyer then pinned down the hearing officer regarding the admissibility of documents and the testimony of those who were not present. Wertz was emphatic that all documents would be admitted, regardless of whether management could prove who wrote the documents or not.

Earlier, Dwyer told me to prepare to testify at the hearing, even though there was a great possibility that I would be disciplined for speaking.

"You know they're going to charge me with something else if we win."

Dwyer already knew that to be the case, and after reading the official transcript of the last departmental hearing, and making particular notes of the type of questioning that Mike Gogal asked as well as the kind he failed to ask, Dwyer and I both agreed that I would not provide anybody else, especially the FOP attorneys, with any additional information about our strategy. I had informed two of the more senior lawyers at the firm about Gogal's actions, but didn't expect much to come of it.

"Try to stay calm, Kenneth. You seem to be very good at that. Just don't expect them to play fair, especially not at this point in the game." Dwyer said.

"I want to file the civil complaint." I said.

"Stay focused, Kenneth."

"Focused or calm?" Dwyer understood my sarcasm and wasn't offended, knowing that if anybody had a right to be sarcastic, it was me.

"Let's just see what happens here."

"Now that sounds like a $275.00 an hour plan." I said.

The strange had reached an all-time high when Dwyer noted on the record that in trying to fire me, the department held an official formal hearing seeking the termination of a permanent civil service employee, but called absolutely no witnesses, all done with the express approval of the hearing officer, over Dwyer's adamant objections. Everything that the department presented was taken as factually undisputed in Wertz's mind, and we were effectively prevented from questioning any of the documents. Furthermore, we couldn't even cross-examine the authors of the documents to ask them if they had, in fact, written them.

Since we were unable to question anything entered into evidence against me, Dwyer began his questioning of me with the background of my employment. He focused on the department's coincidental timing of when I was first deemed a troublemaker, and the date of my first written complaint to and about Chief Faunce.

Finally, the time of reckoning had arrived. Dwyer's face was set aglow, as a sinister grin was freshly painted on the corners of his small mouth. I couldn't deny my own excitement at what would happen after Dwyer dropped our bomb; a bomb that Faunce, Teflon Don, Cevasco, Jimbo, and Wertz thought could never be found. I believed that ol' Jimbo would run for cover, and the department would be forced to choke on defeat. Nevertheless, recent history cautioned me not to hold my breath waiting for it to happen.

My attorney covered the history of my harassment, focusing on the absurdity of the prosecutions against me. He then aimed his questioning towards how Mr. Wertz had ignored the transcript, which would have exonerated me in the last hearing. And, when Wertz tried to defend his actions, Dwyer was ready.

"Well, we didn't have the entire transcript to review." Wertz nodded towards Dwyer with his hands open.

"Would you like to read it now, on record, and adjust your findings?" Dwyer pulled out the transcript and laid it on the table, as Wertz grinned precariously.

"No thank you."

So, Dwyer pressed on, focusing all of his attention on me.

"Mr. Freeman, did there ever come a time when you and Dr. Williams spoke regarding the changing of his official evaluation?"

"Yes."

"And, what did he tell you?"

"He told me to watch my back." I said.

"Watch your back? Why?"

"Dr. Williams said that he received a call from the department asking him to change his report to match Chief Faunce's opinion of me. Her medical opinion, that is."

Jimbo sat in relative comfort, secure in his knowledge that Dwyer had no idea that the two crucial documents that had been shredded. The first, dated August 2, 1999, was from Faunce to her confidant, Mary Cupa-Cruz, the head of Corrections' Equal Employment Division, and the second, dated May 22, 2000, was from Dr. Daniel Williams to Dr. Cevasco.

"What else did he tell you?" Dwyer began shuffling papers, all the time smiling.

"He said that he refused to do their dirty work for them." I said.

Jimbo sat up, moving his stomach around restlessly until he exhaled.

"I'm going to object here. Mr. Freeman continues to make these baseless speeches."

Dwyer didn't skip a beat, cutting Jimbo off and keeping Wertz at bay.

"Don't worry, Mr. Wertz. I'll make them make sense soon."

Wertz allowed Dwyer to continue, and Dwyer didn't waste any time.

"Do you have anything, Mr. Freeman, to prove what you claim that you were told?" Dwyer's grin jumped from Maine to San Francisco.

"Eee-Yup!"

And with that, Dwyer, with a grandeur of elegance, deliberately lunged into his dark brown, rolling-file folder, struggling to unveil his black-market atomic bomb. As the bomb eased out of that brown folder, Jimbo and Wertz realized what was happening and their eyes began burning.

Wertz's mouth formed words without making any discernable sounds. Jimbo was never a poker player and it showed. "How did you get that?!"

Dwyer laughed aloud, his eyes opened wide. "The question should be, why didn't you give *me* a copy of it?"

Jimbo attempted to regain his composure as he squeezed back in his tight arm-chair, dazed and staring harshly at Wertz for what had to be betrayal. Dr. Daniel Williams had written a follow-up letter to Dr. Richard Cevasco indicating that after their telephone conversation he pulled my file and reviewed his notes. After reviewing my case, he saw that a note had been made indicating that he had in fact told me that somebody called him and asked him to change his official evaluation to comply with Faunce's decision that I was delusional. Dr. Williams also noted that the caller was very persuasive.

"Well?" Dwyer asked.

"It's the department's position that we have never received a copy of Dr. William's letter. I'm just as shocked as you are." Jimbo will never be nominated for an Oscar.

"Mr. Wertz." Dwyer wore a look of laughter. "Please enter this into evidence as appellant's exhibit nine." Jimbo shot daggers with his eyes at the clumsy hearing officer, who looked as if he was starring in one of those Southwest Airline commercials that asked the question, "*Do you want to get away?*"

Dwyer continued.

"And in this letter, does Dr. Williams write that somebody from the New Jersey Department of Corrections tried to delicately attempt to sway his professional opinion of you to correspond to the psychological opinion of your Chief, Debbe Faunce?"

Of course, my thoughts were in harmony with what Dr. Phil

would have said, "*Absolutely, Dwyer,*" but my response sounded a little different.

"Yes, it did."

"And what was Chief Faunce's official opinion of you, Mr. Freeman?"

"Chief Faunce claimed that I was 'delusional'," I said.

Jimbo knew that he had to stop the bleeding at some point, but he didn't know how.

"I'm going to object here, again!" Jimbo actually thought that he sounded like an attorney or something whenever he made that statement. But he just sounded goofy!

"The appellant is making another false allegation against Chief Faunce. She has never made such a determination about the appellant's mental state."

Jimbo had visions of another disciplinary charge dancing inside of his big head. However, there was a different vision dancing inside Dwyer's head. Again, he deliberately lunged in that magic folder, careful to smile at me, holding back his laughter. He removed the nuclear warhead and a copy of it detonated in the hearing officer's clammy hand.

Wertz rubbed his forehead as if it were a scratch ticket. He despairingly mouthed, "You have got to be kidding me." Jimbo swallowed hard, but he was no stranger to getting caught in a lie, as Dwyer pushed on.

"Mr. Freeman, will you read into record the one word that Chief Faunce used to describe you?"

"Delusional." The hearing officer entered both documents into evidence. End of story, or so we thought.

It was time for summations, and Jimbo had the floor.

"The behavior of the appellant can not be tolerated. This is his third disciplinary and the sanction of termination should be upheld."

I knew that Jimbo wasn't the brightest light bulb on the Christmas tree, but Dwyer still held out hope for reason. But how do you demonstrate reason with unreasonable people?

Moreover, Jimbo made Homer Simpson look rational.

"Tell me, Assistant Chief Willie. Do you think that these charges are warranted?" Dwyer probed Jimbo on the record the way that Gogal should have done less than a month ago.

"I have put on the record that he should be terminated." Jimbo was defiant and had practiced only one response. Any attempt by him to adlib would have infuriated Faunce, who had given him specific marching orders. But Dwyer couldn't tolerate Jimbo's incredulous self-righteousness.

"I want to put on the record that management refuses to even state whether or not these charges are warranted. I mean, how can you terminate a man for lying about something after he brings in documentation that corroborates everything that he's being accused of lying about?"

The mouth of the court reporter was open so long from her own astonishment that it became a nesting place for the flies hovering above Wertz's soon to be carcass. Not even Wertz, with his skewed loyalty, could have anticipated this level of disaster, yet here we were.

After the hearing ended and the court reporter began packing her equipment, Dwyer and I watched an angry Jimbo yelling at the hearing officer as they hurriedly left the conference room. Both of them stood firmly outside of the double glass doors that separated them from us. The look on Wertz's face was of terror as Jimbo verbally bullied the hearing officer into submission.

"Why the fuck didn't you do something, Dennis?"

"What the hell was I suppose to do?" Wertz said. "They used *our* doctor. How am I going to block his words?"

"Then how'd they get that fuckin' letter?" Jimbo asked.

"Don't try to blame this on me. I didn't give it to them."

"Then who could've given it to him?"

"I don't know, maybe Dick did." Wertz was trying to deflect the blame, but it wasn't working. That pair of idiots couldn't even figure out that maybe, just maybe, opposing counsel's presence wasn't the most advantageous location to have their little "CYA" brainstorm session. But, their vaude-ville impression of Amos & Andy proved quite entertaining.

"You fucked up!" Jimbo's finger came violently close to Wertz's nose.

"Me?"

"YOU!"

"How did I . . ."

Jimbo spied us smiling at them, and cut into Wertz's re-sponse. "Let's go."

Wertz looked at me, then at the floor, again, as the odd-couple strolled down to their master's office. Dwyer was still talking to the court reporter and rather deliberately gathered his effects. I approached him quickly, but it was clear that Dwyer was in no rush.

"Andrew, did you hear them? They're trying to find a way to screw me anyhow." I said.

Dwyer and the reporter both laughed and shook their heads. Dwyer mumbled under his breath "those bastards" as the re-porter simply said, "Wow!"

"Andrew, did you hear me?"

"Yes, Kenneth, I heard." Dwyer said. "Mr. Freeman, relax. We've got that idiot on record acknowledging that their doc-tor's letter is authentic, and then asking the other idiot to fire you anyway." He sighed heavily as he placed his last notepad inside of his file folder. His grin disappeared as he reflected on the absurdity of the events.

"Willie couldn't even claim that the charges were warrant-ed, but he still wanted you . . ." He never did finish his state-ment. I believe that for the first time, Andrew actually lived my frustration.

"I think it's time for us to file that civil complaint." His trademark-grin was resurrected, and the sarcasm was again in full effect. "They're pissed! I hope you realize that they're never going to quit until you're fired?" It didn't take three years of law school for me to understand that.

"Should I quit?"

"It wouldn't work. They want to fire you." We shared a brief reprieve. I sat in a chair that was near the rear of the conference room and read portions of an old copy of the Trentonian newspaper while I waited for the reporter to pack up her equipment. After a short time, Dwyer asked me if I was ready to leave. That was the easiest question I answered all day. Dwyer then turned his attention back to the reporter.

"I'll walk you out." He then directed me to stay with him, and not to approach anybody inside of the Internal Affairs offices. We both knew that Faunce would be pissed after she learned that we presented a copy of her letter and the doctor's letter.

We walked down the staircase and towards the exit door near Chief Faunce's office. As we walked passed, we noticed a pair familiar faces emerging from her office. It was Amos & Andy. Amos didn't acknowledge us, but Andy made a despicable attempt to show that he was still an impartial hearing officer, capable of being unbiased.

"Hello." Wertz's feeble attempt to appear friendly fell on fallow ground.

I spoke to Andrew, who was already laughing.

"Unbelievable!"

"This whole place passed unbelievable a long time ago, Mr. Freeman."

"Agreed!"

There was another figure sitting inside Faunce's office who I didn't recognize at the time, but who had written many things about me. I wouldn't find out who that figure was for another three years.

Moments after I departed Central Office, Jack arrived for a regularly scheduled supervisor's meeting. The rumor mill pounced on Jack with all of the details about the letters that were supposed to have been shredded. Before and during their meeting, Jack was prodded for some inside information to use against me, but Jack didn't make any friends at Central Office that particular afternoon. He repeated sentiments that spread around the state that day.

"I told y'all, he's a quick study. It looks like *he's* the varsity, and you're the practice squad." *Hern, hern, hern!* Jack couldn't hold back his gut-wrenching laughter that pierced any closed door.

Before Jack left the meeting, Faunce huddled inside her office with Teflon Don and Cevasco.

"You fucked up, Dick!" Faunce knew that the documents that she had were already shredded as soon as they touched her secretary's hands.

"That smug bastard just ended your career, you incompetent asshole!" Teflon was not about to take the fall for anybody.

"What are you talking about?"

"Well, the way I see it, somebody's getting fired today. And since it won't be Kenny…"

"Don, wait! I can fix it! Give me a chance!" Cevasco ran out of the office and headed for his telephone list. He called Dr. Daniel Williams in a rampage.

"Dr. Williams? What have you done?!"

"What are you talking about?"

"I need another letter from you saying that I didn't try to make you change your opinion. Please."

"When I look at these notes, I'm almost sure that it was you from last summer." Dr. Williams said.

"I didn't! Remember, I only called about clarity, remember?"

"And, since I'm not sure that it was you, I wrote that I wasn't sure who it was. But I am positive that it was from your department because that's how the caller identified himself."

"But since you don't know, maybe it was Kenneth?" Cevasco was grasping for straws by that time.

"What!"

"Yeah, he's like that."

"Kenneth is going to call me and ask that I say that he's delusional so that you can justify firing him?"

"Yes!"

"I don't think so. Besides, I can recognize Kenneth's voice."

"But could you write that it definitely wasn't me?"

"I'll write that I can't be sure, and that's about all." Cevasco saw that it was better to stop at that point and accept what Dr. Williams was offering. Dr. Williams had no idea that Cevasco would later make him the scapegoat, dramatically hindering any future state referrals for Dr. Daniel Williams.

The following morning, Jack greeted me with that same laughter and with his own jokes.

"You beat 'em, kid." Jack was happier than I was, and his sarcasm gleamed. "Debbe is pissed! They're claiming that you threatened your doctor, made him lie for you, and jeopardized his professional practice. She's really got it in for you."

"They tried to hide the letter, you know."

"It doesn't surprise me." Jack laughed. "You know they were trying to figure out how to suspend you, right? And they might try to charge you for beating them." Jack's sarcasm straddled an infinitesimally thin line between truth and terror.

"What else can they do to me?"

"Kid, you'd be surprised how wicked Debbe can get. Just ask Blake or Sapp." Larry Sapp was kicked out of Internal Affairs a few years earlier because he had the audacity to request to be assigned in a closer proximity to a sick relative for whom he was caring.

"What should I do?"

Jack slowed his laughter slightly, but he kept his smile glowing. He drew on his many years of working in the prison system, and the parallel cautions and dangers that a convict faced daily.

"Pretend that you're an inmate and you're trying to take a shower."

"What?" I asked.

"Take a deep breath and watch your ass." *Hern, hern, hern!* Jack's reverberating laughter had a way of jolting everyone's eardrums, but his message was loud and clear.

TWENTY-NINE

I Don't Want Your Help

"Kenny!" Jack called for me from his office after meeting with Pablo Alicea, but I couldn't respond to his call at that moment. "Hey, Irene, where's Kenny?"

"He's on the phone with the prosecutor's office. Do you want him?" Irene asked. She was a great secretary; she knew everyone's business and managed to seem oblivious at the same time. I had settled in at ADTC, working with the small crew there. Jack was a force when it came to shielding his workers from politics and I had finally found a degree of comfort.

I was working on a case involving an officer who had stolen a credit card and used it to buy some strange items. Worst of all, he stole it from an inmate. New Jersey had recently instituted a "civil commitment" policy for sexual predators, which allowed the state to involuntarily commit those predators after they completed their sentences. It may not have been fair that some that were civilly committed were only classified as predators after their sentences were completed, and after they had been denied any kind of treatment during the length of their incarceration. However, I have an extremely limited supply of sympathy for rapist, and an even tighter supply for those that specialized in the rape of children.

Jack entered my office, followed at a distance by Pablo.

"Kenny, come to my office when you're done."

Jack didn't normally call me to his office for anything formal, choosing rather to say it wherever we stood. I told the investigator that I would have to call him back, then I hung up the telephone.

"What's up, Jack?" He didn't look very happy.

"It didn't take Debbe long after all." Jack said. "Debbe sent up your suspension dates for the fifteen days."

"Well, I expected that much." I said. "You look like I'm not going to survive." Jack looked at Pablo.

"You didn't tell him?"

"Tell me what?" I asked Pablo. "What's up, partner of mine." Faunce had threatened Pablo plenty of times. Initially, I believed that Pablo wouldn't be afraid of her, considering he was retiring in less then a year. Yet, despite all of the tough sounding rhetoric, he was a "Down-Low" A-K.

"Hey, Ken, it's Jack's job to tell you. Not mine." Pablo threw his hands up in the air as if to wash his hands of any drama.

"Forget all of that." Jack was irritated by the absence of Pablo's spine. "You've been transferred, kid. Again."

I smiled as a cold pit grew inside of my stomach that made me feel like doubling over, a combat-boot kick to my groin. I fixed my face and even shrugged my shoulders.

"She can't bother me." I said. "Where am I heading?"

"Watch your back, kid. They're going to send . . ."

"Relax, baby. I'm good. Where to?"

"Rahway." Great. Faunce had concluded that I refused to comply with Alex Atkins' investigation and so the issue of whether Hamner assaulted me was another effect of my delusions and the injury to my arm was a physical manifestation of my bipolar disorder. Hamner acknowledged that he hit me with the door, but Faunce decided that both Hamner and the departmental medical facility that treated me didn't understand how manipulative I was.

Nevertheless, Faunce was sending me back to the days of Jim Crow at the hands of a friend of Governor "Machiavelli" McGreevey. The chosen one who had been promised a promotion to Assistant Chief after both Jimbo and O'Brien retired. The inevitable had finally taken shape.

I reentered my office and stared at the emptiness, and my hapless situation. The logical move for me was to quit. *Makes me wanna holla, throw up my hands.* I couldn't win! *I've gotta take a walk.* I strolled out of my office and crossed the street, headed for the front gate. I entered the main prison and greeted several individuals who weren't all that surprised to see me return. As I walked closer to the prison's barber shop, two inmates approached me.

"Mr. Freeman. We need to speak to you." Inmates didn't normally talk openly to IA, but they knew me from my days as an officer, and my association with Curtis didn't hurt behind bars. "You know they talkin' 'bout you 'round here, right?"

"So, what else is new?" I laughed, but these two weren't amused. They were scouting the area the way you're not supposed to.

"You and the minister good people. Mr. Perkins said you straight." Perkins was an old-timer from One Wing. We never liked each other, but we each had a profound respect for the other. "We got your back!"

Dealing with Cracker Rob and "Snowball" taught me not to discount men simply because of the state in which you find them. Regardless of what you may have heard or thought, a moral code deeply permeated prison society.

"I guess I should ask "why?" Right?"

The pair shook their heads. "They been talkin' about gettin' you back here."

"Why?"

"Somebody's supposed to find you behind Four Wing."

"Oh, really?"

"No shit. With a shank in your back."

The other interrupted. "Fuck dat! It ain't going down! Not here!"

I nodded my head in exhaustion, releasing air from the hidden recesses of my sub-consciousness. "Good looking'." I gave both of them dap, tapping my fist on theirs, and entered the barbershop in a daze.

As I greeted the individuals sitting in the chairs, my mind raced through the specifics of what had just happened. Once again, I found myself being protected by the same individuals I was paid to investigate. Immediately, I reflected on an earlier incident that occurred in the Ad Seg interview area prior to my leaving Rahway the first time. Hamner directed me to immediately interview an inmate regarding an assault by one of the wing officers. But before the inmate made it to my interview room, the escorting officer discovered a makeshift shank inside his shoe. It was common for me to have all restraints removed from my subjects while we sat inside an isolated room, with the door closed. The officer asked me if he'd ever made a threat against me, but he hadn't. I'd never heard of him prior to that event, but now I questioned just how coincidental our close encounter truly was.

"I'm out, fellas. Peace."

After returning to the IA office, an unwanted guest accompanied me—headaches! I entered the old, dilapidated building and fiercely shook my head to try to stop the muscle spasms on the right side of my face, which made one of my eyes close, and caused sharp aches in the side of my neck. *Oh, no!* The pain was unbearable, and a ringing sensation ricocheted in and out of my ears. My eyesight dimmed. Suddenly, I was dizzy and exhausted. *I've gotta get out of here!* Never had my head throbbed this intensely. I was terrified, not knowing if it was the onset of an aneurysm, stroke, whatever. I had to go, but driving wasn't the best idea. Bob Karkoska knew where I lived!

I staggered towards Karkoska's office to ask him for a ride home. "Bob?" Through my blurred vision, I saw his silhouette sitting at the State Police NCIC computer that was against the wall of his office.

"Bob. . . Hey, man, could you give me a lift home? I got to get out of here."

"Bob's not here, Kenny." It wasn't Bob. It was Vincent working at the terminal. We had gone to the academy together and developed a friendship of sorts.

"You okay, man? Kenny"

I staggered out of Bob's office.

"I've got...to...get. . ." The stress of the past two and a half years had finally claimed me as its prey. Without the benefit of my hands to lessen the fall, I collapsed like a weathered tree in the forest. The impact of the fall injured my head, leaving a deep bruise.

"Kenny!" Vincent jumped to the area near my head and began loosening my tie. "Mary! Call 9-1-1! Kenny's down!" Our secretary, Mary, screamed at the top of her lungs, but Vincent remained calm as he checked my airway. "Tell them that his eyes are fluttering, but he's unresponsive."

Hamner rushed downstairs because of the commotion, and seeing my lifeless body on the floor, he inquired further.

"What happened?"

"I don't know. He was looking for Bob and then he just passed out. I think he hit his head."

Emergency Services arrived in an ambulance and took me to the hospital. I was intravenously fed medication to alleviate the pain of the headaches as well as to prevent the possibility of a stroke. I regained consciousness, but was unable to do anything more than observe. My problems had dealt me an agonizing blow, allowing all of my enemies to bask in the pleasure of my demise, and there was absolutely nothing I could do. That's when I decided that I needed real help.

My doctor prescribed Ultram, a strong painkiller, and I participated in an experimental new procedure aimed at pinpointing unidentifiable headache pains.

"Kenneth, I want to run some tests on you. From what you're describing..." Dr. Buglisi paused momentarily to gather her thoughts, never finishing her sentence. "I just want to make sure that nothing else is going on." She scheduled me to see a neurologist named Dr. Blady. I was reassured that Dr. Blady was an excellent physician, and that he would be able to do a more thorough analysis of why my headaches were so severe. The office manager at my doctor's practice, Linda Monaghan, wrote the referral as per my doctor's instructions.

"Does your employer have family leave?" Linda asked.

"I'm not a personal favorite of my employer these days." We both laughed.

"Yeah," Linda said, "I heard. But they can't deny you medical leave. It's a federal mandate. I think New Jersey's got one, too." She pointed towards the posting of the Family Medical Leave Act (FMLA) criteria that was displayed inside of their office. "Your boss is prohibited from retaliating against you."

Linda wasn't naïve, she just hadn't been exposed to the Internal Affairs' storm that I was weathering. "But, they can't do that!" was the all-too familiar cry that emanated from any rational person who heard my story. And Linda was no different. My response to them was inevitably, "You'd be surprised at what Internal Affairs can do and get away with."

THIRTY

If at First You Don't Succeed

I returned to work and, after informing Hamner and Faunce about the threat against me, I filed for FMLA. I attached a separate letter to the front of my request package that rescinded any and all medical release authorizations that the department may have previously had on file, remembering they had claimed earlier that year that I gave them permission to act on my behalf as my advocate. In the letter dated June 25, 2000, I noted:

> *Furthermore, I am requesting advance written notification documenting each and every contact (or attempted contact) from anyone from the NJDOC and/or the State of NJ to any physician, doctor, medical personnel, etc. regarding, involving, and/or concerning Kenneth Freeman.*

"Who in the hell does he think he is!" Faunce was pissed. Her secretary, Colleen, was nervous because of Faunce's temper and because Colleen had accepted my letter without first checking with Faunce.

"He just dropped it off, Debbe. I stamped his copy for

him."

"You stamped it! Why?"

"He said he wanted it for his own records. You know how Kenny can be." Colleen sat motionless while Faunce took her tirade into her own office and slammed the door. Hot tempered, disgusted, and faced with her own vulnerabilities, Faunce instinctively resorted to her ace tactic, and telephoned Hamner with a very specific task in mind.

"Charge him!" Hamner may have been on Faunce's side, but he was smart enough to try to keep his own hands clean.

"Charge him? With what?"

"He violated the sick leave policy, right?"

"What?"

"He didn't request sick leave, right?"

"He was unconscious! How the hell was he going. . ."

"Did he specifically request sick time?!" Faunce didn't ask questions for you to ponder the correct answer. When she used words such as "right" or "specifically", she expected you to simply agree with her in the same manner, with the same enthusiasm, and with the same conviction that Dr. Phil responds "AAABBB-SOLUTELY, OPRAH!"

"He's going to beat us at the hearing." Hamner understood the implications of going against the provisions of the Family Leave Act. "That FMLA protects him, especially since he passed out right here at work. We can't say that we didn't know about his condition."

"Who said he's going to get a hearing?" Faunce asked.

"Debbe, the man cracked his head on the floor. I saw his eyes shaking. Why don't we just…"

"I said charge him!" Faunce was blinded by her own omnipotent power, privilege, and rage. As for Hamner, he didn't want anything further to do with my situation, seeing the backlash that would no doubt result from such an assault on decency. Hamner was no angel by any means, but he was rational, methodical, and from time to time, compassionate. Out ranked and fearing retribution on himself, Hamner just held the telephone in space without making a sound, hoping that his silence would sufficiently protest his dissent.

"Did you hear me, Chris? Charge him!" Faunce said.

"Fine." Hamner said, "We've got another little problem, Debbe."

"Jesus H. Christ. What now."

"It's his PAR. Kenny won't sign it." Hamner said. Faunce knew something was wrong with that scenario because although she would covet any wrongdoing on my behalf, refusing to follow an order was out of character for me. Especially regarding something as routine as the signing a Performance Assessment Review (PAR).

"What happened?" she asked.

Hamner took a deep breath.

"I didn't feel like hearing any of his shit, you know. So, I met with everybody else, and reviewed their performance evaluations with them, you know, how I normally do. I put his assessment inside of his box, and left Kenny a note on top of his assessment instructing him to sign the damn thing, and then, simply to return it to me when he's done. Now, he's making a big stink over it."

"What stink?" Faunce asked.

"The kind in which he's claiming that I ordered him to lie."

"What lie?" Faunce began heating up again, and Hamner knew he'd screwed up. Delicately, Hamner continued with his explanation and justification.

"I sort of, kind of told him to indicate that he and I sat down, and had a formal face-to-face meeting, and that I explained everything about our expectations to him during our meeting." Hamner had a slight nervous laugh. "Well, Kenny wrote that he couldn't agree or disagree with something that hasn't been explained to him."

"How the fuck are you going to survive as an Assistant Chief if you're already screwing up simple shit?" Hamner didn't respond. "It seems to me that he's requesting a meeting. So give him one."

"Debbe, the meetings are mandatory. If we say that he requested a meeting," Hamner said.

"Just give him the damn meeting! He requested one, right?"

"Sure, Debbe. He requested a meeting."

"Tell Skippy to listen in as a witness. And I want a report from you afterwards and don't let him scare you again." Faunce said. "I've never seen so many scary-ass men in my life!" Faunce hung up the telephone with a fierceness that left no doubt that his pending promotion was in jeopardy.

Later that afternoon, Wayne "Skippy" Everett came to my office.

"Kenny. I think Chris wants you to come upstairs."

"Give me a moment." I smiled, and waited for Everett to exit my office. I sat there for approximately thirty seconds, wondering what was waiting for me inside of Hamner's office. I telephoned Davies, who had by now remarried and changed her last name to Davies-Kopp, but she was out of her office. So, like a sheep being led to the slaughterhouse, I strolled up the creaky staircase and stretched my neck, preparing for round 18.

As I entered Hamner's office, I slowed my pace. Hamner was sitting behind his desk and Everett was standing near the built-in bookcase.

"I'm here." That introduction was all that I could muster to say to Hamner.

"Have a seat, Kenny." Hamner was determined to impress Faunce, but I had other thoughts.

"I'd rather stand, if you don't mind." My eyes were drawn to the ketchup spot that decorated his necktie. "I'd like to know what I'm being charged with."

Hamner grinned.

"No, this isn't a charge. You requested a meeting, right? Well here you are." Hamner passed me a copy of my PAR. Not the one that I had written my notes on, but a new, blank copy. There was no way that I would sign a blank copy without noting on the form that it was, in fact, blank. But there was the matter of Everett.

"Why is Skippy in here?"

"Oh, he's my second-in-command as well as my witness." Hamner was fishing, trying to find a way to take the onus off himself. "He's here for your protection."

For my protection? "I don't need him for protection. And I'd like him to leave, unless you interviewed every other investigator with him present."

"But I say, he stays." Hamner finally made it clear what was happening, and his stance revealed that a disciplinary charge was somewhere in the making. Hamner may have been accustomed to these types of tactics, but Everett was more of the choirboy type when it came to pushing Central Office agendas. There may have been some dirt in Everett's past dealings with Richard McHort, but he did everything he could to at least avoid the obvious scandals.

Everett trusted Hamner's judgment, but Everett was a diligent thinker, very intelligent, and much more astute than Hamner. Everett and his wife had made some prudent financial investments, and they were on the brink of a bright future, both professionally and as a family, and Everett's future was more important than hanging me. I liked dealing with him because you could engage his intellect, as opposed to a complete moron, like Allen.

Departmental guidelines and policies made racism practically impossible to prove, short of some simpleton using an actual word or reference. Tessenholtz calling me "Sambo" in the presence of three witnesses wasn't even considered racism. However, showing a disparity in the treatment of individuals in a similar job title was far easier to decipher. Comparisons of what happened to one versus what happened to others were reduced to a quantitative analysis. All I had to present to an independent person was clean water, and that reasonable person would know that the clean water was more acceptable than was the muddied water. My objective with Everett was simply to muddy the waters, and watch Everett find the first exit.

"Am I the only investigator being forced to have a witness? The mandate is that the meetings be one-on-one."

"You requested a meeting, right?" Hamner asked.

"Meetings are mandatory, right?" Ordinarily, you were not supposed to answer a question with a question, but rules are subject to circumstances. Everett was watching and starting to lean forward. So, I continued. "And I just happen to be the only African American investigator, second in seniority to only Skippy. . ."

"Don't forget Wojo. He's senior to you as well." Hamner said.

"No, he's not."

"Wojo has been in corrections…"

"And I have four months seniority in IA over Wojo, along with a ton of respect for him." Everett had to see that I remained reasonable, especially since Vincent Wojohowicz and I were classmates from the Academy. Everett was simmering by now, but I knew that it was time to make him boil.

"But even if he was senior to me, that wouldn't explain why you are forcing the only African American investigator to have a witness for something as routine as a performance evaluation. I've stated that I don't need any protection. Furthermore, your witness is clearly not African American." I turned to Everett, "No offense, I'm just stating a fact."

Everett smiled, but he was suffocating as he stood there, ironically, next to the built-in bookcase, which contained the same annotated policies that supported my argument against disparate treatment. Superficially, my monologue had to appear to be directed at Hamner.

"Add to that your disparaging comments regarding Essie Williams, another African American investigator, that you called . . ." I looked directly into the dilated pupils of Everett, ". . . you called her Aunt Jemima, right, Chris? Discriminatory actions, attitudes, or statements are never appropriate."

Hamner stood up, teeth gritted, face flushed with furious indignation. I had reminded Hamner and Everett of the financial settlement that Hamner paid Essie Williams after Hamner made racist statements about her. Hamner had also agreed not to ever supervise Williams, a promise that would be broken when Hamner was promoted to Assistant Chief.

Hamner's anger was amplified by Everett's uneasy body language along with his involuntary, verbal utterance. "Oh, God! This ain't happening." Everett's mutter wasn't lost on Hamner. He stared at Everett as if he had lost his most trusted ally.

"Fine. Who do you want as a witness?" Hamner was not going to stick me with this one.

"I just want to be treated like everybody else. They didn't have a witness, and I don't want one."

"Well, just name a witness, and you'll get your meeting just like everybody else." Hamner said.

"Disparate treatment. That's what it's called. And I object to this kind of treatment." I turned to leave the office, then I faced Hamner again. "Am I allowed to leave?"

Everett's eyes were counting the balls of lint on the ceiling as he shook his head, probably wondering why he bothered getting out of bed that morning. Hamner realized that he needed help. Faunce had opened up a bag of worms and left him to sort out the slimy creatures with a man who didn't want to get his hands dirty.

"You can go."

And with that, I patted Everett on the stomach.

"Don't worry, Skippy. I know." I smiled at him. Not

because he was an angel, but because Everett's desire to stand was overwhelmed by Faunce's dictatorial rule. Sun Tzu warned that you had to accurately identify your adversary, and Everett was not the one.

"Debbe, he's claiming racism! I told you. . ." Hamner was irate, but Faunce hated anybody yelling, except for herself.

"All I want to know is did he refuse to sign the PAR."

"We never got that far." Hamner knew that he was in trouble. "He didn't want Skippy to listen to his evaluation, so I told him to name his own witness."

"I told you that Skippy was his witness." Faunce sighed. "Well, who does he want, Jack?" Faunce asked.

"He wouldn't name anybody."

"Good. Then charge him with refusing to name a witness."

"He's not supposed to have a witness." Hamner reminded her. "Plus, I never ordered him to have a witness."

"Then order him to get a witness, and charge him if he doesn't comply. He said he needed to feel comfortable, right?" Faunce made it transparent that I was to be charged at all cost. She and Teflon would handle the termination. "I'll give Jack a call now."

Faunce called back and told Hamner to schedule the meeting for 1:00 PM.

"What if he names somebody else?" Hamner asked.

"Don't worry. I'll take care of that." Faunce said. "By the way, when Kenny fell out at work a couple of weeks ago, did he request sick time, or did he just leave?"

"I told you. He was unconscious, Debbe, on a stretcher."

"Damn! So, what did he give you? A doctor's note?" Faunce was searching, and she demanded help.

"Yeah, he stuck it in my box." Hamner said.

"Lose it! And charge him for abuse of sick time. You specifically told him to give *you* a note, not your mailbox, right?"

Faunce knew that, thanks to Teflon, I had about a month and a half of sick time remaining on the books, and that I didn't need a doctor's note for that incident. But, fearing that they might have claimed that a note was required, I brought a note back anyhow. That afternoon, I received a letter from Hamner that read in part:

> *Due to your request for a meeting, I have repeatedly offered you the opportunity to discuss this matter. Due to your repeated statements that you feel I am treating you in a racist manner, any PAR meeting we have must be witnessed by another person.*
>
> *I have offered to have this meeting with any witness you choose, however you have failed to suggest anyone. Please advise me prior to the end of the workday today who will be your witness for this meeting and that they will be available so I can schedule it for 1:00 PM tomorrow June 22, 2000.*

After receiving Hamner's letter, I wrote down everything that happened during our confrontation, and prepared a written response to it. Because of the department's history, I knew it wouldn't be long before they would order me to provide a written report or something about the conversation that I had with Hamner and Everett. There was no doubt that both of them had already written reports, citing what actually happened, which was even more of a reason for me to immediately make my own notes.

I became accustomed to writing down very specific information about conversations I had with anybody attached to Faunce. That way, I wouldn't leave out the critical aspects of conversations and orders if ever I had to formally address an issue.

At the end of the day, I approached Hamner in the presence of the other investigators to ask him about his demand that I name a witness.

"Is this an order?"

"No, it is not." Hamner had a smudged smile, the kind that offered no credibility, just scathing cynicism.

"So, this is completely voluntary on my behalf, correct?" No matter what Hamner's response was, I couldn't win.

"I just want you to feel comfortable, Kenny. Is there anything at all I can do to make you feel more comfortable, Kenny?"

His irritating rancor never penetrated my poker face. I turned to the secretary,

"Give me my review the way that you gave everybody else theirs. That would be a good start."

"But you have to name a witness."

"Have to?"

"Yes, have to."

"Then, I don't know." I believed that I couldn't be charged for not knowing, but once again, I was wrong.

"Then you are ordered to know by tomorrow. We want you to be comfortable."

I was done talking with Hamner. He was only repeating his marching orders and had nothing else to offer. I slipped my jacket over my arm and pulled out my car keys.

"Have a good night everyone." It was time to go, and I couldn't wait to sign-out at the door.

Hamner's voice echoed from inside of the building.

"I want you to be comfortable, Kenny. Are you comfortable yet?"

He needed more than that to make me respond in an inappropriate manner. I drove away without once looking back, not even in the rearview mirror. There was nothing that I could do from that point to stop what Faunce had planned for me. I won, but I knew there was a price I would have to pay for my moot victory.

THIRTY-ONE

And Behind This Curtain (Teth)

The next morning, Hamner was away from the office for an extended period. I was unsuccessful following up on some information that an informant had provided regarding one of the civilian contractors acting as a mule for inmates on Four-wing, bringing in narcotics through the rear gate near the outside mailroom. Allegedly, he was assisted by two officers who would ensure that they were the ones that searched the contractors, thus avoiding any scrutiny. My leads were dead ends with nothing but rumors as evidence.

For lunch, I met with a friend with whom I hadn't heard from in over six months. She paged me the day before and asked me to meet her for lunch at Chi-Chi's Mexican Restaurant, a favorite of mine, stating that she wanted to talk to me about us. I told her that there was never any us, but she wasn't exactly convinced of the finality of it all. And, neither was I.

"Hey, brown eyes. Why haven't you called?"

"I've been busy."

"Too busy to pick up a phone and dial a number?"

"Something like that." My words were few, and our meeting seemed to drag on for hours. I tried not to look directly at her because as upset as I was at her for trying to contact my wife, I still felt a modest attraction.

"I told you that I was sorry." I looked at her as she reached across the small table and tried to hold my hand. I slowly withdrew it and clutched my drink as evidence that there were no feelings left for her. "I wasn't really going to *tell* her. Kenny, you know me better than that." She briefly giggled at her own words.

"Do I?" I was forced to pause as I swallowed. "Do I *really* know you?" As intelligent and rational as I thought she was, when her emotions got involved, she was dangerously unstable.

"I didn't say anything about your other little friend. How was I supposed to act?" She shook her head and forcefully breathed through her nostrils. "You cheated on me, and your wife, with that heifer from Northern. And, now I hear you're doing some chicken-head at ADTC? God only knows how many we *don't* know about!"

Ouch! Her words made me consider everything that I had done in my past. Everything. It made me focus on my anger towards my wife for what she had done in our marriage, and to consider how much of a hypocrite I had been. Furthermore, I was an embarrassment to the faith that I proclaimed on Sunday mornings, and to my children. It amazed me how easy it was for me to justify my own indiscretions, while condemning my wife's and anybody else's unfaithfulness to me, the married guy.

"All I'm saying is that you can trust me, Kenny." She said. "I love you, remember?"

"I'm married, remember."

"Not when you're in me, you're not."

"Always married."

She really started smiling. "I almost forgot how pretty your eyes were. Especially in the sunlight." She loved to flatter me, and I loved pretending as if I didn't want to hear it.

"Married eyes."

"And, I hope *to* be married soon. To you and those browns."

"Never gonna happen. Not in this life, or the next." I'd had enough of my food, which lost its taste somewhere during my first few bites. My words were full of vigor, but there was nothing but indecision behind my statements.

"I'm going to Jamaica next week, and I've got a ticket with your name on it. What'cha think? Me in a thong bikini?" I rose from the table with my leather jacket camouflaging the full attention my member had unconsciously given the thought of her thong. Holding the jacket secure with one hand, I reached for my wallet. "Oh, don't worry your conceited self. I got this, sweetheart." She sat back and folded her arms. "Why don't you use that money to buy a pair of Speedos?" Her income was maybe twice as much as mine, her home was immaculate, and she picked cars just because she liked the colors. All were the result of extremely hard work and persistence—two more traits that I adored.

"I gotta go. Take care of yourself." I knew she wasn't worth the aggravation, but my saluting mid-section recalled other attractive aspects about her.

"Maybe I'll send you and the lovely Missus a postcard." I pulled my excitement to the left side of my trousers, and stiff-legged, I walked towards the exit. "I'm only joking, Kenny. Damn!" She hurried behind me, chuckling, smiling. "Where's your sense of humor?"

"It left when you called my home."

"I'm sorry. But I was only trying to help."

"Help?"

"Yeah." Her smile increased as she got closer, stopping so close to me that I could feel her breathing.

"How?"

"Well...I thought I'd help you get out the house for the night." To be so intelligent, she said and did some dumb stuff. Sad part was, I knew where she was headed. "I wasn't going to *say* anything to her. I just thought the two of you might go through your little corny argument, and you might need a shoulder to cry on, at least for the night."

"You've got issues. Real ones." Whether she did it spitefully or if she was simply clueless didn't matter. I didn't trust her at all.

"I said I'm sorry." She seductively straightened my tie. "We shouldn't end it this way." She swallowed softly, then patted me gently on my chest. "Try to make your marriage work, and… I'll try not to make it difficult." She kissed me on my cheek, then, using her thumb, wiped the lipstick from my face as an idle tear fell from her eye. "I love you."

"Enough to walk away?"

She nodded her head and smiled even more, taking control of the emotions that had caused both of us so much pain. "You should've married me, you know." We hugged each other, not intimately, but in a way that signaled the realization that the end had come, with one exception. "Looks like somebody misses me."

"Don't flatter yourself."

"Too late. I already am." She walked back to the table, grabbed the bill, and exhaustedly plopped in her seat. As I watched her, I remembered the night we sat in Washington Square Park in Greenwich Village. Her legs straddled me as I sat on the park bench. My eyes danced as she recited poetry, both her creations and others. When midnight arrived, we made up silly songs and learned each other's heart. Her intelligence was captivating, and more intimate than words can express. I walked over to her and put my hands on her shoulders.

"You want me to wait?"

"Better not. I'm kind of horny." I nodded my head and said nothing. "We've got some heavy repenting to do."

I couldn't let her take the blame for my lack of judgment. "This thing? I'm at fault here, not you."

She laughed. "You're brighter than that, sweetheart." She

shook her head in disbelief, confronting some hard truths. "I knew what I was getting into before we got involved. Any man who cheats on his wife ain't shit, including you, my love. But it was my choice, and I *chose* to fall in love with those beautiful browns." That look of love left her face. "How did I get so low?"

"Ease up, it just happened." I wasn't used to hearing her curse, but I knew she was upset.

"Just happened? Fuck you!" She scowled as she gritted her teeth and I nervously looked around to see if anyone noticed the elevation of her voice.

"Watch you mouth!"

"My *mouth*?"

"Did I stutter?!"

"Fuck off, you Sunday-morning Christian!"

"What did you call me?!"

"Did *I* stutter, bitch?" Her eyes cleared as she spoke through her teeth. "You fucking me and everybody else, sneaky bastard. Everybody but your wife! So don't preach to me about no damn profanity!" Now, she didn't have to go there. She wouldn't dare speak blasphemies about Christians; rather, she was criticizing me, and me alone, for my behavior while I flaunted the Christian banner for everybody else. The truth about my self-deception was not only hurtful, but the humiliation of it oozed from my self-righteous veins. So, I quickly sought another approach to stop the bleeding. I leaned forward, glared into her eyes, and touched her hand.

"If you ever loved *me* like you said…

"Fuck love and fuck you!" She yanked her hand away and sat tall in her seat. By now, I guess you've figured out that my "pretty browns" had lost their influence with her. "You ain't shit, Kenny! I don't know who's worse—your punk ass or me for screwing your punk ass!" Her thoughts shifted slightly. "It was me! I screwed another bitch's man!" Tears loaded her eyelids and her head tilted downward slightly as she considered her future. "You tell me, how can I expect other bitches to respect me enough to leave *my* husband alone, if I ever get one?"

Her picturesque smile broke through, but it was draped with a flood of tears, perfectly synchronized, each pausing near her soft, rouge colored lips. She refused to wipe them, and her teeth never separated. "I can't *stand* yo' yellow ass!"

I sat close to her and held her hand, shaken by the depths of her feelings when I really hadn't thought much about my spiritual plight. I knew I had betrayed my wife, but hadn't considered that I also hurt anybody with whom I entered into a relationship while married. Unlike my wife, they had no recourse because, as she said, she knew exactly what she was getting into the first time she laid down.

As I sat there, my eyes focused less on her and more on the unfinished chips and salsa left on the table. I began noticing the triangular shapes of the chips, the very deliberate shapes, proving that they weren't made by chance, but by a sophisticated process. Hence, my dilemma with the department couldn't have been completely by chance. Could it have been that God permitted hardship to come my way in order to knock some sense into my thick skull, allowing me to openly confront the promiscuity? (*Teth.*)

"Well, we're not together any longer. At least we've corrected that."

Her head quickly popped up. "What? And you think that that's enough?"

I knew better than to answer her question. In fact, I knew better than to make the statement that caused her to ask that question in the first place. Our little talk succeeded in revealing my own corrupted morality, not the admirable character I pretended to have, but rather the abyss into which I had plummeted.

"I'm sorry. But what do you want?"

"I've got to let Priscilla know that I'm so sorry for what I've done to her. I need her to forgive me."

She must have lost her mind! I quickly began constructing some serious damage control, until she finished her thought.

"Stop your worring. I won't say anything to her." *Whew! What a relief!* "But you should." *This bitch is crazy!* Oops! Sorry for the profanity, but that thought just popped into my head.

By that time, I was ready to send her to see Dr. Quack because if she thought that *I* was confessing to *my* wife, after what my wife had done to *me*, then she was no doubt insane! There was no question that she was correct about everything she said, even her assertion that any man who cheated on his wife "ain't shit". However, she had to be really angry to speak to me with such venom. In fact, in three and a half years, the only time that I've *ever* heard her use profanity was when we were making love. And then it dawned on me, *I really screwed up!* I kissed her hand and left her sitting there, crying, as I headed towards the exit.

"God's not pleased, Kenny." Although I acted as if I didn't hear her, those were the last words I ever heard her utter, and the final time I ever saw her. True to form, she was right, again. I had a bigger problem than wanting Priscilla to forgive me. I had tainted my vow of allegiance to the God who could do a whole lot more than sit and cry at a Mexican restaurant.

My life felt like a true-life "series of unfortunate events". On the one hand, my employer was treating me unfairly, while on the other, I had created so much animosity in my home and social life that I began wondering if I deserved whatever hardship came my way. I may not have *made* my wife behave unfaithfully, but I surely didn't encourage her not to.

I got into my car and turned on the radio when my pager frantically vibrated on my belt. Certainly, I wasn't about to hear more preaching from the restaurant. What she said was already received, even if I didn't like her message. But, it wasn't her. It was our secretary paging me, trying to notify me that Hamner had returned and wanted to see me as soon as possible, if not sooner.

By that time, the first sincere signs of my sorrow and repentance began to flow across my puffy cheeks, finally bringing a taste of some well-earned shame to the area of my life I'd kept hidden for so long from my own conscious. I wanted to make a vow that I would never be unfaithful again, and that I would do everything possible to make it up to my wife, but something inside of me didn't even trust my own words. I needed proof from myself in order to be satisfied that I was making an effort to change my despicable behavior.

As soon as I entered the office, our secretary let me know what I already expected.

"Chris is upstairs waiting for you."

"I'll be right back. I gotta make a call." I headed straight for my office and closed the door behind me. I dialed the telephone and spoke to the lady on the other end.

"Hello?" Her voice was soft and unassuming.

"Priscilla, it's me."

"Now this is a surprise."

"I know. Can you take the kids to your sister's house for awhile?"

"Oh, boy. What did I do now?"

"It's not like that. But we really need to talk."

THIRTY-TWO

Prelude to Havoc

My telephone conversation with my wife was very brief because she deserved to hear what I had to say face-to-face. I hung up the telephone only to have it start ringing while my hand still held the receiver.

"Kenny, I need you to come up to my office. Now." *Click!* The telephone rang inside of my ear from the impact of Hamner's disconnect, and I knew what awaited me in his office wasn't supposed to be cordially delivered.

As I walked inside of Hamner's office, I was surprised to see that Hamner had a guest there just for little ol' me.

"Kenny, how ya' doin' kid?" Jack Dale had been summoned to be my friend-slash-union-representative-slash-whatever-I-needed.

"Well, you know that I can't complain because I might get charged."

Jack laughed heartily. *Hern, hern, hern!* "I hear ya' kid. But maybe you can tell me why I'm here?" Jack asked the question as if I was in charge of something.

"I was hoping that you'd tell me."

"I got a call yesterday from Debbe." He shrugged his

shoulders. "Am I supposed to *watch* you get a PAR or something?" *Hern, hern, hern!* "Who in the hell needs to be
watched signing a fucking performance review? It's supposed
to be private!" *Hern, hern, hern!*

You couldn't help but laugh at Jack's sarcasm, but Hamner
was clearly not amused.

"Could we get started?" Hamner stared at Jack as he wiped
the tears of laughter from his eyes. I stopped laughing long
enough to hear Hamner read aloud what was on the review.
There was nothing new on the review, only what performance
levels any supervisor would have expected from me during the
next year. The reading took less than two minutes for Hamner
to complete.

"Kenny, do you have any comments you would like to
make?" Hamner had that same grin on his face that he had
when he delivered his "I Want You To Be Comfortable" speech.

This time, I had prepared a reason to grin, too. "As a matter
of fact, yes, I do." I reached inside of my suit jacket and pulled
out the response I had written the night before.

 Jack rubbed his forehead and whispered to himself before
bellowing out in laughter. "Oh, God!" *Hern, hern, hern!* A
huge smile radiated through Jack's hand as he tried to cover
his mouth. I didn't cover my mouth as I began reading aloud
what I had written in expectation of some silliness on behalf of
Faunce.

"I would like to put my objections on the record." I noted
everything that I had told Hamner on the day before. Then, I
reminded Hamner about the agreement that he made with me,
in the presence of our attorney's, at the Woodbridge Municipal
Court.

"I believe that your repeated attempts to treat me unfairly
are a violation of the agreement that you and your attorney
made in return for me not pursuing criminal charges against
you for assault. You agreed to treat me in a manner that was
consistent with the manner in which you treated every other

employee. This meeting is proof that I am being treated differently, and I resent it. Therefore, I am considering the possibility of reinstating the criminal charges against you, Mr. Hamner, for this violation." I had predicted that I would be forced to have the meeting with Everett despite my objections. If they were sincerely worried about the racial element, why not assign the on-sight Equal Employment officer?

"No offense, Jack. But I don't understand why the only witnesses that Hamner or the Chief can come up with are not African Americans." I shrugged my shoulders. "I mean, if the true reason behind all of this was for me to be more comfortable and they claim I don't like good white folk."

Jack chuckled and interrupted to add his own flavor. "I'm right with you, kid. I'm white and I still can't figure out this shit." *Hern, hern, hern!* Jack looked at Hamner. "Just give him the damn PAR, and be done with it!"

Hamner pushed the review over to me. I carefully read it just to make certain that nothing was slipped in without my knowledge. I signed it and noted in the comment section "I object with the manner in which the review was conducted." Then, I used that opportunity to infuse some reason into my written comment.

"What would you have done, Jack?"

"Shit. I would have met with you like I'm supposed to in the first place. One-on-one." *Hern, hern, hern!*

My grin had evolved into a full-scale smile.

"Well, Chris, that supports my contention that you are incapable of supervising me without the assistance of a competent investigator, like you Jack."

"Ah, hell, Kenny!" Jack burst into laughter. *Hern, hern, hern!* "Chris, is this thing done yet?" Jack looked at me and shook his head. "What the hell was this all about?"

"It wasn't my call. Maybe you should ask Chris."

"What!" Jack tried speaking through his own laughter, but was practically inaudible. "Debbe said that you asked for me to come over here to make you more comfortable."

"I asked?"

"Hell, yeah! She said you specifically asked for me!"

"Now, Jack." The expression on my face should have said it all, but the words rolled out anyhow. "Did Debbe use the word 'specifically' when she told you that nonsense?" Jack doubled over laughing, understanding fully that Faunce had duped him. Getting up from my seat, I looked at Hamner as I shook Jack's hand. "I'll get out of your way so that you good gentlemen can compare notes."

Jack patted me on my shoulder with his other hand.

"Take care of yourself, kid."

"See you soon, Jack." Jack and Hamner talked for a while after I left Hamner's office. Jack later described their conversation with one colorfully expressive term. "Bullshit!"

A few days later, I went to check the post office box I had rented for one reason—to stop all of the department's harassment notices from being passed through my home's front door mail slot, greeting me on Friday afternoons, and making me agonize over them for the entire weekend. My box ensured that I received notices from Tuesday through Thursday, only. No exceptions.

Inside my box was another of Faunce's thinking-about-you grams. I opened the departmental envelope and read the top enclosure, indicating that I was being disciplined again, but this time for my terrible "abuse of sick time". Faunce had determined that my use four of sick days after falling unconscious and my subsequent ambulance ride were excessively abusive, and would not, could not, be tolerated. Oh, yeah, she also determined that the fact that I only had about forty-five sick days available on the books was irrelevant. Faunce, personally, rejected my Family Medical Leave application so that she could make the charges stick, asserting that she needed access to my personal doctor so that she could "clarify" some matters with him, to which I strenuously objected, and with good reason.

Faunce's letter said that the Personnel Department was handling the request for more information. I contacted Personnel, but nobody there could give me a straight answer as to what was officially required by the department in order to have the application approved. So, I telephoned the head of Human Resources, Margaret Rich. Ms. Rich was a close associate of Faunce and rumored to owe the Teflon Don for saving her career several years earlier when it was discovered she had "borrowed" some departmental property and forgotten to return it.

"Ms. Rich, this is Investigator Freeman."

"Who?" Never having spoken to me in the past, there was no way for her to recognize my voice.

"Kenneth Freeman from Internal Affairs."

"I'm not supposed to talk to you." Yep! That jarred her memory.

"That may be, Ms. Rich, but I received Debbe's letter and I had a question for you. What clarification do you need?"

"Who says we need clarification?"

"Debbe's letter does." I said.

"The matter is closed."

"Closed?"

"Sorry, Mr. Freeman. Your request was rejected. We'll be mailing you information on how to appeal."

I knew that she answered my question, but I had to ask again.

"You are really denying me Family Leave?"

"Well, yes." Ms. Rich said as if it was ridiculous for me to inquire any further about their decision.

"May I ask why?"

Ms. Rich began sounding a little miffed at my questions.

"You can't hide behind FMLA every time you violate policy, Mr. Freeman.," she said. "We just won't let you do it."

"Nobody's *hiding* behind. . ." I took a deep breath, calming myself down so that I could speak rationally to her. "There's no hiding going on. Prior to being charged with anything, I applied for Family Leave because of . . .

"I *know* why you're filing, Mr. Freeman."

I refused to respond to her assertion, or to let her distract me from my point.

". . .FMLA. My own doctor advised that I file the application, which I was told was my right."

"You've chronically abused your sick time, and you're going to be suspended. It's departmental policy."

I couldn't help myself. I had to respond. "So I guess that means that there's no need for me to have a hearing on this subject."

"Debbe said you violated sick leave policy."

"And who am I to want to have a hearing. An *unbiased* hearing, at that."

"Well, that's what she said. You didn't have any permission to just leave the building."

"I've got over forty sick-days on the books." Incredible. I went out unconscious on a stretcher, in an ambulance, and they're claiming that I didn't have *permission*? "Do you even care to know what happened?"

Ms. Rich paused slightly.

"You left work on June 12 without authorization. You were charged sick-time and you never brought Chris a doctor's note. That's a violation and they're going to suspend you for that. You can't just leave work anytime you feel like leaving."

I knew that I had to get to the meat of the matter, and that was the Family Leave application.

"Debbe's letter says that she needs clarification of something about intermittent days, right?" She didn't answer. "Ma'am could you just tell me what kind of information you need?"

Margaret was livid.

"You don't bark at me!"

I sighed out of frustration.

"Nobody's barking. . . I'm speaking calmly, and I'm only

asking what facts you need to approve my application."

"You can't give me any facts! They have to come from your doctor! And you can't threaten *him* and make him send another letter."

Enough was enough! She was well versed in management's illusions. "I think you had better consider your words, Ms. Rich. You know how I tape-record my conversations, don't you?" Although I didn't have my handy-dandy tape-recorder with me, it was always a great bluff.

"You are not allowed to record somebody without their permission."

"Check your facts, ma'am. New Jersey only requires a single party consent, and I consent." I finally had her attention. "Now, am I correct in hearing that my FMLA was denied because of a sick-policy violation charge and not because of some medical clarity?"

Her tone changed to that of Sister Theresa sitting inside of the Library of Congress with an acute case of laryngitis.

"I never said that, sir."

"Yes, you did."

"You misunderstood me." Ms. Rich whispered more Homma-na Homma-na's than Ralph Cramden on the Honeymooners, back-pedaling her way out of her own mouth. "I only mentioned that you have a pending. . . you *may* have a disciplinary charge against you."

Now, a few moments earlier, there was no "may" about it, and in actuality, Ms. Rich's name was prominently placed in the bottom corner of my copy of the disciplinary charge. I loved the response I got from mean folks who thought their jobs were in jeopardy. She even called me "Sir".

"Ms. Rich, could you please tell me what medical facts you require, that is, unless my federally mandated FMLA application was already denied."

"I said it *could* be denied." *Could*, she said. "If your doctor doesn't indicate if intermittent leave is required or not. That's all I was saying."

"Great! Then I can expect you to send me a letter with that information spelled out, correct."

"Sure I can. I was going to mail something like that out to you today."

"Excellent. Then I look forward to receiving your letter. And, thank you for your assistance, Ms. Rich."

That letter, which was dated that same day, spelled out what was required in order to have my Family Leave application approved. They wanted my doctor to indicate, in writing, that neither the severity nor the frequency of my headaches was predictable, and because of that unpredictability, I might intermittently use a sick day. Talk about trivial.

Nevertheless, I was still charged for abusing sick time, even though my Family Medical Leave was approved and I had sufficient sick time on the books, and the fact that Hamner had the doctor's note. I filed an appeal for a hearing on that charge and patiently waited all summer for an opportunity to prove my case. It was a slam-dunk for my defense, or at least it should have been. Problem was, they determined that I didn't need a hearing and found me guilty.

Simultaneously, I was charged with a separate violation because of my performance review. I was being disciplined for refusing to voluntarily name a witness, which Hamner stated he determined was mandatory, to be present at a hearing that I had requested, but that I shouldn't have had to request. Now, if all of this is starting to make sense to you, then welcome to the Matrix.

THIRTY-THREE

Hell Hath No Fury

"Who in the hell approved this?" Faunce said. My FMLA was approved without Faunce's foreknowledge, and she wasn't pleased. Compounding her misery, top brass was upset by a newspaper article that opened old wounds. *The Press of Atlantic City* staff writer Eileen Bennett described how Faunce's husband, Scott, connived to force Lawerence Aston, the former warden at Bayside State Prison, to resign so Scott Faunce could be appointed. The animosity between Scott Faunce and Aston was a frequent topic at Bayside, and Scott was usually on the losing end.

Debbe headed that investigation into Aston's mismanagement, without any intention of being unbiased. The article reported how she and other Internal Affairs officials illegally shredded reports, evidence, and other documents in the Central Office headquarters building.

The department had previously heard and denied the allegations, but was now faced with a massive problem. *The Newark Star-Ledger* had obtained sworn testimony from one of Debbe's henchmen, Timothy Dill, who had participated in the shredding party and admitted that not only had they shredded evidence, but they did so under the Chief's direction as she watched and participated in their destruction. To Debbe, all that mattered was that her investigation opened the door for her husband's subsequent promotion to Aston's vacant position as the head of a major correctional facility. So the news of my FMLA approval seemed to add an enormous amount of fuel to her consuming fire. Nevertheless, Teflon would know how to handle things.

"Don, he got this bullshit Family Leave thing approved by your people."

Teflon Don wasn't pleased either because his name had been mentioned as giving her instructions as to which documents would hurt the department, and were not needed.

"What's his reason?"

"Headaches!"

Teflon looked at the letter I attached to the cover of the FMLA request forms.

"What gall! And he's got the audacity to *forbid* us from calling his doctor? Can you believe that?"

"Fuck it! Just fire his ass and figure out why later?" Faunce asked.

"Sure, if you want to get sued again. This bastard's got you by the balls. How did he find out about the prosecutor's office?" Teflon was accusing Debbe more than asking the question.

"I don't give a shit."

"Well, you'd better start!" Teflon's warning wasn't lost on Faunce, but after building her career on doing practically anything she pleased, I frustrated her.

"What makes him so different? You're supposed to get him fired, right? So do your fucking job, Don!"

"Well, he would've been fired, if your people hadn't released that letter." The Don had no intention of being made the department's scapegoat. "You and your crew can't just shred away your troubles this time. Say what you want about him, but Kenny makes copies, and then the little bastard mails them to everybody and anybody with a title and address."

Teflon Don didn't hate me. Rather, there was a perverted admiration of me and, if he had his way, I maybe could have worked for him. However, he had been the department's hired gun for so long that attacking me was nothing more than the cost of doing business.

"Well, Willie's gone, with *his* incompetent ass." Faunce said. Blame was always placed on those who couldn't protect themselves, and Jimbo wasn't there to do so.

"But you've got Simone's husband there now. And you know what he's capable of." Teflon was referring to Timmy Dill. He was promoted and assigned to Rahway, my unit, as my new supervisor. Dill's wife, Simone, worked directly for the Commissioner and that scared Faunce. Neither Faunce nor Teflon Don trusted Dill, but they tolerated him in order to keep peace with Simone.

Teflon Don sat down and rubbed his face.

"Maybe there's another way." The Don took the time to think about the situation. "Why would you suppose Kenny doesn't want anybody to ask his doctor any questions?"

"He's hiding something." Faunce said. "I told you that he was delusional."

"Will you give it a rest? The man's not delusional! All of our own doctors say he's fine." Teflon couldn't understand why Faunce would help my position by contradicting the department's own doctors.

"Let's give *his* doctor a call anyway."

Teflon Don was never amazed at Faunce's superiority complex. And, like Hamner, he wasn't willing to needlessly ruin his own career. Teflon was well versed in the federal guidelines for the Family Medical Leave Act, as well as the state's own statues, which both prohibited any employer from contacting an employee's private doctor in reference to FMLA without the employee's consent. So, my June 25 letter should have been nothing more than paranoia, right? Well, if you believe that, you haven't been paying close enough attention.

"No. Not us. *We* can't do that."

"Sure, we can. I'll get Chuck on it now."

"No! *We* can't."

"Why not?" Faunce asked.

"Because Kenny's protected by a little thing called Federal guidelines that are attached to every family leave application." Teflon said. "But I've got somebody who owes me a favor. I'll give Julius a call."

Dr. Julius J. Hafitz, MD operated a sleazy office hidden inside of a Senior Citizens building on Greenwood Avenue in the Trenton area. He was a long time friend of the department, and Teflon often called on the doctor to give the impression of legitimacy. Dr. Hafitz often used his "doctor" title to access information that would have otherwise remained private. Dr. Hafitz never allowed any state or federal regulation to interfere with pleasing his master, knowing that if any question was raised about his actions, he had some very powerful people on his side. Moreover, Dr. Hafitz was good at conjuring his own brand of consent, with or without the employee's knowledge or permission, and was extremely effective.

On the morning of July 12, 2000, my doctor's office was formally introduced to my department and their tactics when the receptionist answered the phone.

"Good morning. This is the ImmediCenter. May I help you?"

"Good morning. I'm Dr. Hafitz, and I'm calling in reference to a patient of ours named Kenneth Freeman. I would like to get some information about him."

"And you are. . ." she asked.

"I'm his doctor. And I need to get some information so that I can treat him."

The receptionist pulled my file and read the copy of the letter that I asked my doctor to keep in my file that prohibited the release of my medical information.

"I'm sorry. But we can't release any information without Mr. Freeman's consent."

"Oh, that's fine. He's sitting right here in my office, and he's consenting. It's about his job. We just need to verify some basic information."

"What type of information?" she asked.

"Routine stuff. Who treated him last, for what conditions, if he was prescribed any medications, anything that you might think is important." The receptionist put the doctor on hold and called for Linda.

"Hey, Linda. I've got Mr. Freeman's doctor asking about his medication. Could you take a look at it?"

"Dr. Blady, right?" Linda asked.

"Who?"

"We referred him to Dr. Blady's office for tests. That's the young man with the terrible headaches."

"He said Dr. Hoitra or something." the receptionist said.

Linda took my file and was connected to Dr. Hafitz.

"Dr. Blady's office?"

Dr. Hafitz didn't hesitate in acknowledging himself, although falsely.

"Yes, ma'am. And how are you?" Dr. Hafitz said.

"Fine, sir. Sorry about the confusion, but Mr. Freeman has this letter on his file asking us not to release his info."

"Yes, he told me and he's right here smiling, nodding his head." They both shared a laugh, Linda completely unaware of what Dr. Hafitz was doing. "Could you tell me when was he treated last, and for what? He can't remember the specifics."

"Well, let's see. Dr. Buglisi has been treating him for headaches since December of last year. He was prescribed Naprosyn, but she recently prescribed Ultram after he blacked out. Stress related headaches it says."

"And you say it was Ultram?"

"That's correct."

"Now, how do you spell "Ultram"?"

Linda froze. Dr. Blady was extremely professional, very intelligent, and had dealt with and had prescribed Ultram as well as other pain medications on a regular basis. So, he should have been familiar with the spelling of Ultram.

"Dr. Blady?" Linda asked. Dr. Hafitz didn't immediately respond, seeing that his scheme was blown. "Who is this?"

"I'm with the Department of Corrections."

Linda tried to understand why she had been deceived.

"Why did you say that. . ." *Click!* Dr. Hafitz hung up the telephone, leaving Linda and her staff in a very precarious position. Linda's attention shifted to the June 25 letter that was stapled to the front of my file, and why it was there.

Dr. Hafitz immediately telephoned Teflon and later faxed a letter documenting his deception and unethical violation.

> *As you requested, I investigated the medication that was prescribed for Kenneth Freeman for a headache.*
> *The medication prescribed for Mr. Freeman was Ultram. Ultram is a medication that is given for sedation and relief of pain. The effect of the medication would depend upon the amount prescribed and/or amount taken. Ultram is equivalent to Codeine. 50 mg of Ultram is equivalent to 60 mg of codeine phosphate.*
> *In my opinion, it would certainly sedate the individual and the effect would be according to how much Ultram was ingested.*

Teflon telephoned Faunce with the news. "We've got him! Ultram is just like Codeine!" Dr. Hafitz had established exactly what Teflon and Faunce wanted. Dr. Hafitz's unethical actions were positive proof that I was working in a sedated state on a pain killer with the equivalent potency of Codeine. Dr. Hafitz's actions were reported to the New Jersey State Board of Medical Examiners, who faulted my private doctor's office for releasing the information, but refused to place any blame on Dr. Hafitz for deceiving them.

Faunce couldn't wait to gloat over her handiwork. Within the hour, there was a knock on my office door.

"Hey Kenny. We need to talk to you."

It was Everett and Vincent. Vincent's face wasn't normal. He was definitely upset at what he was about to witness. Everett, on the other hand, seemed completely at ease with what he would say and do.

"Debbe faxed this to me and ordered me to read it aloud to you in the presence of a witness." Everett held up a single sheet of paper and began reading.

> *Pursuant to the firearms policy for the Special Investigations Division, it is your obligation to report any medication that may impair your ability to safely and properly handle a firearm.*
>
> *Your request for FMLA contained information that you have been prescribed medication for chronic headaches.*
>
> *Pursuant to the FMLA Regulations a departmental physician today 7/12/2000 contacted you[r] physician to get clarification on your medication.*
>
> *As a result of that information, you are directed to turn in your weapon until such time you are no longer taking that medication or a determination is made that the medication will not affect your ability to safely handle a firearm.*

With that, my handgun was confiscated, again. Vincent handed me a copy of the letter, then he waited there briefly until Everett left my office.

"Brother, I want to ask why they're dogging you so bad. But I don't think it's wise for you to tell me the answer." Unlike Barney or Mueller, hearing Vincent call me brother brought with it much comfort, and I knew that if I asked for his help, he would help me. But that would mean they would eventually come after Vincent. And that's not how I treated friends.

"I still got a little fight in me, Vince."

"I know. I just hate to see. . ." Vincent sighed in disbelief. "Take care of yourself, man." If I had a nickel for every time somebody told me that, I'd still be poor. But it was nice hearing it anyhow.

I immediately faxed a response back to Faunce focusing directly on the portion of her statement that indicated that I couldn't get my gun back until I was no longer taking that medication. I made sure that my letter stated that I had immediately ceased from taking <u>any</u> medication until Faunce determined which medications were acceptable for me to take and which were not. My letter meant absolutely nothing.

Timmy Dill was trying to redeem himself after his testimony about the shredded documents. He charged me with anything he could dream up. Once, he told me to drop the state vehicle off at the motor pool near Northern State Prison and wait there until the car was finished being serviced. When I returned, he found out that I arrived early to the motor pool, before my shift started.

"Nobody approved overtime, Investigator Freeman." Dill was trying to flex his humming bird-sized muscles. "You worked for free."

"No problem." With that response, I headed to my office to look over a case on which I had been working, when I received a telephone call from Dill telling me to return to his office.

"Did you try to submit an overtime request?"

"No."

"Well, I just got off of the telephone with Debbe and she said that you have to fill one out." And who ever said that "free" meant "not-for-Free"? I could smell that charge from a mile away. Filing a fraudulent claim would be grounds for termination.

"Thanks, but no thanks. I don't want any overtime." Now, you would have thought that my statement would have ended the matter, but it only made it worse.

"You have to request overtime."

"Why? You said I worked for free, Dill. I didn't do anything while I was there, anyhow. So, why should I lie and ask for overtime pay."

"Are you refusing an order, Kenny?"

"No, Tim. Give me the form. I'll fill it out." I wrote my name, the date, and then I wrote, "*I never worked for this overtime pay, but if you want to pay me, go ahead.*"

"Is this alright, Timmy?"

Dill exploded, but he didn't know what to do and didn't want me to see him call and ask for guidance. Later that day, Dill approached me from behind while I sat in a vacant office typing on the upstairs computer.

"Why are you in here, investigator Freeman?"

All I could do was to shake my head. "Timmy, you told me to write you a statement about why I didn't request overtime, and I'm trying to do that now." I never looked around at Dill, who kept asking me if I was refusing his order.

"Timmy, I don't want overtime. I arrived early on my own *personal* time. No charge to the state. That's a good thing, right?"

"That means that you're refusing my order. We finally got your ass." He moved a step away from me, turning to the door. "Vincent! Come in here! I need you to witness Kenny refusing an order!" Dill stepped back closer to me as I sat in the chair. "We're going to burn your ass!"

I stopped typing and shook my head. Dill wasn't a major player. He wasn't even a pawn.

"You don't have a clue about what you're getting yourself into." In hindsight, maybe I should have looked aggravated, hostile, pissed off, because suddenly Dill had reached inside of his pants and confused two pieces of lint for a set of balls.

"Keep sitting there, cause I'll fuck you up!" It took a while for it to dawn on me what that cowardly lion had uttered. Dill was the poster boy for all of the before pictures of every muscle magazine, with scrawny, bony legs and a stomach that extended four and a half inches past his concaved chest.

The threats, assault, charges, everything ran through my thoughts. Before I knew it, I was out of my chair, teeth tightly gritted, and a suddenly more timid Dill was penned up against the wall with my finger less than a nanometer away from his crooked, punk nose. My words filtered through my teeth.

"Say it again!!" Dill stopped breathing, his eyes resembling a deer caught in a semi's fog lamps. "I said, say it again!!"

"Oh God! No, Kenny!" Vincent arrived at the door and saw Dill against the wall, terrified, telepathically screaming for help like a fly in a spider's web.

"Let him go, Kenny." I knew that Vincent was right, but I had had enough of the foolishness, and nobody else was going to threaten me or touch me again, even if that meant I lost my job.

"Say it again!"

"Vince? You, you didn't hear me say anything, did you?" Dill had started feeling safer because Vincent was present, and he started to move sideways, against the wall, avoiding contact with my finger. He finally escaped that room, and stood behind Vince.

"Don't try to get me involved, Timmy. I just walked up here." Vincent didn't want to get involved, but Dill's word wasn't enough. Dill ran into his office and slammed his door. I knew Dill kept his gun in his desk drawer, and a coward with a gun was always a bad combination.

Immediately, I needed to have on record that I warned Central Office, so I started dialing the telephone from Vincent's office, and newly promoted Assistant Chief Mueller answered the telephone.

"Chuck, I'm tape-recording my words, but not your responses. I want you to understand that first."

"Kenny, this you?" MBM didn't quite know what to say.

"I am officially notifying you right now that Timmy Dill just approached me while I was sitting at the computer and said that he would 'fuck me up'."

MBM had to laugh at Dill's bravado.

"Timmy? Fuck you up?" Mueller's laughter seeped through the receiver. "He couldn't beat his own dick."

Although I had to agree with Mueller, I was not particularly in a laughing mood.

"Exactly! But Timmy's got a .40 caliber Smith & Wesson inside of his desk, and y'all just confiscated mine. Don't think I won't defend myself if I feel he's coming my way."

"Timmy's too scared to pull the trigger."

"Remember, twelve not six." Mueller knew precisely where I was going. I'd rather be judged by a jury of twelve, than to be carried by six pallbearers.

"Kenny! Get out of there now!"

"Chuck, if he comes after me. . ."

"Kenny. Right now. I'm ordering you to go to Avenel with Jack." Mueller was extremely calm and forceful in his directions. MBM may have been a buffoon, but understanding the pressure I had been under made him consider my warnings. "Where's Vincent? Is he near you?"

Vincent happened to come upstairs after the commotion had settled. I gave Vincent the telephone and watched his reactions to whatever MBM was saying on the other end. Vincent's responses were simply "Okay, Chuck. Okay."

Vincent hung up the telephone and turned to me.

"C'mon, brother. Chuck wants me to put you in a car and watch you go."

"Let me guess. To Avenel, right?"

"Yeah. Hang out with Jack for a while. Just don't say anything to Timmy on the way out. He's scared as hell."

"That punk. . ."

"Kenny, I don't want to know what happened."

I collected what few items I had inside my office and was escorted out of Rahway for the final time, never to step foot back inside of that dilapidated, wooden house again. Moments later, Jack welcomed me with open arms as I was permanently transferred back to Avenel for the remainder of my career.

"Welcome home, kid! Welcome home!" *Hern, hern, hern!*

THIRTY-FOUR

The Hail Mary of Attacks

Having Jack as my supervisor came loaded with a plethora of benefits. Jack was the opposite of a Faunce pawn. Having been a shop steward for a factory union for many years prior to working for the department, he had plenty of experience dealing with management, and resented the way our local Fraternal Order of Police (FOP) lodge had so willingly jumped in bed with management. Even the FOP headquarters in Trenton was disgusted with our local lodge—off the record, of course—and who could blame them. They had a name to protect.

The greatest benefit of working for Jack was that all of Faunce's attacks had to be long distance shots. Jack's commandment was, "Whatever happens here, stays here." That was one commandment I could live with.

Now, just because those attacks were long distance didn't mean that they didn't take their toll on me. My attorney had filed a civil lawsuit against Faunce, the Teflon Don, and others in the department during that summer. I was told that I was protected by the "Whistle Blowers' Act" and by the Law Against Discrimination, but I knew better than to rely on any laws to protect me from a lawless agency.

The long distance harassment centered around the fax machine and telephone calls. I would hear my secretary, Irene, answer her telephone and then she would call out to me.

"They're at it again, Kenny." Irene would get so nervous whenever Central Office called that I would find myself forgetting about my troubles and trying to reassure her.

"It's cool, Irene. Same thing?"

"Yeah. But they want me to call them back if you leave." I smiled, hiding the degradation and humiliation of the situation. I would stand at my position as ordered next to the unit's fax machine waiting for a notice to come across the machine. Some days I would find myself standing there for over thirty minutes doing absolutely nothing. Often, certain individuals would visit, by chance, as I stood at my post.

Then, after being impatiently patient, we would get the obligatory follow-up call from Colleen or Sharon asking, "Is he still standing there?"

"He's right here. You want to speak to him?" Irene would ask.

"No. It should be coming through now."

And with that, I would find out what new lows they had reached. Some of the faxes ordered me to file discrimination complaints, regardless of whether or not I wanted to file them. Faunce determined that I needed more discrimination complaints for them to reject, and so, they ordered me to file more complaints under the threat of further charges if I refused.

One afternoon, Jack called me into his office with more of the same.

"Hold your breath kid, Chuck's on the phone."

I took the telephone.

"Yes?"

"Right now, you are ordered to walk inside of the conference room, and meet with two of the investigators from the Equal Employment Division who are waiting to take your statement."

The department's top brass deified the Equal Employment Division after the department signed the Holland Consent Decree. The decree was intended to fight against the rampant discrimination and wanton retaliation that occurred throughout New Jersey's prisons not many years prior. But my adventures reminded me that a new regime brought new rules. All failures were blamed on the system, never the individuals running that system.

I grudgingly met with the investigators that afternoon, but I honestly had nothing of any value to say to them. I knew that, as before, I would be disciplined for whatever I said or for whatever I failed to say. All of my failed mandatory discrimination complaints were designed to assist the department in their defense against my pending lawsuit. Faunce figured they could create evidence to show a jury I had filed multiple, frivolous complaints, and to demonstrate how swiftly and professionally and thoroughly my deepest concerns were investigated.

From my own experiences as well as the horror stories of many other employees who were familiar with the department's Equal Employment Division, filing a discrimination complaint in the State of New Jersey was likened to milking a virile bull. You'd definitely draw a smile on the bull's face, but you'd might not want to drink the milk. Which was why I was metaphorically accurate in my contention that the Equal Employment Division was nothing but a bunch of bureaucratic "jerk-offs".

I requested permission to tape-record the many forced interviews and was repeatedly denied, but was told by Equal Employment that I could trust them. I suggested that in an effort to save time, they should simply give me their conclusion first, instead of making me sit through the interviews, only to find that whatever I said wasn't credible. They were not amused at my candor, but they did manage to threaten me with more disciplinary actions if I didn't come up with some kind of complaint. They noted my reluctance to give them anything to investigate encroached upon "Conduct Unbecoming A Public Employee", a very serious violation of departmental policy.

So, I did what I was taught to do as an investigator, or as James Brown put it, I was talkin' loud and sayin' nothin'. I rephrased whatever they would ask me, picked their thoughts for the specifics that they were seeking, and actually managed to look magnanimous in the process. In the end, nothing changed their conclusions. All of the mandatory complaints I was forced to file were, of course, found to be without merit. Go figure.

Finding only limited successes through the mandatory complaints, Faunce ordered a few other investigators to research my background. All of my former employers were notified of my deplorable behavior and negative information was requested of them with all urgency. Failure followed failure, but Debbe never stopped her efforts in trying to destroy me.

September 2000 brought plenty of beautiful fall weather as well as a few more surprises. At home, the final notice from the bank telling me that my house was being foreclosed had arrived. The countless skipped paychecks and paycheck errors had proven extremely effective. While at work, Debbe was back to her old tricks, ordering me to undergo yet another psychological evaluation by their sixth psychiatrist, Dr. David Gallina, MD. Officially, my evaluation was required because Faunce determined that a psychiatrist, and not a physician, needed to evaluate whether Ultram affected my ability to carry a firearm. Unofficially, Dr. "Quack" Kahn and Dr. Cevasco coined a phrase when it came to me and these evaluations—"Psyche Him!" Being consistent in her efforts, Faunce determined that it was irrelevant that I hadn't taken any type of medication since my weapon was confiscated over two months prior.

When I showed Jack the letter ordering the latest evaluation, he laughed for almost an hour. *Hern, hern, hern!*

"Take a look at this, Jack. I'm being evaluated to see if Ultram affects my ability to carry a firearm."

"What the hell would a psych know about your headaches?" Jack's laughter caused him to turn beet-red, but he managed to act concerned, routinely giving me guidance. "Just be your ol' charming self, kid. And, wait for the Superior Court jury to hear about all of this stuff." *Hern, hern, hern!* "You can't make this shit up." Jack was more tickled than worried. I didn't share that luxury because I knew the potential damage any evaluation would have on my case.

On my way out the door, Jack gave me some additional professional advice.

"If he asked me what effect it had on me, I'd tell him, 'Hey, doc... it makes my dick hard and my wife wants to know if I can get free refills! *Hern, hern, hern!*' "

"Thanks for the tip, Jack. But then they'd charge me with having an inappropriate erection!" We laughed to tears at the absurdity, yet the possibility, of it all. And I knew if Faunce failed this time, she would just keep attacking.

Dr. Gallina ended up being a Godsend. He had a long history of working with law enforcement and had seen just about everything imaginable until he looked into my situation. Initially, I was skeptical about talking to any psychiatrist affiliated with the state. But I quickly discovered Dr. Gallina was a man of integrity, professionalism and courage. His questioning wasn't like any other psychiatrist I had been forced to see. Instead, he was bewildered as he sat across the room staring at me and jotting down notes on his yellow pad.

"Doctor, would you mind if I tape-recorded this session?"

Dr. Gallina shrugged his shoulders while the corners of his mouth drooped. "Sure. It's your evaluation and I certainly have nothing to hide." He then leaned forward from his seat.

"Would you like to have the recorder closer to me so that it picks up everything that I say?"

For the first time, I was speechless. Never had I expected that at that juncture of my dealings with the department my recordings would be accepted so freely.

"Thank you, but this is fine."

Dr. Gallina sat back in his chair and deliberately folded his hands on top of his lap. "Why are you here, Mr. Freeman?"

"Strange question, doc. I was hoping you'd tell me." Dr. Gallina spoke to me briefly about the meaning of life, asking me essay-type questions. I kindly responded simply "yes" or "no".

"My notes have that. . ." He scratched his head with the pen that he held between his fingers. That reaction of stopping his own questions and scratching his head happened often during our evaluation, but this time, he spoke to himself aloud, and asked,

"Why would they send me this?"

"Are you asking me that question, sir?" It was obvious that he wasn't, but I thought that I'd throw my question out anyway.

"No, Mr. Freeman. No. I just don't get it."

My investigative bent took over, and I had a couple of questions to ask, even if he didn't answer them.

"Get what?"

"*This*. These letters. They've got nothing to do with headaches or medication." He lifted the top document to look at the document beneath it, and became irritated. "I don't need to see this stuff."

Dr. Gallina paused, then he began shuffling through the stack of documents Debbe had sent to him.

"Didn't you notify your Chief, what's her name, Debbe Faunce, that you weren't taking any medication?"

I nodded my head. "Yup, about two months ago."

Dr. Gallina looked up as he shifted in his seat. He grinned with aggravation, and shook his head repeatedly. "And again, I must ask you Mr. Freeman, *why* are you here?"

I took a deep breath, and responded the same way I had all morning. "Again, sir, I was hoping that *you'd* tell *me*."

My answer disappointed him because he had no idea what he was being paid taxpayer money to do. He made a few final notes while I sat there, patiently answering his questions about my life until he released me.

"We're done, Mr. Freeman."

"Good. Can I leave?" I asked.

"Sure, you can leave." I nearly leaped from my chair and headed for the interior door that led to the reception area. The receptionist stopped me and asked me for some additional information on an intake form I had filled out when I first arrived at their office. I didn't feel much like spending any more time in there, but she was so polite that I had to accommodate her.

"Mr. Freeman. I thought that you'd be halfway home by now." Dr. Gallina approached me from the behind and stood next to me, leaning on the counter where I stood holding the clipboard. I didn't look up at him. "You can relax if you want. I don't bite." He gestured with his hands as his fingers flexed in and out. I handed the clipboard back to the receptionist.

"Have a good day, Dr. Galina." As far as I was concerned, the evaluation ended when he told me I could go. I was not only forced to drive an hour each way to be examined about medication I wasn't using, Faunce was taking one of my sick days because she scheduled it during the work day.

As I walked out of his office into the outside corridor, Dr. Gallina followed me, refusing to give up on finding out why I was sent to him in the first place.

"Mr. Freeman." His walk quickened to match my stride, when I turned to face him.

"I thought that you said our session was over."

"Please, Mr. Freeman. I know there's nothing wrong with you. But, I really would like to know what the hell is going on? Agencies don't just throw away good money without having a damn good reason."

"The evaluation's over, doctor. I've got nothing else to say." I checked my watch hoping to drive home the idea that I had better things to do than to give him another shot at ruining my career.

"Oh, it's definitely over. And you're cleared to get your firearm back. I'll say it on your recorder if you'd like. But I want to know what my office was really asked to do." Dr. Gallina was upset, but his hostility wasn't directed at me. "Will you tell me your side of the story?

His frankness was knocking down my defensive walls, but I remained a bit cautious. He didn't mind tape-recorders, which meant I didn't need one. Liars hated hearing their own words, but Dr. Gallina was inviting me to record him.

"How much time you got, sir?"

"As much as you need." And with that, Dr. Gallina and I spent our after-session talking about everything from soup to nuts. His blood curdled with every instance of retaliation that he heard I had suffered at Faunce's hands. His indignation rose as he realized why the department sought him out.

"Has your civil case been filed yet?"

"Yeah. This summer."

"Fine." He said as he crossed his arms. "By law, I can't give you anything in writing about this evaluation because I'm working for them. However. . ." I had seen enough legal opinions to know that whenever you heard somebody say "however", there was going to be thunder on the other side, ". . . take my business card, and tell your attorney to subpoena my records. I think both of you might well enjoy some of those documents they mailed to me."

As I received his card, Dr. Gallina tossed his caution. "Bullies."

"What?"

"Your weakness is bullies." I had no clue what he was talking about and I didn't care.

"Thanks doc."

"Slow down a minute, Kenneth." He took a couple steps towards me and lowered his voice. "You need to assess why you feel compelled to beat up every bully you run in to. That's going to take a bit of soul searching because sometimes," he grinned as I rolled my eyes and sighed, "experiences from our youth can mold our perceptions of life and others."

"Another childhood thing, doc?" Why does every psychiatrist/psychologist want your problem to bleed from some traumatic childhood experience?

Dr. Gallina laughed, stealing one of my favorite lines. "Something like that."

"I'm fine, sir."

"I know you are." He nodded in agreement. "I'm not afraid of bullies either. But, I don't have anything to prove."

I returned to work with my firearm. No explanation was offered regarding whether Ultram affected my ability to carry a firearm, even after several requests. Eventually, I began using the medication because of the severity of the headaches. I wrote Faunce advising her that I was taking the same medication that required my weapon to be confiscated a few months earlier. I asked for her decision on whether I could carry my firearm safely and asked that her decision be put in writing.

The next day, I received a letter from her. Faunce reminded me of an investigator's duty to notify my superiors if my medication affected my ability to handle a firearm. But she closed stating that if I had any questions regarding the effects of Ultram, I should contact the doctor who prescribed it and stop bothering her with such frivolous matters.

Now, why didn't I think of that?

THIRTY-FIVE

A Symbol Without Substance

The filing of my civil law suit against Faunce and the State of New Jersey, coupled with Faunce's latest psychological debacle, caused the state to enlist their own heavy hitters for the defense. The largest and best-financed law firm in the entire state, the New Jersey Attorney General's Office, handled their case. From that point, the AG's office was calling all the shots, and every action taken against me would be strictly coordinated between Debbe, the department, and DAG Thomas Goan, an ethically challenged deputy.

The Attorney General's Office determined that I didn't need a hearing regarding my "abuse of sick time" charge and was found guilty. I was also found guilty of "refusing to voluntarily request a witness" after the hearing officer, Marilyn Chadwick, called me a month prior to the hearing. An employee of Teflon's office, Ms. Chadwick was personally assigned by the Don to ruffle my feathers, or at least try. She told me that she was "investigating" my defense because Hamner and Faunce were "curious" about how I obtained certain documents in the past and wanted no more surprises. I refused, we argued, and I was found guilty. Ms. Chadwick put on record during the hearing that she would neither recuse herself nor allow the charges to be dismissed. Go figure!

Ellis Allen made some very inappropriate remarks to me in the Spring of 2001 during my semi-annual firearm qualification. Remarks Allen was afraid to deny after I removed my tape-recorder from my pocket and replayed his voice to him. The investigation of my complaint about Allen's comments was taken away from Debbe, who would have doubtlessly screwed everything up, and was now the domain of DAG Goan.

But there was one little problem with that scenario. The Attorney General was officially the attorney of record for the defense, and Dwyer was not about to have his client questioned by the defense without him being present.

Jack was scheduled to go on vacation for about a week, leaving me without any shielding from whatever Faunce decided to do.

"Debbe decided to send McHort to the unit while I'm gone to be the acting supervisor. He's going to be their little spy." Jack said.

"You think I'm scared of Rich?" We both laughed at my inference. Jack didn't like McHort any more than the rest of us.

"McHort and I had a run-in when I was at Mountainview."

"I heard."

Jack started to laugh. "Leave him alone, Kenny. You'd kick his ass." Jack thrust his hands forward, as if to stop me from running out and finding McHort. "So don't hit him when he gets here, you hear me?" *Hern, hern, hern!*

Jack was cautious because he remembered how McHort had investigated me when I was assigned to Rahway, and he knew how loyal McHort was to Hamner, who was recently promoted to Assistant Chief. I wasn't much interested in beating up McHort, even if he did deserve it.

"I'll try not to scare him too much. But I won't pretend that I like him." I was reminding Jack about our conversation regarding how to be more passive, an idea I heartily rejected.

"I'm not telling you to propose to him, Kenny. Just don't give them any rope to hang you with. Okay?" Jack recalled McHort's testimony where McHort stated he was convinced that I had lied about Hamner because "supervisors never lie on their employees", a notion at which a former shop steward shuttered.

"No problem, Jack. I'm supposed to drop off the rest of my things to my lawyer after work." I had been reviewing a huge garbage bag full of the extra documents and the tapes I had made over the years.

"That's an awful lot of shit." Jack's eyes were wide open, as he'd seen the girth of the bag.

"Don't worry. You're not on the tapes." I said.

Jack joked about the prospect of having him on tape.

"Damn! And I wanted Paul Newman to play me in the movie." *Hern, hern, hern!*

Jack prepared to go on vacation, and my problem drove up inside an unmarked police cruiser. McHort walked into the unit, heading directly into Jack's office for an impromptu meeting. Later, McHort emerged from Jack's office and attempted to engage in light-hearted conversation with me.

"Hey, Kenny. I just wanted to tell you that. . ."

I didn't like McHort, I didn't trust him, and I didn't enjoy pretending that we were on our way to being bosom buddies.

"Rich, is what you're about to say 'business'?"

McHort stopped. He looked at me strangely and answered in the only way that he could. He said nothing.

"If it's not business, then we're not having this conversation." My eyes told Jack that McHort wasn't my friend, and I walked down the short hallway towards my office.

In Jack's absence, the unit quickly took on a "business only" atmosphere, which actually proved to be mildly pleasant. We were cordial with each other, always mindful of the limits of our interactions. I knew that Faunce held McHort's reigns, pulling them to control him at her pleasure and my peril.

McHort was promoted to head the department's drug search team shortly after he investigated me, a promotion that placed him directly under Faunce's supervision. And, on May 17, 2001, I was about to discover that Faunce wasn't the only one conspiring against me.

"Irene, could you tell Kenny that I need to see him," McHort said.

Irene peeked inside of my office, afraid of what would happen, whispering in her softest voice.

"Ken. Rich wants you to come to his office. You going?" Irene didn't know if I would listen to McHort, but I had no problem listening to him as long as it was business related.

"Relax, Irene. I'm alright."

She was nervous because McHort had received an urgent fax from Hamner only moments earlier, a fax that Irene wasn't allowed to see.

"Is this it? They're going to get you now, Kenny?" Irene meant well, but all the tension temporarily made her the "Prophetess of Doom". She was suspicious of everything Central Office did, and with good reason. She was condemned to witness everything happening to me, and she had a tenderly compassionate heart—a dangerous combination in our line of work.

I knew they would attack me when Jack wasn't present, but they couldn't have put a well-thought out plan together in such a short amount of time. What I didn't know was that DAG Goan and several other deputy attorney generals were working on my case simultaneously. I entered Jack's office, with McHort sitting behind Jack's desk.

"Kenny, I had nothing to do with this. I mean, I don't know why. . ."

I couldn't take his insincere groveling a moment longer than was necessary.

"Save the speech, Rich. What do you want?"

McHort's phony sense of compassion dropped like a bolder

off a sharp cliff, and the McHort I knew so well emerged.

"You are ordered to report to the Attorney General's office at 10:00am, tomorrow, May 18, 2001, and to answer all questions regarding the incident at the range and any other questions the investigator decides to ask you. You are ordered to participate by completely answering each and every question that you are asked to the satisfaction of the interviewer. Failure to comply with any portion of the investigation may result in your immediate termination. Do you have any questions?"

Now, that wasn't very nice. But it was better than hearing how badly McHort felt about my predicament.

"Do you want me to report here before I head down to Trenton?"

"Kenny, you are ordered to proceed directly to the attorney general's office, no exception. That is a direct order. Are we clear?"

"Crystal." I calmly peered at McHort as my head started to pound. My eyes wanted to shut tightly, but my pride was stronger than my pain. "Is that all?"

"Yeah. That's all." McHort gave me a copy of the written order. The pain shot towards the back of my neck and my shoulder area. Those areas had become the new home of my pounding. They hurt so badly that I longed for the return of the days when the debilitating pain was confined to my temples. In agony, I refused to allow McHort to see any change in my demeanor.

I was scheduled to get a refill prescription on the 18th, but it didn't matter to McHort, and I shouldn't have bothered mentioning it. He had his job to do, and so did I.

I immediately telephoned my attorney and told him what had happened, all to his amazement.

"Mr. Freeman, when are you going to bring those tapes and papers for me to look at? I want to be sure I have copies of everything."

"I'll bring them tomorrow, but we've got a bigger problem.

I'm being ordered to go to the Justice Complex in the morning so that the AG's office can interview me, supposedly about my complaint against another investigator."

"Another mandatory complaint?"

"No. The one I made about the range."

"Doesn't matter. What they're trying to do is to conduct a deposition on you without me being present." Dwyer said. "Let me take care of it. Don't you say a word to them."

"They're going to fire me if I refuse."

"Let me handle it. Listen. Don't go against them. Just don't talk to anybody without me being present. Okay? I'll handle this." Dwyer was already looking for the telephone number of Judge Patricia Sapp-Peterson, who had initially been assigned the case. The name "Sapp" had been a staple in the Trenton area when it came to state politics and law enforcement, with one of our investigators, Larry Sapp, boasting of the amount of JUICE that the Sapp name wielded. Our civil case was reluctantly reassigned to the Honorable Judge Andrew Smithson, to the chagrin of the AG's office. From his cell phone while driving from a separate court hearing, Dwyer managed to conduct a conference call with the judge and a representative from the attorney general's office.

"Your honor, I don't believe that I'm being unreasonable, demanding that defense be prohibited from conducting a deposition on my client without me being present." Dwyer said.

"We object, your honor. We were simply conducting business, and investigating an employee's complaint is simply in our course of business."

"No problem." Dwyer interjected. "But not without me present." The judge reluctantly agreed, ordering that my attorney had to be present during any questioning of me. It was clear that the judge prevented them from questioning me without my attorney, but there was always a loophole that was set to trap me. That loophole, which wasn't closed, was the fact that I had been ordered to go directly to their office.

I didn't mind taking a trip all of the way to Trenton just to prevent another sloppy disciplinary charge from being slapped on me. The way I figured it, I was on-call for that week, and I was driving the unmarked state cruiser. All the drive was costing me was time. And since the interview was scheduled during work hours, it was on their time, unless Faunce chose to use my personal vacation or sick time to justify my absence from the office.

The next morning, I appeared at the AG's office as scheduled. A simple flash of my credentials allowed me to proceed to the fifth floor, headaches and all, but with no medication to take the edge off the pain. I had to be in the wrong place because nobody knew the investigator I was supposed to see. I then telephoned McHort about the situation from an interior office on the fifth floor of the Justice Complex.

"I'm here, but I can't find the interviewer."

"Didn't your attorney tell you the interview was cancelled?"

That was a trap, a trap that I wasn't going to walk into it.

"You're my supervisor. Why didn't you tell me?" I asked.

McHort stuttered, then decided to get some assistance from the only person who could bail him out.

"I'm going to call Chris. What number are you at?"

"I don't know." The secretary allowed me to use a telephone after I showed my badge.

"Well, call me back in about ten minutes."

We ended our call and I looked around the corner of the office. The receptionist asked me if I had finished with the telephone and then informed me that I couldn't remain inside of the office because it belonged to her boss. So, I left that office, and decided to drive to Central Office, which was only about five minutes away. When I arrived, I asked Colleen if the Chief was there, then I telephoned McHort.

"Rich?" I said. "I'm at Central Office."

"I've got Chris on the phone now. Why didn't you just stay there?"

"I needed a phone after she kicked out of her office. I didn't want to get her in trouble, so now I'm here."

"No problem, Kenny. Do you see Chris?"

"No, but the interview was cancelled." I said.

"Yeah, I know." McHort said. "Chris said just come on back to work."

"Cool. I got a chunk of sick time and I still need to make my appointment. You mind if I go home?" Faunce who had approached me from behind broke our conversation. She had overheard me talking to McHort about why I had driven to Central Office.

"Who kicked you out, Investigator Freeman?" Faunce asked.

That was the first time that Faunce had spoken directly to me in almost two years, a silence that I had enjoyed and sorely missed. I motioned to Faunce by putting one finger into the air, to say *hold on one minute*, as I listened to McHort's response to my request to be allowed to go home.

"Who was that, Kenny?" McHort asked.

"That's Debbe. Can I get sick time?" I needed McHort to just say "yes", which would allow me to silently leave without having an argument with Faunce, but Faunce wasn't moved.

"Who's on the phone?" Faunce screamed loudly, angry that any mere mortal dared to motion for her to wait.

"What the hell is going on?" McHort asked. "Kenny? Kenny!"

By that time, I turned my attention to Faunce.

"It's Rich, chief. I'm asking for sick time." I said.

"Hang up the phone and answer my question. Now!" Faunce was adamant and her horns were showing.

"Gotta go, Rich. Debbe's harassing me, again."

Rich sounded bewildered and was more worried that he was in trouble rather than if I was.

"Why? What's going on? Kenny. . ." *Click!* Faunce had reached over and pushed down the button to hang up the telephone.

I looked at Faunce and wondered "What next?" And I found out really soon.

"Who kicked you out?"

"What are you talking about, Chief?"

"That's right. I specifically heard you make the statement that you, specifically, just got kicked out of the Attorney General's office. I want you to name the person who, specifically, kicked you out of the building!"

That was the pretext for another disciplinary charge, and I knew it. My head was aching so severely by that time that my eyesight had begun to rock back-and-forth. The blood vessels in my temples pulsated so violently that my equilibrium was thrown off.

"Why are you harassing me, Chief?" I asked.

Faunce decided to take another disingenuous approach at getting me to walk into her trap.

"I care so much about my investigators, and I want to make sure that nobody hurts any of my investigators." That was her public affairs announcement, which was followed by the same Faunce that we've all come to know. "Now, I'm ordering that you tell me who kicked you. That was what you claimed, right?"

"No, it's not."

"Yes-you-did! You specifically said that they kicked you, right?" Faunce was determined to discipline me, and I was weakened too much by my pulsating pain to care.

"Some lady asked me to leave an office where I used a telephone, that's all."

"That's not what you said." Faunce paused briefly before continuing with her rampage. "What's her name?"

"I don't know who she was. Some lady was nice enough to let me use. . ."

"You're changing your story! You said that she kicked you." Faunce said.

"I said I got kicked out of an office. You're saying…"

"Well then, what was the name of whoever allegedly kicked you out of there?"

My knees quivered from the banging inside of my head, and I felt the same way I did right before I became unconscious a year earlier. I staggered over to a small sofa that was along the wall in the general area, and sat down in order to keep from falling.

I spoke to myself, but loud enough to be heard. "I've got to get out of here." I opened my eyes as wide as I could manage. "I'm requesting sick time, Debbe, so I can leave."

"After you answer my question. Who kicked you out?"

"I don't know." I said, clutching my temples. "Sick time. Do I get sick time?"

"No. You didn't answer my question. Who kicked you out?" Faunce said.

"I said, I don't know! Again, I'm requesting permission to leave."

"Not until you answer my question." Faunce said.

"I did answer your question."

"No you didn't!"

"I said I don't know!"

"You didn't tell me who kicked you out!"

I had answered Faunce's question, but she wasn't interested in my answer. She wanted her answer and nothing else would suffice. I had repeatedly asked for permission to leave and I was finally done with asking. I gingerly stood to my feet, made my way to the telephone, and started to dial for help—9-1-1. The telephone started to ring. I knew that an ambulance would have to render first aid when they saw my condition, but Faunce wasn't having any of that.

"Hang up that telephone!" *Click!* Faunce had struck again!

I turned around with the telephone receiver still against my ear in disbelief. "That was 9-1-1 you hung up on."

Faunce was yelling, out of control and out of her mind.

Although it shocked me that she would have the audacity to hang up a telephone, twice, I wasn't too alarmed by it all. I knew the dispatcher typically recorded the telephone number and it would be only a matter of time before they would either call back or dispatch a unit to investigate the hang-up."Nobody gave you permission to use the telephone."

Faunce was irate, and drunk with all of her own perceived privileges and power. I wondered what the courts would have done if a man had hung-up the telephone on a woman who was trying to call emergency services. I returned to the sofa where I massaged my temples as my eyes began rolling back into my head. My teeth were grinding, and my eyesight appeared as though I were peering through a clouded cylinder.

The telephone rang back almost simultaneously to my taking a seat and I sprang up to answer it, giving me hope that EMS would be there soon. It was Emergency Services. I knew that they would demand to speak to the individual that made the telephone call, and I would tell them of my condition.

"We've got a call from this number, is everything alright?" asked the dispatcher.

Chuck Mueller took the call.

"Everything's fine. It was a mistake." he said.

A *mistake*? MBM hung up the telephone, preventing my access to emergency services as my condition worsened.

Faunce handed me a pencil and a notepad. "If you don't know who it was, draw me a picture of what she looked like."

As ridiculous as her request was, I was still stuck on the notion that Mueller called my 9-1-1 call a mistake, meaning that no ambulance was coming. I picked up the telephone one more time and I placed the receiver to my ear while I began dialing, again. 9-1- .

Before I could dial the last digit, it happened. Faunce had utterly lost her mind and grabbed for the telephone receiver that was not only in my grasp, but also against my face, knocking the receiver against the side of my head. I was startled. I instinctively yanked backwards as she tried to pull the receiver away. A scowl was hurriedly drawn on my face as the exorcist entered my throat, altering my vocal cords in a bass-like restrain.

"Don't you **EVER** touch me again!" Faunce's face quickly tuned into the intensity of my voice. More words were gathering at the corners of my mouth, waiting to erupt like Mount St. Helens. She made contact with me, now I'll be justified in allowing my foot to make contact with her cottage-cheese behind. The years of frustration, harassment, anger, discrimination, disciplines, ... Discipline!

"If you ever *touch* me again," What was I doing? Faunce was trying to provoke me, and all of a sudden, I realized that she might have succeeded. It was time for damage control. I took a deep breath and gently let it out. "That was an assault. You just assaulted me."

The scowl was immediately erased from my wrinkled face.

"I never assaulted you. I grabbed for the phone." The anger in her voice was gone, and for the first time in her career, she put her own fear on public display. My eruption, though brief, had shattered her tough persona and reduced her to her low self-esteem state.

"I won't argue with you." I pointed to Sharon Jarrell and Colleen Downy, the two secretaries that were looking directly at us. "They saw you do it."

Faunce regained her composure and instinctively answered for both Sharon and Colleen.

"They didn't see anything." With a glare from Faunce, Sharon and Colleen frantically searched their desk drawers for missing contact lens, with Colleen even answering a phantom telephone call.

I said nothing else to Faunce, but I stood tall near her, staring at her fear and taming an overwhelming desire to separate her partials from her gums. She stepped backwards away from me and looked towards MBM.

"Go home, Kenny." MBM was looking at the situation from a different perspective. Maybe he just wanted to hang me, but maybe, even after all of the terrible things that Faunce had done to me, maybe I still shouldn't have scared her. The sight of an older woman being terrified by a man simply cannot be justified. I turned towards the door, then I paused and looked back at him.

"Should I take the car back to Avenel?"

"Yeah. Just go." MBM said.

My anger had made my headaches a secondary matter, but beneath the surface, they were demanding attention. I checked for my recorder, which I kept in my inside jacket pocket. I stopped at the guard station.

"My name is Kenneth Freeman. I was just assaulted by Debbe Faunce. Please note that in your…"

"Chief Faunce good people."

Needless to say, I picked the wrong person. I shook my head trying to regain focus while my vision diminished significantly. That had worked in the past, but it wasn't as effective when I needed it the most. Unfamiliar with the Trenton area, I searched for blue hospital signs as I headed towards the New Jersey Turnpike. That way, if I felt that I couldn't make it, I could take myself to the hospital. But none of that mattered.

About a hundred yards from Central Office, without warning, my tunnel vision finally closed with no light at the end. I was blind and my arms felt like sand bags. It was at that point that the pains in my temples, neck, and shoulders all ceased.

THIRTY-SIX

One Straw Too Many

Screams came from every direction. Loud screeching screams. But the screams weren't strange. They were as familiar as my own voice, possibly because they were emanating from my own vocal cords.

I opened my eyes and there was a man pressed against my left arm, attempting to choke me. The car was filled with the gases and smoke from the air bags that had deployed during the impact of the accident. Another man had entered the car through the passenger side of the vehicle, and was conspiring with the first man to attack me.

I screamed repeatedly as I reached for my handgun that was supposed to be on my hip. It was gone! I could barely move a muscle. Panic enveloped me, and for the first time, I saw no way out of a jam. That lifetime of distress proved to last only seconds.

As I realized it was the gases and fumes that were choking me, I noticed that the two men inside my vehicle were actually paramedics, trying to place a restraint around my neck to prevent me from further injuring myself.

"You're alright! You're alright, sir. You just had a nasty

crash." he said.

The other paramedic yelled to the mobile unit.

"He's conscious. He's going to be okay."

As I was placed inside the ambulance, the pain all over my body was intense. It was at that moment that I realized that not only was my gun missing, but also my briefcase and the large bag of documents and tapes that I had planned to drop off at my attorney's office. I tried to force the driver to stop the ambulance, telling him that I wouldn't go anywhere without those documents and tapes.

"Relax, sir. We gave everything that was inside of your car to your two friends."

"What friends?"

"Two guys said that they worked with you. Hutton or something."

"Houston and Reynolds?"

"Yeah, that's the name. They were insistent on getting your bag to hold it for you. They also got your briefcase and your gun."

I was toast. My eyes submitted to the anguish as they sealed themselves shut. The pain was worsening with every breath that I took, making my situation all the more bleak. My entire case was inside of that bag, and my briefcase had been my constant companion, holding my life inside of it.

I remained hospitalized for a couple days, and was prohibited from returning to work for over a month. During that time, I filed criminal charges against Faunce for assault, but Dwyer advised me to drop the charges because he feared that there were too many things going on at one time. A sentiment to which I agreed.

But, DAG Goan was just getting started. First, he attempted to file criminal charges against me for damaging state property, the car, and for filing criminal charges against my supervisor, Faunce. Both of his attempts failed, but he wasn't shy when he put his feelings on paper. In a letter to Hamner, DAG

Goan expressed his outrage that he couldn't use the criminal justice system to have me fired, thereby giving the department "just cause" in their retaliation against me. Then, in that same letter, Goan enumerated the specific disciplinary charges that he wanted filed against me in order to help the state's defense in the civil case. Goan's script guaranteed a guilty verdict if I appealed.

Next, I received a notice from the state's Division of Motor Vehicles informing me that my driver's license privileges were being revoked. Goan had ordered his investigator, Dennis Mazone, to inform Motor Vehicles that I suffered from "recurrent, severe, and multiple seizures", requiring me to prove that my "anti-seizure" medications prevented me from having seizures while driving. No anti-seizure medication, no driver's license.

However, it didn't stop there. The department immediately terminated all of my medical benefits, which meant that my hospital bills, the Ultram prescriptions, and all of my children's medical expenses now had to be paid out of my pocket. I was told that I could "re-apply" for coverage through my department, but that there were no guarantees if I had any pre-existing conditions, such as severe headaches or debilitating seizures. On the books, I was still an employee, but my paychecks dried up while my bills continued to flow.

I was finally allowed to return to work, but I had to be cleared by a medical professional with the focus on my ability to both drive as well as my ability to carry my gun on and off duty. To my surprise, Faunce determined that the qualified medical professional had to be me. She ordered me to administer to myself a complete and thorough physical and psychological evaluation as a condition to being able to carry my own weapon. Hamner noted that I would be fired if I failed to evaluate myself and forward a written report about my medical findings to the state.

While all of this was happening, DAG Goan decided to have another DAG conduct the interview that had been postponed a few months earlier. Disturbed by the proof I provided at our meeting, Goan directed that the department's Equal Employment Division conduct their own laugh-fest, and called it an interview. They found that although Allen made derogatory comments towards me, that I should not have overreacted and caused dissention by recording Allen without his knowledge. In addition, I received more charges dating back to the day of my car accident.

Because of the state's inability to terminate me, DAG Goan determined that I was receiving funding from someone or some organization. To counter my perceived assistance, he requested an investigator from the Organized Crime and Racketeering Bureau, State Investigator Steven La Penta, to assist other IA investigators in digging up as much dirt on me as possible. Moreover, the AG's office gave him plenty of latitude, to research the specifics of my assault by Hamner, to the details of my previous employments, to my enlistment in the Marines. Credit information. Employment applications. Telephone data. Tax returns. Anything that DAG Goan could parlay into an unethical connection, "reasonable suspicion", or an indictable offense. My life was turned upside-down—private matters were flaunted throughout the department, my wife's activities were maliciously exaggerated, and the unfathomable stress of their cruelty inflicted a horrendous toll on our already precarious marriage, destroying our efforts at reconciliation.

A hearing was scheduled for Friday, September 14, 2001, but an anomaly named Osama Bin Laden officially introduced himself to the consciousness of everyday America. In the face of the single worst terrorist attack in our nation's history, the gravity of my complaints faded unnoticeably into the ruins of the landscape.

The hearing was conducted a week later with the same hearing officer, Marilyn Chadwick, who constantly telephoned me prior, demanding that I provide her with the scope of my defense so that she could research my facts. At that hearing, she declared that no charges would be dismissed, prior to hearing any evidence. This time, I was charged for calling 9-1-1 after Faunce determined that no emergency existed, for filing an assault complaint against Faunce after Faunce determined that no assault occurred, for not calling McHort in exactly ten minutes (refusal to follow a direct order), and for informing my supervisor about the questions that Dr. Michael "Quack" Kahn asked me about my daughter three years ago.

After the hearing concluded, it was business as usual in my unit for the next month or so. Jack was worried because he had interviewed for the Assistant Warden/Administrator position at Mountainview Youth Correctional Facility. Jack was a shoe-in for the spot, and it was just a matter of time before he received the good news.

"You know, they're just waiting until you leave, Jack."

Jack's laugh was somber, and lacked the vibrant spirit that should accompany the pending, well-deserved promotion.

"I read the transcript of your last hearing, kid. I can't see how any rational person could justify any of this kind of stuff."

I explained to Irene what would happen when the time came for my termination because I didn't want her to worry when it happened. I told her that it would be similar to the way that they passed orders, except at that time, somebody would come from Central Office and would try to provoke me into a fight with them.

We all believed they would attempt to keep all of my personal belongings just to annoy me. Therefore, I packed up my office the next business day after the hearing, and took all of my personal articles home. I finished all of my open cases so they couldn't criticize my work, organized the evidence locker, and stored my weapon and gear in the locker for ease of accountability. However, Irene still wasn't convinced that the termination would run smoothly, and neither was I.

The tension inside of our trailer was thick. Jack, Irene, and I decided to celebrate Jack's promotion, and the dreaded break-up of our team, by ordering Chi-Chi's take-out and eating lunch together for what would be the final time. We often ordered from that restaurant, mostly at my urging. I had my regular twice-fried steak burrito with extra barbeque sauce and refried rice. Jack ate all of the extra hot sauce and later complained about the department from behind the closed hollow door of the hallway lavatory. Irene never finished her salad, but this time, she just didn't want to try. We all knew that the inevitable was approaching, but we didn't know when it would get there.

November 2001 arrived with the news that Jack was promoted to the position of Assistant Administrator. It was truly bittersweet. Jack was to leave Internal Affairs, and more, in the following days. To add insult to injury, Edwin "Tiny-Dick" Melendez reemerged from his hibernation, and managed to finagle himself into Faunce's favor once again. Jack reminded me constantly of Edwin's work with Blake back at Northern State Prison and that Edwin was a snake.

On November 9, 2001, two days after Jack departed for his new assignment, McHort and another investigator named Al Melendez arrived at our doorstep with a manila package in their hands. As I was typing on the computer, Irene ran nervously to my doorway.

"Kenny, they're here. Rich and Al Melendez from Central Office."

If anything, they were predictable.

"Are you okay?" I asked Irene in a very calm voice, more concerned about her fears than about my future. She nodded repeatedly as she looked over her shoulders. "Good. Head back to your area and do what you would normally do. I'll be out in a minute."

She returned to her desk while I took one final survey of

my office. There was no nervousness. In fact, a stimulating sense of relief had come over me. One thought permeated my mind—*God, I thank you*! I had fought the good fight. I stayed my course, and there was no shame in my professional life.

I addressed my empty office aloud. "Peace!" I then headed for the front of the unit, where I saw both of the Melendez's standing with McHort. McHort still pretended to be professional and unbiased.

"Hey, Kenny. Could you step in here for a minute? We'd like to talk to you." McHort said.

"Save it, Rich." I pointed to the folder clutched in his hand. "Is that present for me?"

"Yeah."

"Perfect! Can I have 'em?" McHort handed me the disciplinary decision, which Faunce had signed one day earlier. It unfolded exactly the way I expected, except no one tried to start trouble with me, at least not yet. My goal was simply to leave the area as quickly as possible.

"Just so that we're clear, *I am* officially fired, correct?" I posed my question to McHort in those terms because I wanted Irene to understand what I was saying.

"I'm sorry, brother." McHort's lamentations were about as welcome as gritty fingernails dragging across a washed chalkboard.

"Am I fired?"

"Yes, you are." McHort said.

"Thank you. And, I'm no longer an employee of the state, correct?"

"No, you're not, brother. I'm so sorry, Kenny." McHort said, as both Al and Edwin Melendez pretended to look as if they cared.

I had what I wanted, and I was done.

"Take care, Irene." I walked out of the front door and headed to my car.

"Hey, Kenny. We need your handgun and we need to inventory your office." McHort said.

"The gun's in the evidence locker, my personal effects are in my car, and I'm gone."

"We've got to inventory the evidence locker."

"You should have done that before you fired me. That inventory is your problem now." I had my termination papers, and you remember what happened the last time I attempted to work for free.

"I'm ordering you to open the locker." McHort must have been snorting those drugs he had seized.

"You can't order me to do a thing. I don't work here anymore, remember?"

McHort and Melendez followed me out to my car, making comments as if I would lose my cool. I didn't even lose my cool when Melendez used his police car to block in my car, preventing me from going home.

The combination for the Evidence Locker was in the keybox and so was the master key. Edwin knew it was there, but they didn't want me to leave without having an incident. They refused to move their car until I reached inside the evidence locker and personally pulled out my firearm, and then *handed* it to them, a certain recipe for trouble.

I went back inside and opened the locker. I removed the gun with one hand and allowed the magazine that held the bullets to drop to the desk, without ever removing my gun from the holster. Once the magazine was dislodged, they were prevented from claiming there was a threat because that model of Smith & Wesson cannot fire without the magazine inside of the weapon. I cleared the weapon of a single chambered hollow-tipped bullet, and then laid it on the desk with the barrel facing me.

McHort wasn't satisfied, and I was through trying to satisfy my former supervisors any longer. As I headed back to my car, McHort yelled to me. "You've got more stuff on you, and I want it."

I turned around and faced him, refusing to let him bate me

into slugging him, and at the same time not wanting to let him think he was the tough guy that Faunce convinced him that he was. "If you see something that you want, take it." McHort took a step back, looking at Irene.

"I'm not scared of you, Kenny." Of course, he wasn't. He just wanted to give me some breathing room.

"Okay then. Anything I *may* have belonging to the department will be sent back as soon as I run across it." With that, I returned to my car, patiently waiting until they moved their cruiser out of the way. After a short time passed, Melendez moved their car and I left, ending my chaotic career with the New Jersey Department of Corrections Internal Affairs Unit, but not my troubles.

A month after I was terminated, I received notice from the department that I was being fired a second time. They claimed that I disobeyed an order from my supervisor, McHort, to open the Evidence Locker. Although I had been fired and, thus, was not a public employee, Faunce was still charging me with conduct unbecoming a public employee.

And if that wasn't ludicrous enough, two months after the second termination, I received another notification that they were firing me for a record third time. That time, it was for, you guessed it, falsification. They searched their archives and found something from back in 1998—three years earlier, I complained to Terry Diller and Randy Cicale about what the Quack had asked me about my daughter. Faunce determined that since I mentioned that incident during an unrelated interview with, you guessed it, Equal Employment, in August of 2001, she had the authority to fire me for a third time. Faunce, again, determined that my unemployment status was irrelevant.

New Jersey's Office of Administrative Law (OAL), tasked with hearing the case, decided to agree with Faunce that whether a person who was not employed can be fired was irrelevant, and would not be considered. What I had learned about our connection to Aburami and the possibilities of IA being culpable in assisting him with overseas activities were deemed unrelated, and was not allowed in evidence. They also noted that whatever the department had done in the past was to remain in the past, and my employment history had no bearing on whether I had been targeted or not. After the dust had settled, I set a record for the first person ever to be terminated three times from the exact same job in three months, a feat only a Rising Star could perform.[4]

With all of this bad news came a hard dose of reality as I moved my family of five out of our home and into a third floor, four-room apartment. Our new residence was a 12-unit building, which was located on a main street across from a liquor store and down the street from a strip-bar.

---

4 NJ Superior Court OAL Docket No. CSV-09731.

THIRTY-SEVEN

A Legend Is Born

The jury selection for a full trial in the Mercer County Superior Court of New Jersey was scheduled for Tuesday, February 24, 2004. But, that date would never arrive thanks to Patricia Sapp-Peterson. In dismissing a case unfamiliar to her, she prevented any chance of Judge Smithson impartially adjudicating the matter. Judge Sapp-Peterson rendered her own brand of Jersey Justice, Machiavelli-McGreevey style, under the careful eyes of her half-dozen official "admirers". All of whom sat motionless in the rear of that Trenton courtroom of shame, taking an exuberant quantity of notes. Judge Smithson called in "sick" that morning and it was imperative for Sapp-Peterson to display her authority, as the Assignment Judge of Mercer County, over the reputable Maverick jurist.

Judge Sapp-Peterson declared that every single incidence of retaliation had to be directly linked to a single event, namely, the very first time I complained about being ordered to change my conclusion about a confidential informant back in December of 1997. She determined that even if I was the target of retaliation for a separate whistle-blowing act that could be proven, the state would prevail if I didn't prove it was caused by my first complaint to Jimbo in 1997. One example was retaliation for exposing the department's attempt to have Dr. Daniel Williams to alter his report. Because of that particular complaint, I was almost set-up and fired. However, Judge Sapp-Peterson refused to even consider it, and against every judicial precedence, she decided to view the department's brief in the best light, ignoring our challenge to the state's facts.

The loss was devastating, and fighting the McGreevey Machine managed to get even worse. After preparing and making copies of nearly two thousand documents we had compiled over the course of my employment, the New Jersey Court of Appeal rejected our case without so much as a comment.[5]

My marriage ended without much fanfare, yet we managed to remain close. It was possible that we may never have reconciled, even if Investigator LaPenta and others hadn't purposely aimed to destroy me. But it would have been our doing. With the way the state acted, we didn't stand a chance. For Faunce, it was just one more dissenter silenced. Yet, for us, it was the dismantling of a young family, our family *and* marriage. In hindsight, our problems weren't too different from those that other marriages had not only survived, but become even stronger and more united afterwards. I still loved her, and I guess there will always be a part of me that craves her affection and her laughter. Our conversations improved significantly as our regard and consideration for each other bloomed like xherry blossoms.

I was exhausted—both physically and mentally. My attorney wanted to meet with me in an effort to brainstorm our next move. I walked into his office, wearing my signature leisure-wear, black boots and baggy sweats. My body language and my facial expression echoed the dejection I felt, the hopelessness of the longest journey in my life that had no end. I smiled

---

5 NJ Appellate Division, Docket No. A-4246-03T3/NJSC Mercer County MER-L-7984.

as I shook Ron's hand and collapsed into the arm chair that adorned his office.

"Kenneth. Man, you've put up one hell of a fight." We both grinned in agreement. "Now, in order to appeal this case to the Supreme Court, you're going to have to ..."

"I'm tired, Ron." Ron stopped thinking as a lawyer immediately. He looked resolute as he carefully considered my plight. I leaned my head back until my neck rested against the wall, breathing easily.

"Sometimes you run out of steam, and money. And those assholes got an endless supply of it." Ron laughed, until he saw the look of defeat on my continence. "You're a good man, Kenneth. They didn't beat you. They cheated."

"I know. But I'm too tired to care." I felt as though I could sleep for months on end, waking only to take a leak, and then falling back asleep for the remainder of the decade.

"You're pretty good at writing. Why don't you do that? You know your case would make a great story!" We laughed hard. Ron rubbed his head and straightened his glasses. "But you'd better save all of these damn records," looking at several telephone-sized bundles of documents resting near the cluttered desk, partially impeding the walking path, "because nobody's going to believe the kind of shit that you've been through."

Ron was right about one thing. Believing that any governmental agency would do all of those things to one of their own, somebody who they considered the cream of the crop, was truly unimaginable. Nevertheless, it happened anyway.

"I still can't believe some of it, and I'm your lawyer!" We sat there silently for a moment in a reverberating disbelief. "I heard that asshole testify that you were the 'Rising Star' of the department, then say that they should fire your ass! And, what's that big head mother fucker's name?"

"Willie?"

"Yeah, Willie! He put on record why they're so pissed about Aburami. Trying to hide that the FBI was looking at him."

IA's snitch, who we had both protected *and* compensated, was a suspected co-conspirator of the 1993 World Trade Center terrorist attack. The FBI's initial questioning of Aburami at the prison occurred prior to 9-11 when Faunce thought that I was a controllable nuisance. But after the second attack used airplanes loaded with innocent, unsuspecting American citizens, and my pending litigation documenting our connection to Aburami, the stakes of harboring the suspect in order to get a marijuana bust increased exponentially, and so did IA's level of embarrassment. I was merely a loose end that had to be tied.

Aburami had networked himself both in and out of the continental United States, and had found an arrogant protector, an expeditor of countless illegal, unregistered telephone calls from the prohibited areas of Northern State Prison. Internal Affairs. I never found out where he was calling or if he had anything to do with the terrorist attacks. Nevertheless, one thing was certain. IA supported him and enabled him to carry out prohibited activities, mailed items that were never searched, and received packages that were never recorded. My research and the interviews I conducted were relayed to Jimbo, detailing the access he was given to areas that an inmate should never have been allowed. Aburami even bragged to me about how *he* was the police, and why he believed he really worked for IA. Aburami struck a balance between snitching on low-level drug deals while protecting larger shipments. In doing so, our "braggart" epitomized the question "Who's zooming who?" Being brash and careless was his veil, camouflage for his true intentions. Ultimately, the sovereign State of New Jersey swallowed the bait—hook, line, and sinker!

"You've got one hell of a story!"

Years had passed since my termination—all three of them—and in an effort to put the past behind me, I stored all of the documents I accumulated over the last seven or eight years of my life as far away from my yearning eyes as possible. I had fought valiantly and had nothing to prove, nor anything of which to be ashamed. From the foreclosure, to the repossession, and even through the food stamps, I found the strength to endure. I kept a detailed journal of my daily dealings with the department—conversations, thoughts, triumphs, disappointments—and preserved them separately in my poetry, which became my version of the Blues. However, all of that changed with two chance encounters.

First, as I was walking out of my apartment building with my little girls during the summer of 2003, Officer Joe Williams, who worked with me at Northern State Prison, was driving along my block when he spotted me.

"Freeman! Oh, shit! How you doing, man?"

I let my girls head over to my car where they played with the neighbor's kid while I spoke with Williams.

"I'm good." I couldn't help but grin at his enthusiasm.

"Man, I read about all the shit they pulled on you. There hasn't been a single honest investigator since you left that bitch."

"Sorry to hear that. But, that's not my problem." Trenton had become a filthy petri dish of malfeasance for me and anybody else that dared to take a stand. It was disgraceful to hear about the level of degradation that the Special Investigations Division had plummeted to in such a short time. Nevertheless, I had served my time in hell and survived with only superficial wounds, while others have left with far more disfiguring injuries. Williams lamented the horrors that continued to mushroom throughout the state, and contrasted those terrors with the impression I had made.

"But you know they talk about you like you're a fucking legend."

"Well, the cops at Northern were always cool with me." I never had much of a problem with the officers or the staff at

Northern, with the exception of Lt. Tessenholtz and his Sambo comment. My problem emanated from my own department.

"Northern? I'm talking 'bout the whole state's talking about the man that kicked the state's ass! McGreevey, Faunce, all them bitches get nervous when they hear somebody brag about you." I couldn't help but laugh and smile at his words, which never ended. "And, you're not going to believe it, but the cops at Northern are turning each other in for all kinds of shit. All that turning a blind eye is done! Cops starting to straighten each other out!" He laughed heartily. "People playing that Freeman-card and shit, waiting for your book to drop."

"What book?" I was puzzled by his comment, thinking that maybe he was just referring to an interview with the *Star Ledger* that never materialized.

"*Your* book—the shit Faunce put you through? All them IA bastards running scared 'cause they say your book's about to drop on their ass."

I had considered writing a book about everything, but I didn't know whether anybody would care, or wanted to hear, about what happens in the Garden State. I had compiled a draft about the interviews I conducted with sex offenders. Mostly tape-recorded in the Adult Diagnostic and Treatment Center (ADTC) and its satellite unit in Kearny, N.J., the interviews exposed me to the sexual predator's mind, ingenious manipulations, and resources—a scenario that would scare any parent. I wrote about three particular individuals whose exploits seemed the most egregious, and was able to compose a single character based on their combined profiles.

Suddenly, the prospect that I could still get back into the battle against my corrupt former employer was definitely more appealing. I had all the research I needed packed away in case files and my memory was still fresh. That August, I began putting my thoughts about the department in writing in an organized manner.

Second, my attention waned as time passed and doubts

about the success of such a venture multiplied. Other matters seemed more pressing and took priority over my writing along with anything else that came to mind. All of that changed when I decided to change up my routine and let my kids take me to Great Adventures Amusement Park on Father's Day of 2005. To my surprise, the park was featuring a special rate for law enforcement officers and their families, and I was swarmed by waves of corrections officers from all around the state. One-by-one, 12 to 15 different corrections officers approached me that day, each with their own words of encouragement and tales of my exploits. Some of the officers I saw that day were complete strangers, implying that they expected me to be taller or more muscular, yet giving me second-hand reminders of my own miseries while offering first-hand testimonies of their own.

I freely fielded questions about what occurred at different times, and I listened attentively to the many problems and concerns with which many of the officers had to contend. They were discouraged by the tone and arrogance of SID, as well as the unit's tyrant-like attitude.

One persistent question reflected the one posed by officer Williams. "They say your book blows up the state," a pair of officers from the prison in Bordentown expressed their anxious anticipation for more information. "What's the title?"

The only thing that I could think of was my screen saver, "When Good Men Do Nothing", which became the impetus for my writing. Edmund Burke had written, "*All that is necessary for the triumph of evil is that good men do nothing.*" However, good men and women all over Jersey had, in fact, done many extraordinary things, putting their careers and all they held dear in peril. But a strong, cohesive bureaucracy like either the Whitman or McGreevey regimes proved to be more than any internal efforts could have overcome. Maybe it was stated best in *The Godfather* trilogy, "*Politics and crime; they're one and the same.*" After considering all of the good officers who suffered similar abuses, that particular title would have been inappropriate and dismissive. But it sounded catchy.

"Oh, yeah! Dat shit gonna be hot!" As the pair nodded in unison, I couldn't help but smile as we shook hands. "Ya' gotta tell us when it's coming out."

"Put it on the DOC website!" We laughed so hard, I almost forgot that I was supposed to be enjoying Father's Day with my kids. I gave those cops my word that I would find them after my book was published, and I wouldn't skimp in describing the true nature of New Jersey's rose-tainted justice.

Their sincere interest and appreciation was inspiring, invigorating, and the catalyst I needed to put to rest the doubts that would arise in the middle of my deepest sleep. I began writing with an urgency I had never felt before, and the notion that my victory was in my grasp and power was in my words.

The end of my journey turned out to be nothing more than a few pages. In addition, that was when I saw for the first time in a couple of years that my journey's end was only the end of a long, horrible chapter in my life. Inwardly, I finally understood the conclusion of the whole matter, and my walk with God had taken on a pleasant urgency. I still managed to err from time to time, but those mishaps were fewer and less intentional as I learned that errors indicated the existence of a standard. Also, I struggled to leave the misgivings of my past in the past, and trust that God had, and still has, a unique purpose for my life. With that, He had given me another chance to make right both the intentional and unintentional goofs in my personal relationships and to apologize to Priscilla the correct way, without using her as my scapegoat.

My nightmare was not the end of the story, even if some of the major and flamboyant characters had temporarily left the scene. With a cleared conscience and renewed vigor, I prepared for round two against my foe. Dr. Gallina was dead accurate regarding an impulse to prove I'm not afraid of bullies, a flaw in myself that I decided not to correct. At least not at this moment. Now, I'm not foolish enough to ever believe that corruption in any government will ever totally cease. Yet, maybe if I grit my teeth, shake my fists, and scream loud enough, my bully will finally apologize, give me back my $800, and like Ol' Big Head Eddie, maybe we'll both find a way to move on with our lives.

Yet, even if they don't, there was an expanding comfort growing inside my gut knowing that after almost eight years of waiting, one thing was certain—I didn't lose. I fought a fair fight against state-sponsored Mercenaries. Nevertheless, it was time for me to crawl out of my hole, shake off the dirt, and do some hunting of my own.

"Hey, Debbe? You've had your fun, but now the rabbit's got the gun!"

Teth

Before I was afflicted I went astray: but now have I kept thy word.
It is good for me that I have been afflicted: that I might learn thy statutes.

GADSON JEFFRIES
PUBLISHING

At Gadson Jeffries Publishing, our goal is to rebuild, re-inspire and restore the spirit of humanity - One Book at a Time.

We publish both fiction and non-fiction books that focus on the fundamental truths of the human experience. Locked inside our hopes, our fears and our secrets is the key that will create a more complete tomorrow.

We hope that you will enjoy our books. Have a thought or comment that you'd like to share? Please, feel free to e-mail us at info@gadsonjeffriespub.com.

Submissions are welcome. Visit our website at http://www.gadsonjeffriespub.com for more information.

GADSON JEFFRIES PUBLISHING
PO Box 5416
Hillside, NJ 07205-5416